Selling on the Edge

(Everything they don't teach you in real estate school, but should!)

By

Mark John Williams

"Be You. Sell More. Rock On!"

Selling on the Edge

Featuring: *The Four Cornerstones, The Six Steps,* and the patented selling formula, *Sales Triage*™

First Edition/Updated 2023

Original ©2013 by Mark John Williams
Printed in the United States of America

All rights reserved. No part of this publication may be reproduced, stored in a retrieval system, or transmitted in any form or by any means – for example electronic, photocopy, recording – without prior written permission of the author. The only exception is brief quotations in printed reviews.

Library of Congress Cataloging-in-Publication Data

Williams, Mark John
Selling on the Edge, (Be you, sell more, rock on!)
p. cm.

ISBN

ebook 978-0-9896241-0-7
Pbk   978-0-9896241-1-4
Hcv   978-0-9896241-2-1

1. Real Estate 2. Selling/Sales

THIS BOOK IS DEDICATED TO MY REAL ESTATE WINGMAN AND BEST FRIEND JOE CONVERY, WHO PASSED AWAY UNEXPECTEDLY AT THE TENDER YOUNG AGE OF 52 IN 2016.

PRAISE FOR *SELLING ON THE EDGE*

"In a business world that is increasingly focused on 'self' and driven by social media, it was refreshing to read a business book that encourages humility in sales professionals. When we approach our clients and transactions with a spirit of humility and forgiveness, we are truly able to reach win-win agreements and place the needs of others ahead our own. Thank you Mark John Williams for capturing this wisdom and insight."

-Mo Anderson, Vice Chairman of Keller Williams Realty International

"Mark, well done."

-Simon Cowell, Client, Creator/Judge CBS's AGT, The X Factor, American Idol

"As an avid buyer and seller of high-end residential real estate for over two decades, I would recommend Mark and Mark's book to anyone who is in real estate or thinking of getting into real estate. Selling on the Edge can not only help salespeople and real estate agents in any city and any market, but with heavy weight topics never before touched in the business and sales worlds, it can help change the way we approach business and even our own lives."

-Nick Loeb, Client, Film Producer/Director, New York ,NY

"I wish I had this book when I got started."

-Barry Berg, Agent, Coldwell Banker Realty, 35-Year Veteran Agent/Top 1% Worldwide, Coldwell Banker Worldwide, Minneapolis, MN

"Mark is nothing like your typical real estate agent. Nada!...and that is exactly why I use him. Congratulations, Mark!"

-Sofia Vergara, Client, Actress, ABC's Modern Family

"This really is everything they don't teach in real estate school, but absolutely should! Bravo, Mark!"

-Chad Rogers, Agent
　　Celebrity Real Estate Agent/Expert, Original Cast Million Dollar Listing

"This book will change the lives of real estate agents everywhere. It's a monumental win for our industry."

-Kara Karns, Regional Vice President of Coldwell Banker Realty International

"Be yourself, make money, and have the time of your life doing it!"

-Sharon Rollins, Agent, Sotheby's International Realty

"If you want to win the Stanley Cup of real estate or an Olympic Gold medal in selling homes listen to this guy."

-Peter Svoboda, Client
NHL Player, Stanley Cup winner, Olympic Gold Medalist, Toronto

"The Edge mindset and principles will quickly change your life… AND your bankbook!"

-Bill Perry, Agent
First Team Estates Realty, 20-year legendary agent, Newport Beach, CA

"Mark's no-nonsense approach to selling is a dynamic breakthrough and a gift to more than just real estate agents. Anyone considering selling houses or selling anything for that matter should read this book."

-Brian Combs, Agent, National Real Estate Trainer/Speaker, Vancouver, WA

ONE-SHEET and QUICK-FINDER

Official Table of Contents		6
Preface		13
Part I:	WHAT MATTERS MOST	14
Part II:	THE FOUNDATION (Four Cornerstones)	31
	1. Gratitude	
	2. Service	
	3. Humility	
	4. Forgiveness	
	INTERMISSION	77
Part III:	THE SYSTEM (Six Core Steps)	85
	Step 1: Be Yourself	
	Step 2: Get Out There	
	Step 3: DIS-Qualify	
	Step 4: Focus	
	Step 5: Own It	
	Step 6: Have Fun	
Encore:	BEYOND THE EDGE	295
Index:	Summary of Edge Rules	301
	Special Thanks	303
	About the Author	304

Official Table of Contents

PART I		**WHAT MATTERS MOST**	**14**
	CHAPTER 1	THIS MIGHT NOT BE FOR YOU	14
	CHAPTER 2	YOU SELL HOUSES	17
		Don't Be a Johnny-Catch-All	
		Twenty Years Ago	
		Some Minor Details Before We Begin	
	CHAPTER 3	WHAT IS SELLING ON THE *EDGE*?	21
		Walk Before You Can Run	
		Two Promises	
		The *EDGE* 100K Guarantee	
		How is the *EDGE* Different?	
		Square Peg in a Round Hole	
		The Keys to the Kingdom	
PART II		**THE FOUR CORNERSTONES**	**31**
	CHAPTER 4	LIVING IN THE GARAGE	31
		You Should Get Your Real Estate License	
		The Ability to Execute	
		No One Cares	
		It Is About Being of Service	
		The Doctor Is In	

| CHAPTER 5 | IF YOU COULD NOT FAIL | 38 |

Tiger

Brainbaggage Be Gone

Why Not You?

Repetition, Repetition, Repetition

Where Should I Hang My License?

Finding Real Buyers and Sellers

Overview of The Four Cornerstones

| CHAPTER 6 | **CORNERSTONE I – GRATITUDE** | 49 |

Gratitude is the Seed of Abundance

Eleven Dollars and Seventy-Eight Cents

Run Your 555s (Five-Fifty-Fives)

| CHAPTER 7 | **CORNERSTONE II – SERVICE** | 54 |

Unconditionality

You Will Be Tested and Tempted

Daily Service Rx

| CHAPTER 8 | **CORNERSTONE III – HUMILITY** | 59 |

Ego Is No Match for Humility

Asking for Help

The Alleged Murderer

Uncle Wilfred

Coachability

Awareness

| CHAPTER 9 | **CORNERSTONE IV – FORGIVENESS** | 67 |

Amanda Madsen

Set Your Rocks Down

Make a List and Pray for Them

Throttle Back

One Day It Could Be Too Late

A Little Test Before We Go Forward

Your Favorite Music Album of All Time

==========INTERMISSION========   **77**

CHAPTER 10	IT'S ALL GONNA WORK OUT	78

Be a Giver

Thanks, Mom

Don't Make This Huge Mistake

PART III   **THE SIX STEPS**   **85**

CHAPTER 11   DANGER! WARNING: DO NOT ENTER   85

It's Not Because He Wasn't Good Enough

· You Now Have a System

Main Mission and Main Moves

CHAPTER 12   **STEP ONE – BE YOURSELF**   **91**

Main Mission: Bring Out the You in You

The House Was a-Rockin'

Know Thyself

Find Your Passion Arenas

The Magical Lead-Generating Website

Write It Down

CHAPTER 13	**STEP TWO – GET OUT THERE**	**111**

Main Mission: Get Your Fail On

Homeless Guy in the Parking Lot

Engage, Crash, and Burn

Your Success Tree

The Best Friend Exercise

The Five to One Drill

CHAPTER 14	**STEP THREE – DIS-QUALIFY**	**125**

Main Mission: Determine a Reason NOT to Work

With Someone

Learn How To Say No

You Decide Who Gets to Work With You

Gut Check

How Much Agents Really Make

Talk Them "Out" of It Instead of "Into" It

Denial Isle and One-Itis

Buyers Are Not Liars

CHAPTER 15	**INTRO TO SALES TRIAGE™**	**140**

Buyers and Sellers Also Have a System

Find Trauma Victims and Save Them

Develop Your DQ Not Your IQ

Hawk and Aaron

Hurt Level

Pre-Op

Insurance

Operate

Post-Op

CHAPTER 16	**ADVANCED SALES TRIAGE™**	**159**
	Death Valley	
	The Point of No Return	
	Gut Check Trumps All	
	Pre-Op: Three Important Aspects	
	If You Don't Do a Pre-Op, You Will Regret It	
	Actions Never Lie	
	Show Me the Money – Insurance	
	Go All In – Operate	
	The Runaway Buyer and the Never-Enough Seller	
	Post-Op Summary	
CHAPTER 17	**THE INNER GAME**	**187**
	The Vine Man	
	Forget About Winning	
	The Edge Is a State of Mind	
CHAPTER 18	**STEP FOUR – FOCUS**	**203**
	Main Mission: Avoid Weapons of Mass Distraction	
	So You Can Do What You Must Do	
	Weapons of Mass Distraction	
	Find Trauma Victims	
	The 80/10/10 Focus Rule	
	Your Three Ideal Lists	
	Analysis Paralysis	
	The Terminator for Real Estate Agents	
	Are Your Goals Really *Your* Goals?	
	Success Triangle	
	If Everyone Else Is Doing It, Stop Doing It	

| CHAPTER 19 | THREE PERSONALITY PITFALLS | 229 |

The Babysitter

The Control Freak

The Big Spender

| CHAPTER 20 | THE BLAPPA BLAPPA BLAPPA INCIDENT | 240 |

Pistol and Janice

The Rule of Five Friends

| CHAPTER 21 | **STEP FIVE – OWN IT** | **248** |

Main Mission: Take Full Responsibility for Everything In Your Life

Owning It Gives You the Power to Change

To Turn It Around, Listen to Your Heart

Reality Check

A Warning to the Newly Licensed Agent

Reality Check Summary

| CHAPTER 22 | BUILDING YOUR DREAM TEAM | 261 |

The Besty

The Wingman

The Hero

Why We Call Them "Crabby"

| CHAPTER 23 | **STEP SIX – HAVE FUN** | **276** |

Main Mission: Detach From the Outcome

The Art of Acceptance

Turn It Over

How Detaching Turns Into Winning

                    Reward

                    Recharge

                    Having Fun Gets You Back to Step One

ENCORE   **BEYOND THE *EDGE***   **295**

        CHAPTER 24   EXECUTE   295

                     Get In Over Your Head

                     Stay Coachable Forever

                     Don't Just Listen to Your Heart, Act on It

        CHAPTER 25   BELIEVE IN YOURSELF TO BE YOURSELF   298

                     The Memo

                     Now It's Your Turn

                     Dance

INDEX   **Summary of Edge Rules**   **301**

                     Special Thanks   **303**

                     About The Author   **304**

Preface/Intro

SO, WHAT'S THE DEAL?

Traditional real estate training is like jamming a square peg into a round hole. Not good. New real estate agents fail because they try to do things that other people tell them to do instead of following their own instincts. Years go by and after trying to be someone they are not, and doing things they don't like doing, frustration sets in and the end is near. The one-time joyous, inspired, and eager new agent is now bitter, broke, and out of the business. *Ninety percent of all new real estate agents are gone within their first twelve months.* Why? It's not because they aren't good enough. It's because they never learn what really matters. **Selling on The Edge** will teach you what really matters. You now hold the keys to the kingdom. The next move is yours.

Imagine having an abundance of amazing clients without having to chase them, sit open houses, or do things you don't like doing like memorize scripts, knock on doors, or attend pesky network meetings. Traditional prospecting and training techniques are old. They don't work. Buyers and sellers in today's market can spot a "salesman" and someone trying to "sell" them a mile away. In today's competitive world of selling houses, you simply cannot afford to look like a salesperson or you will be toast. **Selling on The Edge** will teach you how to develop relationships authentically, never look like a salesperson again, easily find an abundance of real buyers and sellers, and have plenty of time and money left over to do the other things you love.

SELLING ON THE EDGE WILL TEACH YOU WHAT REALLY MATTERS

PART I opens with WHAT REALLY MATTERS when selling houses. This sets the tone of the entire program and gives the agent a clear picture of what matters most and, more important, what matters least.

PART II introduces The FOUR CORNERSTONES of **Selling on The Edge**, which will help you establish and build on the foundation essential for long-term success in real estate sales. Your critical, formative first 12 months will make or break you in this business. The Four Cornerstones provide your positive path. If you take the time to learn and USE this program, I promise, you WILL make it!

PART III unleashes a simple but revolutionary 6-step selling system that will change the way agents look at selling houses and the way the industry looks at training. It will even change you! The **6 Steps of Selling on The Edge** form the core of the entire program and will show you the way to success right out of the gate.

Selling on the Edge is designed to bring out the YOU in you like never before, so you can develop your full potential and share your unique gifts with the world. Using your own special strengths and passions, and learning to follow your heart and gut, you will soon be achieving things in real estate that you never thought possible.

BOTTOM LINE

No one can do YOU better than you. Maybe you've heard the line, "Be yourself, everyone else is taken"? Isn't that what we all want? To be free to be ourselves? To do things your way? To work for yourself, on your own terms, and not have someone telling you how to be? Congratulations on picking up this book. Your ship has come in and you have hit the motherload. Your life and bank account are about to change. Say goodbye to cold calling, useless network meetings, tricky scripts and tiresome training manuals. It's time to start selling...on *the Edge*! Now let's dance!

Part I

What Matters Most

CHAPTER 1

THIS MIGHT NOT BE FOR YOU

I am not a motivational speaker. This is not a motivational program. If that is what you were hoping for, then unfortunately this is not the book for you. Pump sessions are fun, but they never last. If you are a savvy veteran real estate agent who has been crushing it for years, then this book is definitely not for you. You don't need it. And probably won't take the time to read it anyways, UNLESS you are extremely coachable and want to know how I sold over fifty million in one calendar year working about half as hard as you pal. Ok, calm down don't get all uppety like I'm being cocky, just needed to wake you up, get your attention. Just f'n with ya, (not about the fifty million) but take a punch, relax, just making sure you're locked in here. You locked in?

Do I have your attention now? Good! ...Cuz we're adding a little something to this month's sales contest. As you all know first prize is a Cadillac El Dorado. Anybody wanna see second prize? Second prize is a set of steak knives! Third prize is you're fired. You get the picture? You laughing now? Hahahahaha, ok I did it again, I'll stop with the movie references, (That is the classic opener from *Glengarry Glen Ross*, the movie, written by genius David Mamet.) but please go see it. It will help your career long term so I wanted to plant those seeds now. Ok, shoot, my ADHD is on fire...and yeap, still no website or magnet mailers. OK, fine I may get a website for this book, but why? That is what publishers are for or Amazon, right? Get it? I stick to my role. You soon will too. How about if I told you to never go to an inspection ever again? Would you listen? That really throws agents for a loop. Ok, fine you can go to part of it for 20-30 minutes tops, but will explain more on that later too. Just want you to keep an open-mind and ask you to take everything you think is important and throw it out the window. (Fact: top agents rarely attend an inspection for more than 15 minutes, if at all.) Why? They are not inspectors. Keep an open mind friend we are getting you rockin' big time! You are doing good just need you to hang on, this is only a test. By the way what brokerage are you at? Trick question - STOP! No one cares.

My clients don't even know where I work or what brokerage. The reality is they could care less. When they call, they are calling me. For fun, I sometimes ask them if they are aware of where I actually "hang" my license and most of them respond with "Huh"?.. Lesson, your clients buy you, not your broker. So, beware of "brokerages". Most just want your cash and do nothing for you. More on that later. Let's stay focused here! We're heating up, open up that mind! Stay focused Jack.

Speaking of focus, ever seen the Jack Reacher movies? Or read the books? Jack Reacher was always my ideal realtor role model lol, even though he had nothing to do with real estate. (Just stay with me for a minute. Point coming soon.) My Dad used to read the books. Reacher, for those of you who never saw the movie or read one of the books, was a badass ex-Army guy. Just go watch the movies, be easier to grasp, but in a nutshell Reacher character: Ex-Army Major, hero, badass, who travelled country taking odd-jobs in seemingly dangerous situations, always to end up saving the day, with only his T-shirt, jeans, and toothbrush. What else do ya need really? My friends called me the "Jack Reacher" of real estate because I didn't have a fancy car, no website, dropped the suit, and hardly existed in the real estate world, yet I started putting up numbers and competitors were like "who in the actual... is this guy?" Agents could be called a lot worse, so I ran with it. That eventually became my business plan: T-shirt, jeans, sh'tty car, toothbrush, fierce integrity, protect my clients 'til the end, and oh yeah, a listing contract. LFG Jack!

Now for you commercial agents out there reading this or if you are really interested in selling "commercial" real estate, then this book is definitely not for you. Sorry. That commercial stuff is a different animal, those books are somewhere down in aisle C just past the cheese dip, turn left and never come back. Take your triple net cap-rate bullsh*t and beat it pal. (Or go watch *Wallstreet* again for the 93rd time. Or is *Boileroom* still the goto? My advice is nothing beats *Glengarry Glen Ross*!) OK, kidding, love commercial agents all day long, this book just not going to help you. Point being in your first couple years we're gonna run lean, stick to the basics, not go blow tons of money on sh*t you don't need, and stay focused on one thing. Houses. Got it Jack?

The confusing professional term for a house or condo – for anyone who is new – is "Single Family Residence." I still don't understand what this weird term means. What is a "Single Family" anyway? Isn't that a TV show with the sexy Columbian woman? Or is it the cartoon series with the fat guy? I never understood the term, *Single Family Residence.* It's terms like these that drove me crazy when I was getting started. The good news is, I've thrown out all these wacky terms so anyone can easily understand this program and will quickly be able to get started selling houses.

I created this program because I wanted new agents everywhere to have a better start than I did and learn what really matters instantly. I've seen thousands of agents, both new and seasoned, waste precious months, years, and even careers, trying to master nonsense terms, techniques, factoids, contracts, and techy crap that does nothing for them but waste their time. The ones that made it big were the ones that learned what mattered most. **Selling on The Edge** will help you learn what matters most and, equally important, what matters least. The result will be more trips to the bank to cash your commission checks instead of getting stuck in *Death Valley*, the final resting place of all failed real estate agents.

With that said, if you are here to get good at selling *houses*, then we are clear for takeoff. If you're interested in selling anything other than houses, then please return the book now. I want to be honest and crystal clear: I don't know diddly-squat about selling commercial real estate, selling apartment buildings, buying hotels or restaurants, leasing strip malls, or renting office space -- and neither will you from reading this book. This book is for anyone who wants to sell *houses*. Got it? Bueno.

Chapter 2

YOU SELL HOUSES

Don't be a Johnny-Catch-all.

New residential real estate agents fail because they try to sell everything they can instead of just selling houses. Most get their license initially because they just want to sell houses. Then a few months go by and they haven't sold anything, so desperation kicks in. One day a friend calls and says, "Hey, I hear you got your real estate license now. I'm looking for office space to rent, can you help me?"

The new real estate agent has no other clients because they are new and says, "Sure, why not?" And this is the beginning of the end of their career.

This program is for people who want to sell houses. Most new residential real estate agents are all over the map and start trying to help people with things they have no business getting involved with. It's like going to a knee surgeon and saying, "Hey, I know you're a knee doctor, but can you help me with my root canal?" What do you think the knee doctor would say?

You have to understand the public's perception of you when you are new. You have to understand what they typically think of when they hear the term, "real estate agent." It could be a million different things to them. They don't know what you do yet. When you are new, it's your job, first and foremost, to make sure you don't get caught up in things you should not be doing – and to make sure people are clear on exactly what it is you *do*. Get specific, fast. From this point on, unless it is a house or a condo (which may be called an "apartment" in New York City), you stay away.

So what do you do? You sell houses. In your first twelve months, when anyone asks you to help them find a carwash for them to buy, or sell their coffee shop, you politely tell them:

"Sorry, I can't help you with that. I sell houses."

Some of these other things may look tempting. They may be a lucrative opportunity, but so is the world series of poker. So why are you not doing that for a living? Simple, it's not your bag. You sell houses.

Edge Rule: You sell houses.

(Over the course of reading this book, you will learn a series of what I call "Edge Rules." You will see them frequently as you continue to read. They are all also conveniently listed in one section in the back of the book.)

TWENTY YEARS AGO

Twenty years ago, I was a *magna cum laude* college graduate who somehow ended up broke, out of work, and living in a friend's garage in a not-so-lovely part of Los Angeles—and then it hit me: I should get my real estate license!

And this is where our journey begins.

When I got started twenty years ago, no one told me what really mattered. I didn't sell a house for three years and I quit the business at least ten times in those three years. I had to take odd jobs to support myself and it was a brutal start. I did everything from selling cell phones out of the trunk of my car, to working at Circuit City, to trying to do TV commercials. (You may recognize me from my featured extra work in a Nicorette commercial. No?)

And, yes, I even wasted years chasing non-residential deals like the ones I warned you about earlier. It was a disaster! The truth is, I had always wanted to sell houses, and I barely made it because of one simple fact: No one told me what really mattered – and, even more important, what mattered least. I didn't know what I didn't know, and, needless to say, I almost didn't make it. Thanks to crossing paths with some amazing people and making a few adjustments, I was able to hang in there, get some momentum, and the rest is history.

So why am I here now? To help you. Service. I am here to help you, the newbie, right out of the gate so you can make it in your first year, build a great foundation, and have a long-lasting, satisfying career making more money in real estate than you ever thought possible, with plenty of time and money left over to do the other things you love.

Selling on the Edge is a simple selling program with six core steps. If you follow them, keep an open mind, and stay coachable, you will make money.

I've met an untold number of residential real estate agents who had loads of talent and sales skills, yet quickly faded away, and it broke my heart. It wasn't because they weren't good enough. For a long time, I didn't understand why agents would fail and what was missing in the real estate training world. Once the answers hit me, I made it my new life purpose to help new agents everywhere survive those challenging first few years selling houses and make it big. My mission is simple: To help you, the new agent, have a stellar first year and beyond.

I am not here to change you. I am simply here to HELP by pointing you in the right direction. No strings, just the joy I will get when I find out you kicked some major ass selling houses and didn't waste years trying to figure it all out. You, my friend, are going to make it. Congratulations! You are about to get your *Edge* on. As you are about to find out,

The Edge **Is a State of Mind.**

SOME MINOR DETAILS BEFORE WE BEGIN:

1. Go pass the state real estate exam.
2. Finish this book.

First and foremost, you need a license to sell houses. So whatever state you're in, you need to take that state's test along with the national portion and PASS both parts in order to be licensed to sell houses. Got it? Bueno.

If you are *thinking* of getting your license, then my advice is to just go get it. By the time you finish reading this chapter, you could be registered for the courses and you are set. Cruise through the courses fast and then just go pass the test. Now! Call and get a test date. Don't worry if you fail, you can take it again! And again.

You need a license to sell houses, so let's get that part out of the way as quickly as possible. Capisce?

Second, set a goal now to *finish* reading this book the first time within thirty days of picking it up. I said "first time" because I know after the first read you will want to go back and read it again. It is loaded with material that may be hard to master with one run-through, but the more you study the program, embrace it, and start making it your own, the easier your next twelve months will be and the more money you will make.

You've found your way to this program for a reason. You are different, you are a seeker, and you brought this program into your life because you are destined for greatness. How do I know this? Because everyone has greatness in them and this program is designed to simply unleash that greatness and bring out the YOU in you. You made a great investment with this program, but if you don't actually read it, then it's not going to do you much good. So your only two goals for now are to get your license ASAP and to finish the book within thirty days. And if you already have your license, then you only have one thing to do within the next thirty days. Finish the book. I told you this stuff was easy.

Edge Rule: Just finish it.

Now let's look more closely at what **Selling on the Edge** is all about, why it works, and the "Edge $100K money-back guarantee that you have for the next twelve months.

CHAPTER 3

WHAT IS SELLING ON THE EDGE

Selling on the Edge is a selling program which consists of the ten most essential things every new residential real estate agent must know. If you want to sell houses, these ten key things will not only change your bank account, they will change your life. My goal is to help you avoid the huge mistakes I made and prevent you from quitting before the miracles happen. I also want to keep you from wasting years (like I did) from focusing on things that do not matter and will not help you in any way whatsoever when you're new.

New agents fail because they don't know what to DO in the beginning. From day one, I want you to know what really matters most to make it in this business – and what matters least. And, guess what? What does NOT matter in your first year is things like: fancy scripts, websites, marketing, your signs, contracts, email drip campaigns, magnet-mailers, online lead-generating tools, social networking, and all the other stuff traditional training firehoses down your throat.

Don't get me wrong, these things will have their time and place. But initially you have to learn a foundation. If you don't build a foundation, learn a selling system, and understand what matters most, you will regret it.

From this point on, I'll often refer to the entire **Selling on the Edge** *program and its 10 essential points* simply as "**the Edge.**" **The Edge** is changing the way agents look at selling homes and it is changing the way the industry looks at training. Find one other real estate training program that will tell you that you do NOT have to sit open houses if you don't want to. You won't. The key to that statement is, "if you don't want to." If you love open houses, then by all means, do them. For me, I hated sitting open houses and the truth is that most agents do, too, so why would I waste a Sunday doing something I absolutely loathed? Answer: because some manager told me that's how it had to be if I wanted to make it. Not true!

With **the Edge**, you'll have the freedom to do what YOU like to do. The key to this program is you. By developing your unique strengths, discovering your passions, and learning how to follow your own heart and gut, you will be well on your way to selling lots of houses – as well as greatness in all areas of your life. Buckle in, it's about to get good!

Many agents bomb out of this business in the first 12 months. Why? Because they get overwhelmed with things that are not important in their first year. They end up NOT making any money and *boom* another one bites the dust, exist stage left, adios, back to your day job. Traditional training techniques that were developed 20, 10, and even 5 years ago have gotten old. **The *Edge*** *will withstand the test of time because it is based on principles that have stood the test of time.*

Part I introduces the four Cornerstones, which are Gratitude, Service, Humility, and Forgiveness. The Four Cornerstones will help you develop the solid foundation and state of mind essential for long-term success. Part II unleashes the 6 STEPS of **Selling on the Edge** which form the core of the entire program:

One – Be Yourself

Two – Get Out There

Three – DIS-Qualify

Four – Focus

Five – Own It

Six – Have Fun

Unlike flashy sales tricks and short-term motivational seminars, the principles and steps of Part I and Part II will ensure your success right out of the gate and foster a wonderful life and selling career. Hang tight, we are getting there, but first I need you to understand the big picture. And the big picture is that **the Edge** is more like a state of mind than any one technique or series of scripts.

"But don't I need a script?" No. Buyers and sellers know these old-school scripts and flashy sales tricks better than most agents. With **the Edge**, there are no scripts. Have you ever had someone call you on the phone or met a salesperson and you knew they were just reciting some script? Of course you have, we all have. Buyers and sellers can spot this a mile away and it immediately makes them uncomfortable.

Your new journey is NOT about learning fancy scripts or building fancy websites, buying fancy signs, putting your face on a bus bench, memorizing contracts inside and out, or flashy "Always Be Closing" sales moves. Some of these things may be useful later in your career. In the beginning, they're all pointless until you learn and master the fundamentals. When we are new in real estate, we are in our "formative" years. If you learn what really matters early on and build the right foundation, establish the right mindset, and learn the right system, you'll have a much better chance of success, long-term. So what really matters, you ask? You are about to find out.

TWO PROMISES

One of the reasons I created **Selling on the Edge** was that I felt the real estate training programs on the market today were difficult to understand. Another reason was that many selling programs made completely unrealistic claims about the results you would get. For example, "Make a million dollars" or "Generate hundreds of leads per month with this program." Since we all want instant results, new agents get sucked in and invest, but it never pays off.

I wanted to deliver a program that was honest, achievable and totally realistic in terms of what you could expect. I feel that if you follow the steps of this program and stick to the fundamentals, you will be well on your way to $100,000 in your first twelve months. I hope you shatter this number, but I wanted to be realistic. This is do-able, real, and not out of the reach of a new real estate agent. So I came up with what I call the EDGE 100K GUARANTEE.

THE EDGE 100K GUARANTEE

If, after reading this book, studying this program, and using it, you don't make at least $100,000 in the next twelve months, you can send it back and get a full refund. Yes, that is correct, you have twelve months to use it or send it back. No questions asked. (ebook, kindle and auto downloads due not apply). I am offering you this guarantee for twelve months from the date of purchase. You have one year to use these products and learn this program. At the end of your twelve months, if you have not made at least

$100,000 – or you have, but you're still disappointed with the program – then you have my word and a guarantee here in writing that I will return your investment. No. Questions. Asked. (*Does not apply to eBooks, Kindle, or auto downloads.*)

My second promise to you is that your life is going to change. Your life in all areas will change by leaps and bounds in the next year if you keep an open mind to these concepts and start practicing this program. $100,000 is my hook and guarantee, but you are in for a surprise, my friend. If you follow the six steps on this path and use the cornerstones as your lighthouse when things get rocky or you lose your way, I guarantee your life is going to change for the better in all areas. My goal is that one year from now, you will be well beyond anywhere you could have possibly imagined. This is promise number two.

Yes, you will have more money. However, along with financial success, your life will get better in all areas. You'll feel better, look better, smile more, and laugh more, all because you are finally bringing out the real YOU in you. The goal of this program is to help bring out the authentic you and always put THAT person smack dab in front of clients – as opposed to some phony, salesy, slick, flashy salesperson. When you are real, authentic, not perfect, and can just be yourself, you will be amazed at how many people want to work with you. Simply because they now trust you. You are not trying to be someone you are not. **The Edge** will teach you how to be you. The authentic, real, raw and honest you.

No one can do you better than you. This integrity and refreshing twist on selling will attract serious Buyers and Sellers to you, as opposed to your having to chase them down the way traditional training teaches. Your unique differences and unique self will ultimately brand you and set you apart.

Edge Rule: No one can do YOU better than you.

HOW IS **THE EDGE** DIFFERENT?

So how and why is this system different and better than anything else out there today? Three reasons:

1. It teaches how to become an expert at finding real clients faster than any other system out there.

2. It is the only selling system where you will never, ever be accused of sounding, acting, or looking like a "salesperson." This means more people will want to work with you.
3. No real estate or previous sales experience is required to understand and master this program. Anyone can understand this program. Anyone.

The Edge will teach you how to get to the winners faster! That means finding "real" clients faster. A "real" client is someone who is going to buy or sell in the next ninety days, with or without you. They are ready to make a move. If a real Buyer sees the right thing, they are going to buy it now. A real Seller is not only going to put their home on the market any minute now, they are going to list it at a realistic price. **The Edge** will teach you how to find and identify these people and get to them faster than other agents. Think of an Easter egg hunt if you knew where all the eggs were!

How does it work? For starters, you'll find the winners quicker by spending less time with the losers. Now don't take this the wrong way, I don't think anyone is a loser, and people who are never going to buy or sell are not literally losers, but is you get stuck wasting time with them, you will lose any chance you have at making a living selling houses. You, my friend, will be the one losing. The biggest reason people fail in real estate is that they spend all their time with people who are never, ever going to buy or sell.

The Edge will teach you how to quickly assess who is real and who is not. **The Edge** will help you quickly identify these "Linda Lookie-Lous" and "Kenny No-Doughs" and DIS-QUALIFY them so you can get to the real deals – the ones I call the winners! You will have a system to do this. The system is called **Sales Triage™**.

New agents are prime targets for the following characters: "Linda Lookie-Lou," "Timmy Time-Waster," "Kenny No-Dough," "Johnny Low-Baller," and my favorite, "Billy Bullshitter." These time-wasters are not bad people, but they will do one thing indeed: they will suck you dry if you get stuck with them. While you are parading them all over town, catering to their every need and thinking that someday they are going to buy or sell, the real clients are passing you by and someone else is snatching them up. These time-wasters prey on new agents because traditional selling systems have made it possible. These characters have learned they can get free information, see lots of houses, and waste as much of an agent's time as they like. Why? *Because so many agents simply put up with it, especially the inexperienced newbies.* YOU WILL NOT!

These losers have learned that inexperienced realtors will work for free and have figured out how they can take advantage of this. So people who really have no intention of ever buying or selling will waste the time, the effort, the energy and even the money of the new agent, just because they can. Why do these time-wasters do this? The short answer is, who knows? But the real reason is that, deep down, everyone in the world would love to own a house, but the reality is that ninety percent cannot. However, this does not prevent from dreaming and waking up one day saying, "Hey honey, let's go look at houses today." They call Johnny New Guy Realtor and run him all over town and Johnny New Guy Realtor things that someday this person is going to buy. But they never do, and after four months of New Guy Realtor's wasting every weekend showing these bogus buyers half of southern California, the bogus buyers finally say they've changed their minds. New Guy Realtor is crushed and another one bites the dust.

Not you, my friend. You will be ready. You will have **The Edge**. You see, in real estate the person who knows the most is not the one who makes the most money; it's the one who can get good at finding real clients and quickly eliminating the time-wasters. Not with the use of any fancy script or technique but through learning to follow your heart and gut.

And learning to follow your heart and gut and saying whatever you feel is a lot easier to do than memorizing a script. The fact is, scripts are hard to use, and if you're trying to follow a script and remember what to say next, you are not listening to your client. You're in your own head and the client will sense this. Not good. Clients don't use scripts, so what if they say something you are not prepared for? Do you have a script for that? With **the Edge** you will. It's called the TRUTH!

Edge Rule: The only script we use is the truth.

I was starting out in real estate and my sales manager sent me to a training program. What they gave me was a three-inch-thick binder of over 150 different scripts. One for this, one for that, one for this objection, one for that objection, how to greet the customer, how to close, to show, to stand, what to say if they said hello, goodbye; what to say if they said they didn't like the house, if they didn't like the yard, and on and on. I sat up night after night trying to learn these scripts, and guess how much money that made me? Donut hole. Using these scripts, I came off as fake. Buyers and Sellers saw right through it.

My manager said, "Don't worry, just master those scripts and it will get better." That is exactly what I tried to do. More months went by, I finally had every script memorized, and one day I was in a big listing appointment and the Seller asked me about pricing the property. I paused for a minute, remembered the "pricing a property" script and started to talk. This is what came out of my mouth . . .

Well, Mr. Seller, have you ever been to an auction? You see, people bid on houses like at an auction and on eBay and if you price it right, you will find that everyone will want your house, but there is no auctioneer and sometimes you can bid it over and get more money; however, eBay will, I mean, well, not the auctioneer, umm, wait, or was it eBay? Ah, um, OK, you should just – wait, sorry, where was I? I mean, what exactly was the question?

I was so busy trying to recite the script that I completely forgot what he even asked me and, needless to say, I didn't get the sale. Complete disaster. I decided: no more scripts for me. A few months later, though, we had another training program offered and I was jazzed because this technique didn't require long scripts. It was called "mirroring and matching." The gist of it is, you move and speak like the client. You *mirror* the client. This is supposedly going to make the client thing you're like him or her and this will help you get their business. *Oy vey.* Oh well, I thought, why not try it; the trainer said everyone else was doing it so it should work for me too, right? Wrong.

Here I was sitting in front of my potential new customer, all ready to use my terrific new mirroring and matching technique. I walked in, said hello, and sat directly across from this prospect. He leaned back in his chair, so I leaned back. He asked me about my background; I asked him about his background. So far, so good. It seemed to be working. The conversation was going well.

Then he reached up to put his hand on his chin like people do when they're thinking. I did the same thing. Bad move. He suddenly stopped talking, looked at me funny and said, "Are you mirroring me?" I kid you not. Busted! He went on to say, "Oh you *are*, and yes, I know all about the mirroring and matching technique; it's been around for years. It never works but it looks good on paper." And he politely kicked me out. WTF?!! I gave up. None of this stuff worked, and I was going broke in the process.

Scripts were not me. Mirroring and matching was not me. None of this stuff had anything to do with my sincerely wanting to help people. I could never do any of this stuff because it was me trying to be somebody else – and that is why I was failing.

SQUARE PEG IN A ROUND HOLE

Most sales systems and traditional training programs try putting square pegs in round holes. They try to force the real estate agent to be someone they are not and do things that they don't like doing. The result is disaster.

I have news for you. You cannot "sell" a house. If the person does not want it, there is nothing you can do to make them buy it. The old school training – the famous "A-B-C," Always Be Closing, is over. No one wants to be "closed" or "sold." You can't mirror your way into a sale or say the perfect scripted one-liner that is going to convince someone to buy or sell a house. **Selling on the Edge** is a refreshing, authentic new way to sell without ever looking, sounding, or acting like a "salesperson." There is no convincing or selling with **the Edge**.

So how can this possibly work if there are no scripts? "How will I know what to say or do?" You will learn to say exactly what you feel like saying and what you feel is the truth. For example, if you think a house your client is looking at is junk. With this program, you will have permission to tell them, "It's junk!" The result of truth and honesty as your only script is that your clients will learn to trust you, and THAT will give you your first edge. You will learn to follow your heart and your instinct and by really listening to these two magical gifts and acting on those instincts, you will sell more houses. By speaking the truth from your heart and gut, and saying what you feel, you will come off as authentic because you are *being* authentic. It is you being you and no one can do YOU better than you. Once you tap into this magical secret and embrace it, the sky's the limit!

After selling real estate for fifteen years now, my passion for teaching has surpassed my passion for selling. I've seen people with incredible talent crash out of this business in their first year or two, and it wasn't because they weren't good enough. It was because they didn't know what they needed to know.

This program is going to show you that YOUR way of doing things will be the best way, because no one can do you like you. And that edge combined with some basic signposts and a simple road map will get you to the Promised Land! **The Edge** will give you permission to be YOU and help you develop a selling style that works for you, because you are going to design it. **The Edge** will empower you, it will help you make more money, it will change your life . . . but none of that will happen if you don't use it. Ever heard the phrase, "use it or lose it"?

THE KEYS TO THE KINGDOM

If you finish this book, yet never end up *using* any of the steps that it outlines, then I have failed you. The keys to the kingdom are worthless if you can't find the kingdom. In other words, if you have the keys to the kingdom, but refuse to put them in the door and turn the knob, you will never get in. Right?

Question: *Why would someone who held the keys to the kingdom (and everything they ever wanted in life) go through their entire life without ever turning those keys in the doorknob?*

Answer: *They couldn't find the door, or something was blocking them from getting to it.*

The *Four Cornerstones* will not only get you to the door; they will eliminate any roadblocks that are preventing you from getting there. The *Four Cornerstones* will set you on the right path to success and keep you on it like a lighthouse or compass. In your first few years, you can expect to face challenges and adversity, and there may be days when you will want to quit. However, by building a solid foundation, you will be OK even when the heavy winds start blowing.

Real estate markets go up and they go down. Every time it gets good, new agents come pouring in, thinking it's easy money. These are the first to disappear when the market goes bad. Why? They have no foundation and no system. They have no idea what to do when the market goes bad. They didn't invest the time in learning a system that works for them. It's like this: fishing is easy when the fish are jumping in the boat, but what about when they aren't? Learning how to fish is probably a good idea if it's something you want to do long-term.

Having a foundation is what will ensure your longevity. You will have a foundation made of brick, not sticks or straw. Remember the story of the big bad wolf? Even when adversity comes, and someone tries to huff and puff and bloooooow your house down, the *Four Cornerstones* will ensure that you stand tall and have a solid foundation to weather the storm.

The Six Steps of **Selling on the Edge** are the keys to your kingdom and the *Four Cornerstones* provide both the foundation and a road map to get you there. With the right road map AND the right set of keys, the kingdom is yours for the taking.

PART II

(The Foundation)

The Four Cornerstones

CHAPTER 4

LIVING IN A GARAGE

I was sitting in my apartment, having just passed the State Real Estate Exam. I didn't know where I was going to work or in what company I would hang my license. All I cared about was those big commissions I'd heard about. I wanted to sell million-dollar houses and figured I'd be living in my Malibu Beach home in two years. Boy, did I have another think coming. I didn't make a penny for almost three years in the business because I was concerned about one thing. ME. I was selfish, self-centered, cocky, and thought I knew it all. Not a winning combination.

Let me share a little bit about my background and what led me to the day I decided to get my license. I really thought I did know it all. I mean, come on, I was almost 30 and living in a garage. Top of the world. A few years earlier, I went to college, graduated *magna cum laude*, landed a cushy job selling phone hardware for AT&T and things were rolling. As you can see, I was King of the World. I mean, hey, I did manage to get fired from AT&T because I wasn't showing up for the mandatory meetings, but why would I? Oh well, their loss. Who wanted to work at a big Snore City corporate job anyway? Certainly not me. Fired from first job out of college. Way to go, Mark.

Then I went to work at an audio/video retail store because why not? I mean, here I was, *magna cum laude* college grad big shot, working retail pimpin' stereos. After that I hit the big time, got snatched up by a CD wallet-manufacturing company, only to finish off my post-college run working at a Circuit City in Westwood, California. Twenty-eight years old, living in a friend's garage because I couldn't afford my own apartment. What in the heck went wrong? I was destined for greatness, but five years out of college I was borderline homeless, feeling like a soon-to-be-thirty-year-old loser.

One night close to bedtime, everyone was asleep in the main house, so I used my cell phone to order a pizza to my wonderful garage suite. I gobbled half, shut the garage door, lights out, and went to bed on my mattress on the floor, leaving half the pizza sitting out on the cardboard box on the edge of my bed. I was exhausted.

About 3:00 a.m. I woke up all of a sudden, hearing scratching at the door. Ricky Raccoon came through one of the cracks in the door, stared at me point blank, and hustled across the garage and onto my mattress. He wanted that pizza! I jumped up, still half-asleep, and freaked out, about three feet away from a raccoon on my bed. I proceeded to fend off the freaky little fella with a hockey stick in one hand while trying to open the garage door with the other. Finally, he scattered off. I sat down on my floor mattress, looked out the now-opened garage door at the stars, grabbed myself a slice of cold pizza, and pondered my bleak future. Then it hit me . . .

YOU SHOULD GET YOUR REAL ESTATE LICENSE

When I was working in Minnesota at the audio/video retail store, I was lucky to cross paths with an amazing man named Barry, who was a top real estate agent in Minneapolis and one of the top Coldwell Banker agents in the world. One day while I was working at Audio King, Barry came in and I helped him choose a stereo system for his kids. When the purchase was all said and done, he handed me his card and said, "Mark, have you ever considered getting your real estate license? You should, you'd be great." I didn't think much of it at the time, though I admired Barry and knew he knew things I certainly didn't.

Almost seven years later, triggered by my Ricky Raccoon encounter, Barry's suggestion that I get my license echoed in my head . . . and that was that. I would do it. I figured I was more than qualified to make it big selling houses, wasn't I? How different could selling houses be from selling stereos? Just a bigger item. No big deal, right? Wrong!

I was expressing READY, FIRE, AIM mentality. I assumed that I would jump right in – and I knew it all, so I'd be up and running in no time. Just sell one house and I'd be back on my feet! I could easily sell houses; why hadn't I listened to Barry's advice years ago? I was going to kick some ass.

If you are a guy – and even if you're not – you know that from about eighteen to the early thirties, we can really be cocky. We can really think we are quite the sh*t. Bulletproof. Oh-boy, my ego, my lack of humility, my sense of entitlement, my long history of stubbornness and my soon-to-be negative attitude would be some of the many reasons that I got massacred and almost didn't make it in this business. Where did it all go wrong? Three years after getting my real estate license, I still hadn't sold a thing. I was a joke. I couldn't close a door. The only redeeming development was that I had managed to get out of the garage and into a small studio apartment. I was now almost thirty and couldn't believe I wasn't married with kids and a mortgage like normal, successful people.

Oh well, God had other plans for me. And maybe, just maybe, He does for you, too.

Faith without works is dead.

-James 2:26, Bible

The Cornerstones are values and principles that I failed to incorporate into my daily life and grasp their importance until much later in my career. I knew of these values, but I was not practicing them in my life or work. It's not enough to know what they are. That's like a thief saying to the judge, "Yes, Your Honor, I know what honesty means, so don't sentence me." After looking hard in the mirror, I realized I simply was not living them. I felt like a fraud. Just knowing what Gratitude, Service, Humility, and Forgiveness *mean* does you no good if you're not *practicing* these principles in your life.

Thankfully, after enough failures, humility began creeping into my life and I manned up. I was realizing that my monumental failure was nobody's fault but mine. It wasn't the market, the clients, the other agents, the business, the trailing, the location, the coaches, the traffic, or the big city. It was one thing that was screwing it all up. It was me! I realized maybe I could salvage my dream of selling houses if I started taking responsibility for everything. And I mean *everything*. Living in a garage at almost thirty years of age fending off raccoons was one of many wake-up calls and turning points where I would start to grasp what the missing links were and why I was failing. Yes, they were dark days, but what I didn't know at the time was that God had bigger plans for me. The experiences of these dark times started formulating the lessons that became the foundation and core principles of **The Edge**. It was time to get to work. It was time to execute.

THE ABILITY TO EXECUTE

The earth beneath the Rocky Mountains must be pretty solid to hold the mountains up. That is what the Four Cornerstones are to **The Edge** Selling System. The Four Cornerstones will make or break you in this business because they will make or break your ability to *execute* the Six Steps of **Selling on the Edge**. If you have all these wonderful tools that can change your life, but you don't use (execute) them, then what good are they? Many of us don't know what keeps us from greatness, but the Cornerstones will eliminate the roadblocks – which is what I call limiting beliefs. If you can understand the Four Cornerstones and make them a part of who you are, then executing the Six Steps of **The Edge** is a no-brainer.

With no limiting beliefs, no roadblocks, wouldn't you agree that it would be a lot easier to execute? What if Tiger Woods felt, deep down, that African-American/Thai people were not good at golf? What if Steven Nash felt he was too short to play in the NBA? What if Kelly Clarkson thought her voice wasn't that good? What if Tom Brady had listened to his college coach, who said he was never going to be more than a second-string quarterback?

I don't know anyone who has never had a moment of self-doubt, but these people's greatness and all success stories show that they overcame limiting beliefs. You are going to learn to identify your own limiting beliefs and get them out of your head for good, so you, too, can do things that you never thought possible! But first it's time for a reality check.

NO ONE CARES

OK, so I know you just got your license and you are feeling on top of the world, but guess what. No one cares. They will someday, but right now, they don't. You are new. You are now just another of over 400,000 yahoos who decided this year they wanted to sell houses, so they ran out and got their license. Whoop. Dee. Doo. This is how potential new customers see you.

As for your friends and family, stay away from them in your early years. It's not worth it. You'll ruin relationships if you push it. First, you have to prove to them that you are in this for the long haul before you even think about working with them. Eventually they will come to you when they see you kicking ass a year or two from now.

Edge Rule: Your first year in real estate, don't even attempt to work with friends and family.

I know what you're thinking. You're thinking, "So if other people will think I'm new and inexperienced and not work with me, and my own family and friends are off limits my first year, how will I possibly get clients?"

You are going to get them from what I call "passion arenas."

A passion arena is a hobby or event you love to be at on a regular basis – that will generate an abundance of real buyers and sellers. For example, for me, one of my passion arenas was my Ice Hockey League. We'll get into this in Part II. For now, it's all about the Four Cornerstones. Got it? Don't be jumping ahead!

With the Four Cornerstones of **Selling on the Edge**, you're going to learn the power of Gratitude, Service, Humility, and Forgiveness in your new venture. In fifteen years, I have yet to come across any other selling program that incorporates these principles. You may not understand now what this has to do with selling houses, but you will soon see that they are essential for starting your career off correctly and going on to long-term success. The Four Cornerstones will lead you down the right path so that you're always doing the right thing and focusing on the right thing.

If you want to rock it big time selling houses, you have to learn to focus on one main thing: other people. Other people. You and your world? No one cares. None of your clients are going to care about you and your needs. Can you handle that in the beginning? Do you need to be the center of attention? If so, you need to quit now.

For some reason, new agents get started and think their job is to become everyone's "buddy" and be friends with all their clients. Not anymore. That's old school training. You don't need to be liked by anyone to make it big in this business, but you need to be respected. That is **The Edge**, my friends. Many, probably most, of your clients WILL like you, I am sure. My point is that having a foundation based on solid principles and sticking to a well-designed system, you will earn the respect of your clients; and, yes, even your friends and family.

The Edge is a state of mind.

IT IS ABOUT BEING OF SERVICE

You, my friends, are going to have a foundation. On top of that, you'll have a selling system. And you're going to learn what matters most to make it big selling houses. And the first thing is: it is no longer about you.

So what is it about? It's about being of service. Service combined with Gratitude, Humility, and Forgiveness will give you magical powers in your new chosen field. However, young grasshopper, the Four Cornerstones are not easy to master and will take time and effort.

THE DOCTOR IS IN

In order to get you in the right frame of mind, I want you to do some exercises in imagination. If you recall from the beginning, I don't want you to refer to yourself as a real estate agent or realtor, because everyone does that. You are going to be specific by telling people you *sell houses*. Ring a bell? For this exercise in imagination, I don't want you to look at yourself as a real estate agent. You are now a PhD in selling houses. It is now YOU, M.D. You are now a doctor and your job is to save lives. That is how I want you to look at your real estate career from now on. I know it may be a little unorthodox at this moment, but you bought this book to learn how to win big and make it long-term selling houses. Part of humility (a Cornerstone) is being coachable, so just try it, as we move forward. The doctor is in! Look at potential clients as patients needing your service. You are not selling them anything at this point.

What does a doctor do when a patient comes in? First thing out of the doctor's mouth is what? "What seems to be the problem?" or "Where does it hurt?" or "What brings you in?" A doctor never sells, get it? (Except plastic surgeons.) Neither will you. A key difference with **Selling on the Edge** is that there is no convincing or putting the hard sell on or talking people into things they don't want. Getting fun, isn't it? Congratulations, you are now a doctor.

New agents get started and think they have to start "selling" homes. They meet someone who claims to have a house to sell and the realtor immediately shifts into salesman gear, which sounds like, "Blah blah blah, I'm a realtor, I work for this great company, and I passed my test on the first try." What if the first thing out of your doctor's mouth was, "My office is the Number One office in my specialty, and look at my degree, and here is my SL500 that shows how much money I make." You would probably think that doctor was a freak and you'd want to get out of there. Well, that is what potential Buyers and Sellers will think of you if you start "selling" them.

If you put the doctor in your shoes, it may sound something like this: "Why do you want to sell the house?" or "What seems to be the problem with your house?" Getting this? OK. This mindset will be helpful up ahead where you will learn **Sales Triage™**, in which you will come up with your own unique way of saying things. If you can just look at the situation as a doctor/patient setting, as opposed to your having to sell someone, magical things will start to happen. By "magical," I mean like as if you couldn't fail.

CHAPTER 5

IF YOU COULD NOT FAIL

(SELLING ON THE EDGE VISUAL)

THE 6 STEPS:

1. BE YOURSELF
2. GET OUT THERE
3. DIS-QUALIFY
4. FOCUS
5. OWN IT
6. HAVE FUN

FOUNDATION: FOUR CORNERSTONES:

GRATITUDE, SERVICE, HUMILITY, FORGIVENESS*

As you can see, anchored at the bottom are our Four Cornerstones. Without a proper foundation, mindset, and belief system (CORNERSTONES), the Six Steps will be worthless. Without a proper foundation, you will not be able to execute the Six Steps or use them to their fullest. It's like a body without air, water, food, and sleep. Even Michael Phelps would have a hard time with that one.

For example, there will be times in real estate when you make mistakes and it will take humility (CORNERSTONE) to admit you are wrong. If you do not understand humility and can't admit you are wrong, this will jeopardize your success. Maybe not right away, but eventually the foundation will crumble. Your behavior will catch up to you. Real estate is a small world and word travels fast on who's who. So I want you to get used to taking the high road right away and doing the right thing straight out of the gate! The CORNERSTONES will give you the strength, the courage, and the proper mindset to operate from the right place. The CORNERSTONES will put your ego in check and you'll intuitively know what to do if you have Gratitude, Service, Humility, and Forgiveness as your core beliefs and values. Using these CORNERSTONES may initially be a blow to your ego, but having them as your foundation will give you **The Edge**. The result will be more money and a more fulfilling life.

What does forgiveness have to do with selling houses, you ask? In real estate you will work with many people and at times you may feel someone has wronged you. It will be natural to be upset. If you hang onto that feeling and let it fester inside you, I promise you, the resentment will eat you up and you will not be able to perform at your highest and best level. This will jeopardize your success. Mastering the art of forgiveness will free you of resentment and allow you to soar to the highest level – and that is what I want for you.

As we continue, you will begin to see that the CORNERSTONES are a belief and value system that will keep you running on a high level. If you can always keep the CORNERSTONES in the back of your mind, understand their importance, and incorporate them into your core self, you will not only have an edge in selling; you will have an edge in life. The CORNERSTONES will give you guidance when you are lost and they will give you courage when you feel you have none.

If I asked you the following question:

"What would you do right now if you knew you could not fail?"

What would you say?

You see, the belief that you cannot fail is your foundation and your mindset. The mindset that you cannot fail stems from being of service, with the thought and belief that you can never fail because your main purpose is to help others. Without that mindset, you might be afraid to take action. Afraid to jump, so to speak.

The CORNERSTONES will free you up not only to jump but to move, speak, dance, sing, and sell like a rock star! The CORNERSTONES will give you the UN-limiting beliefs you will need to sell on **The Edge**. It is essential that we start with the foundation and get you in the right frame of mind. Make sense now, amigo? Good! Are you starting to feel it? It's getting juicy. If we get your head on straight by building the right mindset and value system, the rest is cake.

TIGER

I know Tiger Woods has had his share of ups and downs, and people love him or hate him. However, his mindset is simply this: "I will win. Every time." He essentially has NO limiting beliefs. Did some of his cornerstones crumble in his personal life? Yes, but if you recall, he used HUMILITY to win over the world again by not only admitting that what he did was wrong, but asking for help. WOW! And he did it on national TV! As much as he screwed up, his humility has saved him from being completely wiped out. I could show you in the first edition of this book where, years ago, I predicted he would make his way back to his winning form. With that winning mindset, I knew he would do it. I was sure he would go to the top again. And guess what? (Original book written 2013 claiming he would be back and now in version 2 here and just Moments ago, as I write these amazing words, Tiger Woods, after an 11-year drought, has just won the 2019 Masters!)

I used to study the openings of golf tournaments with Tiger when he was walking onto the first tee box and I would watch the other players. Tiger's physical walk alone would wipe out 90 percent of the competition. He would almost have it won before the competition even began. How did he do this? I would argue it's because his CORNERSTONES were in place and solid. This allowed him to be happy and loose and totally himself, and no one could stop him. It was never a question of IF he would win; his mindset was, "By how many strokes?"

Tiger spends an equal amount of time on training and developing his mindset, and you will, too. Don't disregard the CORNERSTONES. Without them, you will be missing a critical part of the program and suffer the consequences until you commit to learning them. I know, because when I started, my mindset was a disaster.

BRAINBAGGAGE BE GONE

I got into real estate because I wanted to make more money and my focus was one thing, "What's in it for me?" Not a good foundation. I was taught that other agents are my competition and if someone else wins, I lose. Also not good. I was taught that Buyers are liars and Sellers are criers. Definitely not good. I had loads and loads of limiting beliefs, mainly from my own issues and my own limiting thoughts. Even with the best-selling techniques or training, I wouldn't be able to execute, because in the back of my mind were tons of limiting beliefs. Or BRAINBAGGAGE, as I call it.

Mastery of the FOUR CORNERSTONES will wash away the BRAINBAGGAGE. You will have a clean slate to start fresh and from the right place. Eliminating Brainbaggage will allow you to soar and flight high. We are all as worthy and deserving of success just as much as the next guy. So why not you?

WHY NOT YOU?

I want you to walk into the nearest bathroom, find a mirror, take a deep, hard look into your own eyes, and ask yourself this question: "Why not me?" Do it again! Look into the mirror at yourself and say, "Why not me??!!" Maybe even pump your fist or jump up and down. Get pumped up!

You deserve good things just like everyone else, so why not you? You deserve a nice car, an amazing sexy significant other, a sexy body, a million dollars, and a fantastic two million dollar listing or tons of success and happiness or whatever you want! I say it all the time. "WHY NOT ME?"

This definitely keeps Brainbaggage in check. Keep your Brainbaggage under control or your limiting beliefs will invade you like a cancer. In all my years, this is the simplest technique I have ever learned to keep me thinking right. Be aware of your thoughts and if it's Brainbaggage, then recognize that and eliminate it by asking yourself, "Why not me?"

It's probably just me and you are probably not like this at all, but for me, I never felt like I deserved the good life. I saw it going on out there. Saw lots of success in Minnesota, in L.A., with many friends, with others in the news; but, for some strange reason, I always felt less than. Not really worthy. I grew up with humble parents and a middle class, hardworking family that was very happy. They never told me I didn't deserve the best, but when you grow up in a certain environment, you are accustomed to that environment.

Look at people who grow up in the projects and feel they are stuck there for life. That's my point. They are not. Yes, sometimes it takes a miracle, and some are more fortunate than others. I will not disagree with you on that, but the first step in changing your life is the thought that you are just as worthy and do deserve everything you want in life and you are just as entitled as the next guy. So when self-doubt or self-sabotage or all that famous Brainbaggage starts to creep in, hit the pause button on your brainwaves and ask yourself, "WHY NOT ME?" With a fist pump and an F-bomb in there or spice it up however you want? Say it! "Why the F not me?!" Why not you, my friend? Why not you?

To make it big in real estate, you will need to eliminate any and all of your limiting beliefs. Brainbaggage be gone! I don't know what your limiting beliefs or your Brainbaggage may be at this point. You probably don't either. As we move forward, your Brainbaggage will start to surface, but don't get discouraged. Be grateful. Why? Because you are now becoming AWARE of it. In order to eliminate it, we first must identify it.

I have learned that when stress, worry, and fear surface in my life, this is a sign that I'm having limiting beliefs. It's how I know to check my mindset before I go any further. Other symptoms include getting nervous, anxious, or impatient. All are signs that I'm not staying true to the FOUR CORNERSTONES. So I pause and ask myself what I may be doing or not doing to cause this stress. You see, as we go on in **The Edge**, you will learn all about taking responsibility for EVERYTHING in your life. When something is off, it's up to me to fix it. The CORNERSTONES keep me grounded, keep me on the *right* track, which I like to call "The High Road."

"Always take the high road. If you take the high road and lose, you still win." -Lois Williams (My Mom)

You will be tempted to take *many* roads in real estate: the high road, the low road, the side road, the easier road, the other road, the shady road, the immoral road, the left road, the right road, but if you use Gratitude, Service, Humility, and Forgiveness as your road map, your compass, and your lighthouse, you will always end up on the high road. In life and in real estate that is called doing the right thing: taking the high road. I credit my Mom for that one and I never leave home without it!

REPETITION, REPETITION, REPETITION

The way I had that word – and that concept -- imprinted on my brain, it sounded like French: répétition. *Reh-peh-TEE-see-ohn.* Let me explain.

I had the privilege of attending the Royal Academy of Dramatic Art in London when I was in my twenties. I'll never forget the experience because it was there that I learned what it took to master something and become the best in your field. You see, the Royal Academy of Dramatic Art wasn't just your ordinary acting school. It was one hundred percent dedicated to Shakespeare. William Shakespeare. The Brits figured that if you could do Shakespeare as an actor, you could do anything. And let me tell you, they were right!

RADA, as it was called, was one of the top acting schools in the world and don't ask me how, but I managed to get in and study there for a period. The biggest lesson I took from my time there was from an amazing teacher named Peter Oyston. There were dozens of great teachers at RADA, but Peter taught me my greatest lesson that I still use to this day. He was an Australian who spoke with almost a French accent. His biggest lesson that he stressed over and over was that if you wish to master anything, you have to practice over and over and over and over. And once you think you have it perfect, then do it again, and again, and again. He would yell at me in his highly unusual Australian-French accent as he rolled his Rs and had that soft C-sound at the end, "Répétition repetition répétition!" It would come out RRRReh peh TEE see-ohn! RRRReh peh TEE see-ohn! RRRReh peh TEE see-ohn! Try it. Say it a few times, FAST! FASTER! It's fun.

He directed our group and we went on to give one of the best performances of RICHARD III that the school had ever staged. And I played RICHARD! I got the part because I practiced over and over and over, repeat, repeat, repeat, and eventually I could do it in my sleep.

The Edge is designed to be run over and over and over like athletes practice over and over and over. At times you will crash and burn; you will fail miserably and, like me in the early years, you'll want to quit. Maybe on a weekly basis. It can be a hard, lonely business but I am going to help you make it. You will know things that most realtors don't know until ten years into the business. I promise you, if you keep working on your foundation, using your CORNERSTONES to reset your mind and put you in the right place, then you will eventually break through. "RRRReh peh TEE see-ohn! RRRReh peh TEE see-ohn! RRRReh peh TEE see-ohn!"

Selling on the Edge will help you master the art of being yourself in the work field. There may be days when you will crash and burn, but you'll learn from these moments because **The Edge** has a built-in regenerating system. The CORNERSTONES are a filter system to flush out any toxins or limiting beliefs that sneak back into your mind. It can happen. I've been doing this for fifteen years and at times, even now, I lose my way, inch toward losing my focus on what is important. Sometimes I find myself worrying more about a commission check than being of service and, yeah, the wheels come off the bus!

But because I'm aware of the CORNERSTONES, I can go back and learn from my mistakes. Even Tiger Woods shanks a few into the lake every once in a while, so don't beat yourself up when you have a bad day. Keep your CORNERSTONES solid, healthy and underpinning your actions and I promise you, you'll do things and achieve things that you never thought possible.

WHERE SHOULD I HANG MY LICENSE?

When I first got started, my training was about stuff that didn't help me sell houses. It was like the Ambien of Real Estate Training. I passed out the second the trainers began. I was firehosed with licensing issues, legalities, square footage facts, procedures, policies, requirements, regulations, listing laws, insurance codes, REOs and OMG what were all these things?? None of it mattered if I didn't have a client. You could end up going to real estate school for the rest of your life, learn all the real estate contracts and laws and details, but in your first year, it just doesn't matter. All that matters is learning how to develop authentic relationships and then finding real clients fast. That is it. No one was teaching that. I knew I had to get out or die.

A great real estate company will teach you how to fish. They won't feed you fish, they will actually teach you HOW to fish. Find a company that will teach you how to fish and that's a winner winner salmon dinner!

Beware of any company that claims they are going to "feed" you clients and leads. With the exception of two or three companies out there, most of these giant companies that claim they will feed you leads never come through. They are really only concerned with two things: (1) their top agents, and (2) their new people not getting sued. If you're new and you're at one of these companies, you will know it because you are NOT selling anything! Abort, my friends. Abort. Before you waste any more valuable time.

Edge Rule: Time kills deals.

If you are already at a firm, hanging your license there and it is not going well or you are not giddy with joy and money, you have to make a move now! Why? You don't have time to waste. This is not a sabbatical or a place to make friends, you're here to make cash and if you are not happy and it's not working, then get out! Make a move. Don't wait for it to get good. If it doesn't feel good, it isn't going to get good. The faster you can learn to follow your initial instinct and act on your gut feelings, the faster you will start making money. A great real estate lesson that you must tattoo on your soul is that time kills deals.

Time not only kills deals, time also kills agents. Waiting for things to get better and waiting for something to happen will fast-track you to Death Valley. Death Valley is always lurking around the corner to swallow up failed real estate agents. A rolling stone gathers no moss. Don't sit around and let time take your deals out or take you out. Just make any kind of decision, then turn and burn and get outta there! Once you land at the right company, you will know it. You will feel it in your heart, gut, body, soul, and bank account!

I have seen friends stay at certain companies for more than two years and not sell a thing. Why do they stay? Answer: Fear of making a wrong decision. So they make no decision. If you can't make decisions, your clients won't either. Remember the **Edge Rule**, "Like attracts like"? If you are indecisive, you will attract indecisive clients. If you are clear, confident, and know what you want and what you don't want, you'll attract similar clientele.

Before you agree to give a giant percentage to a broker, before you go to work at that office, ask them one specific question: Why am I paying you? The only advice I have is never to give up more than 25% of your commission, your first year, to anyone.

Edge Rule: You don't get what you're worth, you get what you negotiate.

If you're going to give more, then you make darn sure they explain EXACTLY what you will be getting for that additional commission you are giving up. I love many of the companies out there, I really do. Some are amazing. Many have incredible training programs, especially Keller Williams, Coldwell Banker, and many local boutique companies in the smaller neighborhoods. However, if you are going to give a percentage to a broker, you have to make sure that you're going to get something in return. Need I add that a cubicle doesn't warrant half your commission? And if any manager tells you that "our name will help you get business," you should get up and walk out immediately. Going to a particular company because you think their big "name" will benefit you is not a reason to go to an office. People will use you because they like you. They don't hire people just because they are at some huge firm. This, however, is what they will tell you. Just beware. Again, the question you ask your broker is:

"What exactly are you going to do for me if I am going to give you a giant portion of my commission?"

If their answer is anything other than "teach you to find real Buyers and Sellers" (teach you HOW to fish), then they gave you the wrong answer. Reasons to go to an office include: you like the manager, you like the team leader, you like the "vibe," your gut says it's a good fit – and, most important, they are crystal clear about what they are going to do for you.

FINDING REAL BUYERS AND SELLERS

There are great trainers out there and great programs for selling. There are also great companies that I fully support as places to start. However, when it comes to real estate training, apart from a few exceptional companies, the industry as a whole needs a makeover. They need to catch up with Buyers and Sellers – who are more savvy than you think. It's important to never underestimate any Buyer or Seller and what they may know. Old school training teaches silly things like "Buyers are liars and Sellers are Criers." Not true. That is a limiting belief. It illustrates my point, that you have to protect yourself from what other agents and brokers may try to pass on to you. If it's not working for you, you have to question it. If not, then keep moving until you find something that works for you. Like **Selling on the Edge**.

When I was failing miserably, I got mad, I got pissed, I got restless. Why not follow my heart and my gut instead of what others were telling me to do? My thought was, I had about ninety days before I'd have to get a job, so why not go out in style? Trying things my way.

This is what I want YOU to think and act as we move forward. You make great decisions, and only you know what really works for you. It's time to follow those instincts! This program will help you do that if you'll be patient and understand it's about building a foundation and then tackling the Six Steps.

You now know our simple game plan: Build our FOUNDATION and master the SIX STEPS.

We are not going to discuss contracts, or how to do a title search, or what the difference is between a short sale and an REO, or how to calculate your buyer's mortgage payment, or land lease laws or a cap rate on an eight-unit apartment building, or the differences between condos and townhomes, or what type of Errors and Omissions insurance is the best, or what your website, signs, business cards, or stationery should look like, because, guess what? Right now in your first year, NONE OF THAT MATTERS! Yes, that's what I just said: NONE OF THAT MATTERS.

Someday you can learn about that stuff, but it won't be from me. Why? Because none of that will help you make money in the beginning, if ever. So many agents think they have to be educated on every single thing before they do their first sale. I am here to tell you that is nonsense. Three things help you make sales: (1) Being yourself, (2) Getting out there, and (3) Learning how to find REAL Buyers and

Sellers. "REAL" means they are ready to make a move now, they need to make a move now, and they have the money and decision-making capability to pull the trigger NOW! How can you find this out? Just ask them. I told you this program was simple.

OVERVIEW OF THE FOUR CORNERSTONES:

GRATITUDE
SERVICE
HUMILITY
FORGIVENESS

Didn't we already cover these? *Répétition repetition répétition!* Remember? Let's look deeper into the CORNERSTONES…

CHAPTER 6

Cornerstone I
GRATITUDE

Gratitude is the seed of abundance.

Have you ever noticed that the people who are the most grateful are the ones who seem to have everything go their way? Whereas for the ones that are drama queens/kings, always bitching and moaning, things seem to only get worse?

Edge Rule: Like attracts like.

It's the law of attraction, it's birds of a feather, it's misery loves company, it's whatever you choose. Choose good, more is coming your way. Choose negative, look out because the shitstorm is a-comin'!

If you focus on the good stuff and feel grateful for what you have now, you're going to get more of the good stuff. It's just the laws of the universe. I didn't make this stuff up. Understanding this important **Edge** rule is critical to developing an attitude of gratitude. Like attracts like, so that means negative attracts negative. Look at your friends. Are most of them like you? You don't have to answer that yet.

I know you probably haven't sold a house yet, or you failed the state exam the first time and you're still trying, or maybe you are currently broke and don't have money to buy business cards. I get it. I was there. It's OK. Let's look at what you do have. You with me? Let's not focus on what we don't have or what we lack, and instead put our attention on what we DO have and what IS going well. Gift number uno: You are alive today. You get to be here right now. Some people don't. Some people left too soon. Maybe you have a sick relative or an ill parent. If so, I am very sorry for you and my heart goes out to you.

When I was new, no matter how bad things got, I would always remind myself that at least I have my health. So let's start there. Health is something to be grateful for every single day. So focus on that for a minute. Feeling good. Just breathe. Right now, take a breath.

Feel better? You should, because if you really want to break it down, each BREATH is a gift. I didn't always think this way. But it wasn't until I did that I started to soar in real estate. When I was grateful for the things I had, it gave me new energy – and that energy is what will attract others to you.

Gratitude does one main thing. It puts you in a positive light. People are drawn to the light. Gratitude is attractive. In order to attract customers into your life and work in real estate, you must be positive. We keep a positive attitude by focusing on the good things in our life. What you focus on expands, so if you look around in your life and realize how lucky you are and how many great things are in your life, the abundance and good stuff can't help but expand.

Maybe you're saying, "I understand all this, but what does this have to do with selling houses?" Everything! There will be days when things don't go your way selling houses, working with difficult clients, or struggling with the other agent, and you will be tempted to become negative. When you become negative, cynicism kicks in. Next thing you know, you're focusing on all the reasons you are failing, how much you hate real estate and why your life sucks. I want to remind you that your life does not suck and no matter how bad it gets, you will be able to find just one tiny thing to be grateful for and then focus on that. I was on my last leg when I came across a few cents in a jar that turned around my attitude and eventually my life.

I was a couple years in the business, hadn't sold a thing, and was sitting late one night with my friend Joe May in my apartment. Neither of us had any money. It was shortly after I had managed to make enough at my three part-time jobs to upgrade to a studio apartment. I had just moved in and never bothered to empty the boxes because I had no furniture to put anything in or on. Joe and I were sitting around digging through the boxes and I found this jar with change in it. I counted it out: about eleven dollars and seventy-eight cents. Joe asked, "What's in the jar?" I said, "About twelve bucks." We burst out laughing. "Hey, at least we have twelve bucks!"

We laughed even more as we realized we were going to spend my last twelve bucks on alcohol and cigarettes. It was so pathetic, we couldn't help laughing at our nonsense. Then the laughter took over. We went on talking and laughing the whole night away. The shift in focus from what we didn't have to what we DID have changed everything. The new outlook made us laugh and the laughter led to our having a great night and even writing a song about it – a song called *"Spendin' My Last Dime on Booze and Ciggies."*

The song inspired our creativity and we started sharing other ideas. Ideas and strategies and what we could do to have a better life. We were just two guys trying to figure out life and that night turned into one of the most memorable ever, with my friend Joe May. What started out as a depressing moment turned into something special, all because of gratitude for eleven dollars and seventy-eight cents. It made me think. Focusing on what I *didn't* have was never, ever going to do me any good. I had to remember that if I was going to make it selling houses.

Many new realtors will get sucked into the "water cooler gang" where all the agents hang around complaining about how bad things are, how bad the manager is, how bad the market is, and how terrible their clients are. I am here to tell you that what you obsess about comes about! The more you focus on the negative and the on what is *not* going your way, the more you will be headed down the wrong road.

Edge Rule: Don't give in to negativity and cynicism.

Why is negativity so popular? Answer: Because it's easy. Our ego loves it. Talking about how crappy everything is and how much someone pisses us off gives our ego a boost and provides a false sense of wellbeing. By saying how bad everything and everyone else is, we don't have to look in the mirror. Maybe the solution is right there. We'll discuss your part later, but for now you need protection from the Negativity that can take you down for the count.

Negativity and pessimism are the number one cancer for a real estate agent and for anyone, for that matter. You have to have your armor up. You will be attacked by *Captain Negative* as you start your career and you have to be ready. Captain Negative is everywhere. Just turn on the news, read a paper, check out TMZ. It's all the dirt in the world. It's popular. Why? Because dirt sells! People love to obsess over everything that is wrong in the world, how bad things are, why the world is ending soon and why things are horrible. You will not. You will have protection from these onslaughts of negativity. You will have armor and it's called Gratitude. Wear it everywhere. Gratitude will not only protect you from negativity, it's like a double-edged sword. It is also the seed of abundance. So if you wear your armor and choose Gratitude, then abundance will shortly follow.

Gratitude really is a choice. Don't think so? Think again. You can put two people through the same difficult, even horrifying, situation and one comes out shining and the other goes off the deep end. Why is that? Choice. Gratitude is a choice. Gratitude is indeed your armor that will ensure you are protected from all the negativity out there. Keep your armor intact and it will always protect you. How do you do that? When you find yourself feeling negative, simply stop, realize it, and ask yourself what you are grateful for right now, this very instant. If you choose to go down the slippery slope of negativity, even once in a while, then beware – because it's dangerous, and if you choose that path, I guarantee that you won't be here twelve months from now.

Edge Rule: Choose Gratitude.

RUN YOUR 555s EVERY MORNING ("FIVE-FIFTY-FIVES")

Every morning before you leave your house, I need you to set aside five minutes. Yes, only five minutes. I want you to write out five things and five people you are grateful for. Then meditate on your appreciation for these 5 things and 5 people for 5 minutes. That's called running your Five-Fifty-Fives!

This is a simple way to reset your heart and soul and put you on the right path of gratitude as you head out the door. It is very easy to wake up cranky, check your email, find out you are late on a bill, then open the fridge and realize you have nothing to eat. Now how is your mood? Getting crankier by the minute, right? Then . . . you bust out the door, stub your toe, jump in your car and rush to the bank for cash, only to find there is a line twenty feet long in front of you. You get in a fight with the teller because of a fee that you found on your latest statement; then, completely miffed, you drive off, only to get stuck in the worst traffic you've seen in weeks as you arrive forty-five minutes late at your desk. This, or something similar, is how many people start their day. You aren't going to do this anymore. If you are going to make it big in real estate, you have to learn to control your mind and what you focus on.

Move on purpose, be aware of your thoughts, choose to slow down and be grateful.

I keep my attitude of gratitude in my career by reminding myself that every deal I do is an absolute miracle and a gift. Every client is a gift. I have had multiple repeat customers, as you will too someday, and it can be very easy to take these clients for granted. Don't do it. I remind myself that I am especially grateful for these people and that I am the lucky one who gets to work with them.

If you are married or in a relationship what happens if you stop being grateful for your significant other? What happens if you start to take them for granted? You know exactly what happens. It's a flipping dizasty, that's what happens. Master Gratitude; develop this CORNERSTONE, and abundance will pour into your work and your life, in all areas. It's a choice. Choose it.

CHAPTER 7

Cornerstone II

SERVICE

A spirit of Service will always ensure you do the right thing.

UNCONDITIONALITY

As an agent selling houses, it is your job and your duty to do the right thing for your client. How does Service ensure we do the right thing? If our primary purpose is, first and foremost, to be of service, then we will always put the needs of others before our own and that will lead us to do the right thing.

Service is also sharing your gifts with others. The catch is that the sharing has to be done unconditionally. Aha! There's always a catch. Unconditionally. That is a big-time adult word. Give and serve unconditionally. That's the true spirit of service. Service while expecting something in return is not true Service.

I am not saying that you will work for free, but I am saying that you won't get the reputation of only being interested in one thing: COMMISSION! If you want to make more, you have to serve more.

"If you want more, give more."

-Ralph Waldo Emerson

BIG COUNTRY

My friend, wingman, and business partner, Joe Convery – "Big Country," as I like to call him because of his six foot three stature – no longer has to prospect. He has more referrals coming to him than he can manage, from guess where? From all the people he helps. He has mastered the art of service in life and in his business, and it has come back to bless him ten thousandfold. Joe is the first to be there when anyone needs a helping hand. It's not because someone is going to buy or sell a house; most of the people he helps never end up buying or selling – but his reputation is sky-high as someone who helps others unconditionally. Everyone knows his name and everyone he helps refers him. Joe has taught me that

Service not only ensures that you always do the right thing; it will attract an abundance of buyers and sellers your way. Joe's integrity and spirit of service *attracts* buyers and sellers, so he never has to *chase* them the way traditional training teaches.

> *"I never prospect. I just help others . . . and they remember."*
>
> -Joe "Big Country" Convery

OK now, before you run out there and become a non-profit public servant, I want you to understand what I am saying. Joe helps people with authenticity. He knows that if service is the basis for all his work, he cannot fail. It's a law of the Universe. If you want more, give more. If your purpose is service, you can never fail. Let's go back to the doctor and patient mindset. The doctor's obligation is to do what is best for the patient, not to figure out which surgery will make him the most money. But trust me, realtors are tempted with these decisions all the time. Focusing on what is in it for you will be nothing but a slow death for you as a new agent. It can take years to get a reputation as a great agent, like a Joe Convery, but it can take ten seconds to ruin your reputation.

Service shall set you free *and* it prevents commission breath. When you walk into any meeting from now on and think, "How can I serve this person?" or "How can I help?" then you can't lose. Service ensures you do the right thing – and doing the right thing will always benefit you in the long run. I am not saying you're a volunteer agent and work for free at helping everyone. No. You will find out that you might not be able to help everyone and that will be OK. You can't. No one can. And if someone is out to suck you dry, that is not going to work either. The Six Steps of the **Edge** will help you determine who to help and who to avoid . . . but I don't want to get ahead of ourselves. At this point we are building the foundation.

I need you to make it your first year in this business. Agents who make it in their first year go on to make it long-term. Eighty percent of new agents call it quits within twelve months and it's not because they weren't good enough. It's because they don't get the appropriate guidance. They get lost, they don't find the right training, and slowly fade into the mist. Part One of this program is about building a solid foundation to set your mind right early on, so you can make it in your first year and many years beyond. Think of something you are really, really, REALLY good at. Got it? Something you are just awesome at.

Golf? Guitar? Cooking? Playing with kids? Sailing? Pinball? Writing? Think about why you're so good at it. My guess is you started young. You had a good teacher. You learned the basics and the fundamentals early on and that allowed you to really shine later on down the road.

YOU WILL BE TESTED AND TEMPTED

Early in my career I had some friends who wanted to buy a house. Interest rates were extremely low, so lenders were giving money to anyone with a pulse. I felt uncertain of my friend's future income potential and I told him that. You see, he was an actor, and I was concerned that if something went wrong on his show and the money stopped coming in, he'd be in big trouble when his loan rate went up.

Believe me, I wanted to make a commission. I needed the money bad. He and his wife were eager to buy, but my gut and heart said they would be in trouble and they should wait. Was I being of service? I don't know; maybe. Was I being helpful? I don't know. I was just being honest. I had seen actors come and go and no future looked very secure in that business. It was how I felt so I told them the truth. I told them to wait. They said, "But this other agent said we can easily afford this house and our lender said we can handle the mortgage." I told them I disagreed and what I felt in my heart. And after some heated debates, they finally listened. We found them a rental property and that was that. They never bought a home. No commission for me.

What had I done? I was starting to think maybe I was not cut out for real estate. Was the only way to make it to be heartless and dishonest and, as they said in some training class I had been to, ALWAYS BE CLOSING? I couldn't do any of that. I guessed I just wasn't a "closer." Maybe I should start looking at other career opportunities.

Six months later I got a call from that same friend, telling me his show was picked up for another season! I thought to myself, "Boy, am I an idiot, he's going to lay into me about not buying the house." I said to him, "Wow, that is great news, congratulations! I guess I screwed up, telling you not to buy that house." He said, "The fact is, I'm calling to thank you for talking us out of it." I was confused. "But you said the show was picked up for another season." "Yeah, it was," he said, "but my character got written out of the show."

KABLAM! I didn't make a sale, but I felt good because I did the right thing and I won. I felt like I won big! I held my ground with my gut instinct and true belief, and it actually helped someone! I followed my heart and by doing that I saved my friend's ASS! That feeling was worth more than any commission. I felt great. I took the high road and because of that my friends were going to be OK. This was a moment I'll never forget. My friends never did buy a house, but guess what did happen? They went on to refer me to more clients than you could ever imagine. Go figure.

In your early years you will be tempted to take some quick case or maybe pop a fast deal, but I suggest you first investigate what is best for your customer and hit the pause button before you operate. Put yourself in a spirit of service and then proceed. Signs that you are not operating from the position of Service are as follows: WHAT'S IN IT FOR ME? GREED. IMPATIENCE. COMMISSION BREATH. If you are aware of the symptoms, you can spot them early and remedy them. So keep your eyes open. Look at this business as a service industry. You are here to help. Your reputation for service combined with gratitude will soon brand you as one of the best in town and your reputation and bank account will only go up from there. I guarantee it.

What can you do on a daily basis to exercise your service muscles? I call it your daily service prescription. Take your daily dose and you will stay well!

DAILY SERVICE Rx: *Each day do one random act of kindness.*

Do something for someone each day that is a random act of kindness – an *unconditional* random act of kindness. Remember that "unconditional" is the catch here. Many people pose as givers, there for service, but they will have their agendas. To each their own. You can't control others' actions, only your own. We are here to make you great.

"Become the change you wish to see in the world."

-Gandhi

The Four Cornerstones are some of the most powerful concepts not only in real estate, but in life. Having them as your foundation is why you will be different. You now are ready for the next Cornerstone. And buckle in, because this one gets a little more challenging.

Correction: A *lot* more challenging.

CHAPTER 8

CORNERSTONE III
HUMILITY

Ego is no match for humility.

Ever had some macho person try to put you in your place by telling you, "It's all your fault – oh boy, you really screwed things up!"

Try answering, "You know what . . . you're right. I am so sorry. I can see how I really screwed things up and I am deeply sorry. Maybe you can help me – let me know what you think I can do to make this better?" And watch Mr. Macho Man melt in his chair for how bad he feels for yelling at you.

Ego is no match for humility.

What do most of us do when someone screams at us? We put up our defense wall, our protection circuits, we feel offended, we shift into fight or flight mode. We yell back and things get worse. But humility can diffuse almost any difficult situation and make it better if you can learn to use it and live it.

Humility is going to change your life. It is my most challenging Cornerstone, but that's why it is also the most gratifying. I admit it. I have taken years to be able to master Humility, and it is something that, had I learned about it in my first few years, might have saved a lot of deals from crashing. My ego and my UN-coachability were preventing me from going to the top. Humility was something I struggled with and I want you to learn from me.

Humility, however, is not easy to master or understand. It is a major Cornerstone for a reason. Gratitude and Service can be fairly easy to understand and even execute for most new agents, but Humility is where we start to separate the women from the girls and the men from the boys. It will take some practice and some studying to really grasp this concept. You won't learn about Humility in any other real estate program because no one else teaches it. This one Cornerstone can carry all the others on its back and you will soon see its critical importance in getting to the highest level in selling houses – or any field, for that matter.

If you are anything like me, when someone tells you what to do, your first reaction is to tell him or her where to go! Most agents are very independent and got into this business because they didn't want a box, they didn't want to be tied down, and they certainly didn't want to be told what to do. So, let's make a deal. I won't ever tell you what to do and you don't tell me what to do. Deal? Deal.

So what does this have to do with anything we are talking about? It's simple. If I can't *tell* you what to do, then the only way this is going to work is if you are open to suggestions. If you are humble and willing to consider some outside-the-box ideas, you can learn to get very good at this business very fast. Humility means you're willing to admit you don't know everything. To me the ultimate act of Humility is asking someone for help.

ASKING FOR HELP

When we were kids, we did it all the time. Calling for our Mommy, asking our Dad to help. Never being afraid to ask for help is something kids do naturally, and everyone accepts this because they are kids. However, somewhere after high school and into our mid-twenties, it shifts into being "UN-cool" to ask for help. By forty it's unthinkable for most people to admit they need help. Pride and Ego seem to edge out anyone's ability to ask for help. This, in my opinion, keeps all too many people from rising from good to great.

Stubbornness and Ego are like muscles that will build up over time if you overwork them. The only thing that will help bring Ego down to size is Humility. What does this have to do with selling houses? Everything. To grow quickly in this business, you'll need to be willing to admit you know things you don't know. If you can do this right out of the gate, you'll have the foundation of Humility that will get you not only *to* the **Edge**, but beyond it. Beyond the **Edge** is a whole new level. We will discuss what it takes to get beyond the **Edge** in Part III.

Humility is a way of life. If you can incorporate this major lifestyle Cornerstone into all areas of your new career, you will do things that most people never even thought possible. I have seen it. I am living proof. I discovered Humility the hard way, but once I understood it, now I never leave home without it. It has saved my ass thousands of times, not only in real estate but in my life as well. And guess what, amigo? It will save yours. Without Humility, none of the other Cornerstones would be possible.

Edge Rule: Humility – Never leave home without it.

Humility paves the way for all the other Cornerstones. It takes Humility to be of Service, to be Grateful, and it certainly takes Humility to Forgive others. Humility gives us this magical power because it does two very important things that allow us to grow. It keeps us learning-based (coachable).

"Learning and growing, growing and learning. That's what it's all about!"
-Philip Williams (My Dad)

My Dad used to say this over and over when we were kids, and I never forgot it. The minute you feel you have mastered everything, you no longer will grow, because we can always learn something new. We can learn a better way to live, act, eat, love – and, yes, even sell. You've always been right about that, Dad. Thank you!

The Edge, as you will continue to see as we go on, is a state of mind. To have it means being learning-based: willing to listen, willing to try things a different way, willing to DO things a different way. This is the state of mind I need you to have when we get to the Six Steps of **Selling on the Edge**. If you are not willing, not coachable, then no training program will help you. If you think you know it all, you may even have some short-term success, but in the end, nobody likes a know-it-all and you will be gone within twelve months of getting your license. You'll be on your way to join the other failed agents in Death Valley who thought they could circumvent this critical Cornerstone.

THE ALLEGED MURDERER

I was in escrow with a client and on the day of closing we found out that a previous owner, multiple owners ago, had been charged with murder but never convicted. Let me explain. This was not the current owner of the house we were buying and not the owner before that, but the owner previous to that one had been accused of murder, tried, and acquitted. Acquitted means the defendant was found *not* guilty. All of this happened over a decade prior to our escrow.

On the day of closing, this information came to our attention. It was something we hadn't known. It had not been disclosed to us. That previous owner was never convicted of murder, there had been no murder committed in the house – but it freaked out my client and she wanted to back out of the sale. Understandably so. I agreed with her. We cancelled the sale.

The only problem was, she had already released her good faith deposit to the sellers. She ended up losing this deposit of well over $50,000 and guess who she blamed? You guessed it, yours truly! Yet how in the world would I know who lived in this house ten years ago? The sellers never told us and claimed not to know. The other agent didn't know. And I didn't know. It didn't matter, I was the agent representing Buyer, so, by default, it was my fault. Bottom line, my fault. Period. End of story. Sometimes your goose is cooked and you know the bear-down is coming. My client tore me a new you-know-what. She fired me, said I was a terrible agent, said she was possibly going to sue me, and sent me scathing emails saying that as a professional I should have known.

My Ego wanted to tell her she was on crack. My Ego wanted to tell her I battled hard to get her the house of her dreams. I wanted to tell her I couldn't be expected to know what kind of random people lived in that house three or four owners previously – the sellers didn't even know about it, so how would I? Was I supposed to know every criminal record of every person living in Los Angeles and where they lived at some point in the past? And anyway, the guy was *accused* of murder, never *convicted*! Hello?? Who cares?? That's what my EGO wanted to say.

Thank God I didn't.

I knew that Ego would not help anyone, especially me, in this case, so I did my best to come from a position of Humility. I told my client, "You're right and I am sorry. I should have known this information." I said, "I will understand if you sue me and/or my company for your deposit back." I went on, "I'll understand if you don't want to work with me ever again and I am deeply sorry for putting you in this terrible situation." I put my head down, turned around, and left, fully expecting to be sued or something bad to come my way. A month went by . . . two months . . . six months. My friends and co-workers said I could expect to be sued any day, but that day never came. I didn't hear a peep from my former client.

Then one day out of the blue, over a year later, I received this email from the Buyer:

Mark, I wanted to reach out to you to say I am sorry. I have still been looking for a home over the year with other brokers, and I realized one thing. You are very good at what you do and I am sorry for firing you. The situation was no one's fault and I'm sorry I blamed you. You helped me find a house I loved, but in the end, I simply was not ready to make that kind of move.

My ego was involved and as far as who lived there in the past, it didn't have much to do with my backing out. It was just not the right house or time for me. So I wanted to tell you that in working with multiple different agents over the last year, I realized you are great at what you do and I wanted to reach out and let you know how much I always appreciated your help. I hope to see you in the future and wish you the best moving forward.

Exactly six months after I received this email, this very same client used me to help her find and purchase a two million-dollar home. We are still friends. She is one of my best friends I ever met in Los Angeles and I love her and thank her for always sticking with me. She is one of the most successful people that I know, and the magnitude of humility that it took for her to reach out to me blew me away. I made up my mind that I was going to do anything and everything to help her, and that is what I did. In the end, we found her a house that was better than either of us had imagined. However, none of this would have happened without Humility.

UNCLE WILFRED

Humility is a lot of things, but it mainly starts with compassion. That is, an understanding of how the other person feels or sees things. Ego will want to argue, defend, and say, "You're wrong and I am right," but that won't help you sell houses. Compassion for how the other person feels and then being humble enough to check your ego at the door will put you ahead of everyone in this business. Although clients may do things that will drive you crazy, you still have to put them first and try to see things from their perspective.

New agents fail because they get emotionally involved with the sale. They focus on WIIFM ("what's in it for me?"). They smell that commission. They get commission breath. They forget what's numero uno: the client.

A client may change his or her mind or decide to wait on selling, or in whatever way may not do what we expect. I promise you, if your ego takes over, you will start telling that client what to do from your Ego and not from Humility, and you will lose that client. You may tell your other agent pals how you just told some difficult client where to go, and you may head home that day feeling all high and mighty. Trust me, that feels good, for about 30 seconds. Then you might as well look for another job because you will soon realize that client is NEVER coming back.

Edge Rule: Never put a client in their place. Never.

I know what you're saying right now. "But Mark, what about this one client who I promise you is wrong and they screwed me and it really *is* their fault and I want to let them have it! . . . Blah blah blah!" I understand, but just hold tight. You will soon see how to deal with these people without telling them where to go. It takes Humility first and foremost, and you will learn in Step Three of the **Edge** (DIS-qualify) how to take care of all these people in your life without ego. Losing your sh*t and letting them have it does no one any good. In those moments, just remember my Uncle Wilfred's lesson. I call it *Wil's Rule*.

Wil's Rule: Never react. Pause, WAIT, and then . . . respond.

If you tell someone off, your ego may get a rush, but in the end you will lose. You will lose the client, the commission, and any future referral that this person might have given you. It's your choice. React? Or respond?

The best agents have the ability to *not* react in difficult situations, and this takes Humility. So while you're new, how can you get to understand humility or even put it into practice? My late Uncle Wilfred had a great strategy for that. My Uncle Wil was probably the most compassionate man I ever met. He was a priest, but that wasn't what made him compassionate. In his lifetime, he worked with untold numbers of people and their struggles and tragedies, and helped them with many problems. I asked him how he managed to maintain his cool with all these people wanting his help and dumping their troubles on him. "Didn't you ever lose your cool or your mind?" The answer was No. He did not. Before he passed away, he taught me his secret. He taught me many things but this was one of the greatest lessons ever.

Uncle Wil taught me that the most successful people are the ones who can *pause* in the heated moments. In other words, the most successful people are the ones that can pause the longest between something that disturbs them and their reaction. This moment in between is the difference between Humility and Ego. I am sharing this Cornerstone with you so that when you hear and see things in real estate that could drive you crazy, you won't react. You will pause. Pause, wait, and let Humility respond. Thanks, Uncle Wil.

COACHABILITY

Having Humility means you agree that you don't know it all and you are humble enough to ask for help. It also means you are willing to listen and learn from someone else who may just be able to help you. Being open to suggestions and guidance from the right people is paramount for being successful. This Cornerstone can apply to any area of your life.

My great friend Tim got married at a very young age to an amazing woman, Jennifer. A few years into their marriage, they hit some rocks in the road. Tim and Jen were always deeply in love, but marriage can be tough even on the best of couples, and I will never forget when Tim told me that he was reaching out for help to counselors and other married couples. You, Tim came to me initially when I was also very young, proud, and stupid. I told Tim to dump her, just get a divorce and move on. I may sound like an idiot – because I was an idiot, at the time. You see, my pride made me uncoachable and my idiocy at that young age made me think that asking for help was a sign of weakness. Tim taught me that in fact, asking for help was a sign of strength. It takes courage to humble yourself and admit you need help.

I was amazed that Tim had the wisdom at that young age to know what to do. He and Jen have now been happily married for over fifteen years, have three amazing kids, and one of the best relationships I have ever seen.

Coachability and Humility will be instrumental as you begin your new career, so they are Cornerstones of the **Edge**. Coachability not only applies in sports, but in life, at work, with relationships, and especially when you are embarking on something new. I don't want you to have to hit bottom before you become humble and coachable. Ask yourself what you can learn from your friends and potential coaches. It will only deepen your relationships and your life.

You may have used other selling styles or tons of experience selling other stuff, and you may think what I'm telling you is nonsense. But if this is going to work, you have to humble yourself and listen to my direction. If, after a year, you think my approach is nonsense, then OK, we part friends and you can try it your way.

AWARENESS

So what can you do to practice Humility? Simply be aware of how you are reacting to tough situations. Can you practice Wil's Rule or does your Ego want to launch a can of whoopass on everyone that rubs you the wrong way? If you can practice and art of *pausing* and then WAIT until you shift from Ego to Humility before REACTING, then good job, you're being aware. That takes practice. Are you aware right now? Are you willing to take this suggest or is your body and brain saying it's bullsh*t? either way it's good, because you are aware.

Being aware allows us to respond as opposed to reacting. Awareness gives us that slight moment of pause to practice Humility and shut down Ego. If you're going to rock it big time in sales, it's key we leave Ego behind for good. Two things for humility to start working in your life:

1. Practice awareness.
2. Practice Wil's Rule.

Before my Uncle Wil passed away, I asked him what he did to remind himself to keep aware. How did he always respond so compassionately to others with grace and humility, even at times when they were charging at him? He said the key was simply in the part where he would "WAIT" before he responded. He chuckled, leaning back in his chair and pointing to a sign on his office wall that said **W.A.I.T.** Underneath those letters were the following words: **Why Am I Talking?** -Fr. Wilfred Illies (1923-2003) Rest in Peace, Uncle Wil.

CHAPTER 9

Cornerstone IV
FORGIVENESS

"Let us forgive each other – only then will we live in peace."

-Leo Tolstoy

AMANDA MADSEN

It was 4:45 a.m. when sixteen-year-old Amanda's father kicked in her bedroom door, grabbed her by the throat, punched her in the face and lifted her out of bed by her hair. He proceeded to drag her out onto their front driveway and threw her to the ground. It was the morning after Amanda's sixteenth birthday party. Her father walked into the garage and came out with a sledgehammer in his hands. All of the presents that she had received from her friends the night before were lined up on the driveway. He raised the sledgehammer over the first gift. "So, how do you like this gift!" And then SLAM! Down came the hammer, smashing the gift to bits. He went on down the row, destroying every gift until Amanda's mother came running out to stop the madness. At that point he dropped the sledgehammer and glared at Amanda. "Don't you ever be late again!" he told her.

A mere sixteen years of age, abused, humiliated, and left helpless, with nothing but the warm embrace of her mother, Driana, to hold Amanda as she cried and cried. She never forgot that story. Neither would I. Shortly after that terrible day, Driana decided enough was enough, took Amanda and left.

Amanda's father had been passing on learned behavior, for he had been abused by his own father. He *thought* that Amanda had stayed out thirty minutes past her curfew on the night of her birthday, and he thought he would teach her a lesson she would never forget. Amanda never did forget. However, she learned something that would help her move on. She would learn to forgive.

Cut to twenty years later and I find myself blessed with Amanda and Driana as two of my closest friends – whom I consider family – in the world. They have both taught me the most amazing life lesson that has become the final, most important Cornerstone of **Selling on the Edge**. Forgiveness.

I don't know about you, but I don't know if I could forgive someone for doing to me what Amanda's father did to her. I just don't know, but Amanda did. A few years ago, Amanda met with her aging father and forgave him for all the years of abuse he put her and her mother through. She told him she understood why he acted as he did, and that she loved him in spite of it and forgave him. She forgave him to help herself. Up to that point, she had hate, fear, anger and resentment bottled up inside her, and it spilled over into all areas of her life: her relationships, her work, her friends. One day Amanda told me, "If I am ever to move on with my life and be who I am meant to be, I need to forgive my father and start being happy."

"So what are you going to do?" I asked.

"Get over it," she said.

I smiled, and she added, "Everybody else has."

> *"Get over it. Everybody else has."*
> -Amanda Madsen

At that moment we laughed uncontrollably because of what she said and the way she said it. It was just so simple, and we both knew the power, humor, joy, love, energy and empowerment in those few words. "Get over it. Everybody else has." Brilliant.

For Amanda, that was that. She set her emotional rocks down like an old heavy suitcase, forgave her father, and time eventually would heal and refuel her inside and out. I love Amanda because she's a victim who became a survivor who became an achiever. And it all started with forgiveness.

SET YOUR ROCKS DOWN AND MOVE ON

Amanda is now engaged to an amazing man, she has a wonderful job, she is always in the most positive mood and is still one of my best friends who teaches me new and powerful things every time I see her. We can all learn from her story and courage, and the lesson is that forgiveness is never easy, but it will set you free. I share this story because if Amanda can learn to forgive after what she went through, don't you think you can learn to forgive? OK, so someone screwed you out of a thousand dollars, or didn't show up for your big event, or put you down in front of your spouse, or your mother told you what to do again and you're 38 years old – why not just let it go? Set your bag of rocks down so you can be free to be you. The one who benefits the most from forgiveness is not necessarily the one being forgiven. It is you.

Edge Rule: Set your rocks down.

Forgiveness is by far the toughest one to do. That's why we get a whole chapter on this one. You must understand this before we proceed. You must do more than understand it. You must actually forgive or at least try to start moving toward forgiveness. If you don't, it will be like trying to go from point A to point B where there's an impenetrable brick wall in the middle. I need all of the walls and roadblocks removed, or you will have a hard time moving forward. I need your head on straight before we dive in deeper. Any resentments, estrangements, hurts you may have, I ask you to pray for those involved as I did for you, and maybe you can learn to forgive and love them more. If you are upset at yourself, then you have to forgive yourself as well. This can be the most challenging of all: forgiving ourselves. Just try it.

This is where I need you to be before we go on. You bought this book to make money selling. Well, this is the hard part. It is building a strong foundation that will give you the **Edge** to sell more than you ever thought possible. You agreed to be coachable just through the end of this book, so here is what I am asking you to do: if you can't forgive immediately, then start with a prayer for those you hold resentments toward.

MAKE A LIST AND PRAY FOR THEM

Ever try praying for someone who has wronged you? It's powerful. Maybe you don't want to call them or tell them directly that you forgive, but you know that your resentment is eating you up? Try writing their name down on a sheet of paper and then simply saying a prayer for them. Pray that they'll be happy someday or that you forgive them and wish them the best in the future. It's challenging, but Forgiveness shall set you free.

We can all learn from Amanda. Maybe it's time to get over it. Although I don't mean to minimize any abuse or tragedy that you may have gone through, it may be time to set down the rocks of resentment and let it all go. Holding onto that hate and anger and resentment will do one thing. Hold. You. Back. It will hold you back from achieving what you were meant to do and being the person you were meant to be. If this system is going to work, I need you to be YOU in the best possible way. The whole core of the **Edge** is about bringing out the amazing you and all your fantastic potential and sharing that with the world. If you're full of resentments, you cannot be you. Not the you that God intended you to be, anyway. So set your rocks down, make a list and practice forgiveness. It will change your life.

THROTTLE BACK

Growing up in Minnesota, I loved everything that had to do with water, since it was the Land of 10,000 Lakes, "Oh, dontcha know?!" So along with hockey in the winter, in the summer I loved waterskiing, jet skis, speedboats, anything fast on the water. Pushing those speedboats up to full throttle could get a little dangerous, but that's what we did. And I loved it. I loved speed.

Speed was great in sports and for F15s, but in life it was not always the best thing. When I moved to L.A., I had all these unrealistic expectations and I used to really get down on myself for not being where I wanted to be at the age I was. L.A. is a fast-paced town and everyone wants what they want when they want it. In "La La Land," patience is not a popular word. When you're selling houses, if you try to push it, you'll get pushed out. You have to realize that you cannot control certain things, and I struggled with this when I was first getting started. I was taught to hard sell, always be closing, keep on 'em, follow up more, and chase, push, sell sell sell and eventually you will sell a house. I'd try this. I'd fail. And I'd beat myself up. I'd tell myself, "I'm no good, not meant to do this, others are so much better, blah, blah, blah." Brainbaggage was running wild.

Well, leave it to dear old Dad to put things in perspective and set me straight. One day on a visit with my parents in Minnesota, I was telling them I wasn't happy with my progress, had become very negative and really wanted to quite real estate. I complained about how hard it is and how cutthroat and on and on and on until I finally quit venting and shut my mouth. After a moment of silence, my Dad said, "Hey, Mark, maybe you should just throttle back a bit."

His advice hit me right in the heart. I knew exactly what he meant. It was my father's way of saying, "Take it easy on yourself. Relax." Because of my competitive nature, my inclination in all areas of life was to amp up, put the heat on and really push it. I'd go full throttle on everything and everyone, even myself.

Not good. That didn't serve myself the best and surely didn't serve others the best. It didn't do me any good and it won't do you any good. If you have crazy expectations of yourself and others, and tend to beat yourself up, take some of my Dad's advice and throttle back. That's forgiving yourself for overdoing your expectations.

Have huge dreams, think big and go for it, but part of the **Edge** is learning to forgive yourself as well as others. If this is hard for you, start with some simple things like laughing at yourself every time you screw up. I do every day. Laughter puts us in the right frame of mind and helps us stay loose, stay humble and be more forgiving of others and ourselves. Starting now, as you get out there and start meeting people, selling houses, developing relationships, if you have a bad day, just forgive yourself!

Forgive yourself if you screw up, learn from your mistakes, and move on. It's not necessary to dwell on and wallow in how we screwed up or that we messed up or that we're a bad person and how we are going to pay for this . . . and worse just begets worse, like a wave you ride down the drain. Make a mental note of what you would do differently next time, throttle back and have a nice laugh – at yourself! Try this every day and just watch how more joy comes into your life as you learn to forgive numero uno, YOU!

"We must take our craft seriously, but we must learn to never take ourselves so seriously."
-Clint Eastwood

Just keep in mind that most people – including you – are doing the best they can at any given moment. Next time you want to jump all over someone, whether it be you or someone else, for how they messed up or let you down, just remember what my Pops said: "Throttle back."

ONE DAY IT COULD BE TOO LATE

My good friend Kathy had not spoken to her mother in over four years and it got to the point where none of us even knew why they weren't speaking. Both of them were two of the most stubborn people I had ever met, so for whatever reason, neither would budge for years. Kathy's husband Jack miraculously convinced her to take the high road and find the humility and compassion to reach out to her Mom. Kathy finally agreed, called her Mom and asked her to meet.

Once face to face, Kathy said she was sorry for losing four years together, and that she wasn't even sure about how the estrangement started. She told her Mom she loved her and they both broke down in tears. They hugged and loved each other for the first time in four years. Three weeks later, Kathy's Mom died of an unexpected heart attack.

Kathy was 33 years old. Can you imagine if she hadn't made amends with her mother, and would have had to live with that for the rest of her life? What would life have been like for Kathy, knowing she had a chance to say she was sorry, make peace, and tell her mother she loved her, but missed that chance?

We all have someone in our life that we need to forgive before it's too late. Can you think of that one person now? Can you at least think of the possibility of reaching out to make peace? If that is not possible for you to do, then you can put this book down because it's going to be tough to move on from here. Resentments are the rocks that will ultimately hold you down and hold you back from greatness. I understand you may think we have come to a roadblock that you cannot overcome, but I think if you try, you will. Humility will give you the power to forgive.

The road to forgiveness starts with humility.

If you cannot forgive, then I ask you to simply say a small prayer for that particular person. Look at them as someone who is in trouble and needs your help. Take a moment now and write your prayer down, maybe right here in the book.

Daily Rx for Forgiveness

I recommend this monthly. Once a month, make a list of people you are upset with, or feel have harmed you in any way, and just pray for them. Maybe it was a sibling, a neighbor, a client, another agent who upset you, or anyone you feel is getting under your skin. Maybe even give them a call. Practice humility here to forgive or at least open the lines of communication before it turns into something worse. Practicing this will strengthen your self-confidence and ability to face tough issues head on. It will also improve your relationships. Watch how people react when you're the one who humbles yourself, says you're sorry and takes the high road. They will be flabbergasted that you had the courage to do what you did and your actions will inspire others.

In the end how they respond is not your problem. Their life may not be affected either way, but I guarantee yours will. Forgiveness will set you free. When you are totally free of resentments and roadblocks, then you can be the best you possible and that will give you an **Edge** like none other.

A LITTLE TEST BEFORE WE MOVE ON

If you can master the Four Cornerstones (Gratitude, Service, Humility and Forgiveness), you won't need much more help moving forward because mastery of the Four Cornerstones will change your life. These are concepts that people take lifetimes to master, so don't beat yourself up if it takes some time to learn them. The good news is that you are now very much *aware* of them and their importance. If you can incorporate them into your core, your life will change for the better in all areas. If you don't believe me, just try all four of these Cornerstones for the next 24 hours and watch what happens. Try it.

If you hate your job, as of now be grateful for whatever salary you receive and be grateful you're employed. Think of how it would be if you were not. What if all of a sudden you lost your job? Go ahead, you can do it. Fake it if you have to. It's only for 24 hours.

If you hate your family situation, try for the next 24 hours to focus on being of service to everyone in your family. Literally BE of service to your family. Offer to babysit or help them with a ride to the airport. Another idea is to try just a phone call to say hello. Or a random act of kindness like picking up their room.

If you are furious with someone at the office who has wronged you, over the next 24 hours use what you have learned about humility to forgive him or her without any conditions. If your head is telling you "NO WAY!" and you think you can't do this, just TRY it for the next 24 hours. There is no downside of doing this. You have nothing to lose and everything to gain.

Here is one more for humility: go and ask for some help or advice. Asking for help takes major amounts of humility, as most of us don't want to admit we need any. But just as an exercise and a favor to me, if you are struggling with any area of your life, within the next 24 hours, go ask someone you admire for his or her help. If you don't want to use the word "help," then I am OK with "advice." Humble yourself and listen to what they have to say. Take it all in, and no matter what they say, do exactly that. That's called being coachable. Don't question it, don't argue, just try it. If you don't want to listen to Nike and "just do it," then listen to me and "just try it."

YOUR FIRST AND LAST HOMEWORK ASSIGNMENT

Put the book down now, go do the four exercises set out below, and come back tomorrow. I'm serious. For the next 24 hours you have your first and last homework assignment. Do these and I promise you I will never ask you to do another thing for the rest of this book.

FIRST, you are going to be grateful for one thing (Gratitude).

SECOND, you're going to help someone with something unconditionally (Service).

THIRD, you are going to ask someone for help or advice (Humility).

FOURTH, you're going to forgive someone even though ego telling you not to (Forgiveness).

This mission, should you choose to accept it, will self-destruct in 24 hours.

OK, I'm not kidding, put the book down and go get your GSFH on! To remember these things easily, I came up with an acronym, **Go Serve Humanity my Friends**! Gratitude, Service, Humility, Forgiveness. You have 24 hours to do these four activities. Write down in the space below the Four Cornerstone actions you are going to do, or get a journal if you want so you can check them off. See you tomorrow. Place bookmark in book, close book and go get your GSHF on!

Gratitude:

Service:

Humility:

Forgiveness:

24 HOURS LATER?

How do you feel? Better, don't you? OK, you now know where your head needs to be before we get into the selling system. Gratitude, Service, Humility, Forgiveness. Whenever you get lost, you can go back to your foundation and you will always land on your feet. If you can't deal with that right now, then try this one: act "as if." Act as if you *could* be Grateful, of Service, Humble, and Forgiving. And if that doesn't work, my friend, then use the popular phrase they throw around in Hollywood all the time. It's an oldie but a goodie: Just fake it 'til you make it!

YOUR FAVORITE MUSIC ALBUM OF ALL TIME

You're not going to find most real estate selling systems discussing Gratitude, Service, Humility and Forgiveness. This is why this program is on the cutting edge of selling systems. It incorporates these deep, intense, heavy-duty concepts because I want to train you deep in your core, not just on your surface. Be patient, we are getting to the Six Steps very soon, but first we have to lay the proper foundation. Most systems I tried when I was new were light, fluffy, no substance, no depth, quick fixes – one-hit wonders, if you will.

My goal in writing this program was that it would be like your favorite music album of all time. Something you will have forever, something you can always go back and listen to and never get sick of it. Something that, after the first listen, you might not even feel it, might not like it or understand it, but for some reason it pulls you back. Before you know it, the songs get better and better each time you listen. Each time you listen, you hear new things that you didn't before. And ultimately it blows your mind!

There is material in here that may be extremely foreign to most people, and it may not make sense on your first run-through. I know my ADD writing style will send you from story to story, back to a lesson, then step back to a different story. I assure you that every single story, every step, every page has been painstakingly and strategically placed for one very important reason: To ensure that you make it in this business of selling houses and beyond!

Ever listen to Led Zeppelin Four or Pearl Jam Ten? (Two of my favorite albums.) Well, twenty years later, I hear things I never heard the first time. Much like a great album that overlays many different sounds, songs and instruments that you might not hear or like initially, but later on find yourself loving, the **Edge** will surprise you each time you read it with more and more to help you succeed. I know that is a bold statement, but I guarantee that as you go back and reread this, you will discover things that will open your eyes and give you *a-ha* moments when you most need them. The more you study this system, the more you will make it your own and that is my ultimate wish for you. Mastery. Mastery is not only grasping this program inside and out, it is making it your own. This is a foundation to set you on the right path, so you know what really matters right out of the gate. In the end, you will be making your own music.

I know there is a lot in here and it may be difficult to grasp in your first few months. My wish is that the more you study it, the more you "listen" and read, the more you will not only enjoy it, but learn from it. I know that is a lofty goal for any book, but I say that to let you know that I have put my heart, my soul and my passion into this book to give you the depth and quality to make it in this very challenging business. Time will tell if I have achieved that goal. Rock on, my friend!

INTERMISSION

Go take a break and let the Four Cornerstones sink in and digest them a little bit. I'm serious. Put the book down and go get some air, recharge, and pick it up tomorrow or in a few days. I need the Cornerstones to simmer and penetrate your subconscious over the next 24-48 hours.

I mean it. Take another 24 to 48-hour break right now. See you then.

Hey, STOP! Put your bookmark on this page and go away! Go relax, enjoy the weekend and let the Cornerstones sink in . . . too much too soon doesn't work, let's throttle back for a bit and go enjoy some sunshine, a cold beer, a nice hike, or whatever you'd like. Congrats, you are doing great and you have earned a nice break. Go recharge your batteries, your brain, and your soul!

Gratitude – Service – Humility – Forgiveness . . . Take a moment now to acknowledge that you have built one of the most powerful foundations that any real estate agent can ever have. I promise you there is no other training program on the planet that incorporates these principles into a real estate agent training program, so congratulate yourself because it's on, my friend! Take out a sheet of paper or your journal and write down the following words and put a date next to them:

It. Is. Happening.

What is happening, exactly? Your life is starting to change. You now have a rock-solid set of values and foundational Cornerstones that will begin to go to work in all areas of your life. By keeping the Four Cornerstones near and dear to your every move, you cannot fail. Gratitude – Service – Humility – Forgiveness. Breathe them in. Innnnhaaale . . . Exhaaaaale . . . Now please go enjoy your life and I will see you in a day or two.

INTERMISSION

(Please wait at least 24 hours before turning this page.)

CHAPTER 10

IT'S ALL GONNA WORK OUT

Welcome back. Normally, who a book is dedicated to is separated from the rest of the book. Well, not in this one. It is important to understand the act of appreciation and gratitude, and because it is at the heart of this system, it must be in every part along the way.

Before we get to the Six Steps, I pause here briefly to show you who I wish to thank and who I am grateful to. I do this with hopes that you too will learn to hit the pause button from time to time and reset your attitude of gratitude. Gratitude is a wave you're going to ride to the end. It is how you begin and end your journey to the **Edge** and it is the seed of abundance, so it is beyond vital to keep it at the forefront of your mind and your actions. Gratitude along with Service, Humility and Forgiveness are the Four Cornerstones of this system. The lifeblood. The foundation. Real estate agents that grasp these concepts outlast the ones who disregard them and go for the quick fixes. When there's no foundation, we all know what happens. A huff and a puff and he blooooooows your house down. Not good.

If you want to make it big in real estate, you must look at these Cornerstones like air, water, food, and sleep. Yes, like air, water, food, and sleep. Without those four things, what happens? Nothing good, I assure you. A lot of people ask me which of the Cornerstones is the most important, and if I had to pick one, it would be the one that carried me when I was in my darkest days. Gratitude.

Gratitude must be looked at like air for your selling life. Why? Because the minute you succumb to negativity and pessimism, I promise you they will eat you and your career alive like a Big-Mac. Agents get caught up in the economy going south and the water cooler chats about how bad everyone is doing, and the next thing they know, they turn negative and unappreciative of everything and everyone. Gratitude is the lifeline that can revive you during your darkest hours. When adversity comes – and it will come – if you breathe in pessimism and negativity, we all know what the result will be. However, if you shift your mindset and focus on what you are grateful for, then *breathe in gratitude*, what you exhale will be abundance, joy, and I promise you . . . it will all work out. Try it now. Take a hit!

Edge Rule: Gratitude is like air. Breathe it in or die.

BE A GIVER

If gratitude is the air of this program, then the Cornerstone of Service would be water. Being of service and taking action to truly *give* to others is what keeps people in this business for the long haul. If you want something you don't have, have you ever thought of first trying to help someone else who wants the same thing? For example, if you want to be a better tennis player, go help someone learn the game and watch what happens to your own game. If you want to make more money, go help someone else make more money. If you want your personal relationships to get better, be there for someone else who is having a hard time with their partner and just listen. If you want more laughter in your life, go to a hospital and cheer someone up. If you want a nicer house, go help someone improve his or hers. Try this theory out with anything you want more of. Give away that which you want – and watch how you will start to get everything you ever wanted and a hurricane of abundance will pour into your life.

Edge Rule: Give unconditionally of whatever it is you want.

You are here because you want to sell more houses, right? OK, so right now you're probably saying, "How can I sell more houses by helping other people sell houses? I don't know anything yet about selling houses!" Sure you do. Try teaching them what you've learned so far in this book and program. If you see someone who is struggling, ask whether they would like your help. Share with them the Four Cornerstones and how you are using them in your new career. You *do* have something to give. Even if you have not sold a single house yet, you have something to give. Be a giver and watch how *Hurricane Abundance* pours back wealth, happiness, and success into your life. Abundance always comes when the givers step up and come out to play. It might not be right away, but I promise you it will come. Givers make the world go round. I know they have changed mine, and if you stop reading here, you still now know the most important takeaway from this book. Give unconditionally of whatever it is you want. (. . . and then put on your raincoat!)

This one **Edge Rule** is something I didn't learn until it was almost too late. Had I learned this in my formative first months or even first year or two, I would have had a much better start. However, you can benefit from my experience, so please take this moment to realize the power of this concept. It is one of the most powerful mindsets and belief systems you will ever learn. Ralph Waldo Emerson said it over a hundred years ago in its purest form:

"If you want more, give more."

THANKS, MOM

I want to acknowledge my gratitude to all the givers in my life. I do this with hopes that you will carry the same state of mind with you as you move forward. It's important that you keep reading this section and you will soon discover why it is placed in the middle of the book as opposed to the front or end as most authors do. This book is dedicated to, and inspired to, all the givers in my life, especially Dad, Mom, Chris, Brian, Rachel and Nicole. In addition to the super six I just mentioned, I want to acknowledge all of the people in the world, in my life and in your life, who want nothing more than to see us get better and to make our lives a little brighter, just for the sake of it. The Givers. Can you think of anyone in your life that fits this description? Someone who has given unconditionally to you over and over throughout the years? As you read the following list, I ask you to really think of the people who have given to you in your entire lifetime so far. The people who have helped you just because. Look at the list below and think of these people who may be in your life and specifically how they have given to you.

Parents and grandparents, sisters and brothers, nieces and nephews, aunts and uncles, spouses and sponsors, girlfriends and boyfriends, in-laws and exes, teachers and trainers, coaches and consultants, professors and partners, co-workers and co-dependents, priests and pastors, ministers and mentors, soldiers and sages, wingmen and wingwomen, heroes and higher powers, volunteers and veterans, and most of all, our friends and best friends who have given to us unconditionally from their hearts and souls, just for the sake of giving.

There are more givers in the world than there are on this list. But these are some of the people I wish to thank and I ask you now to make a list of all the people who may have helped you along the way. You can do this in the space below. Why? Remember that part about humility and being coachable? OK then, so just roll with it!

As you write your list, take this moment to thank them all. This will get you in a huge spirit of gratitude and appreciation, which is where I need you to be as we embark on our next part of our journey to the **Edge**: The Six Steps.

WHO ARE THE GIVERS IN YOUR LIFE THAT YOU ARE THANKFUL FOR?

Write every name of everyone you can think of from the day you were born that inspired you, gave to you, and helped make you who you are! Ask yourself who was really there for you at some of your darkest moments, that you may have forgot about or may have taken for granted. Let's thank the givers in our lives. Without them, none of us would be here. None of us.

(Write their names in the space below)

1.

2.

3.

4.

5.

6.

7.

8.

9.

10.

11.

12.

13.

14.

15.

16.

17.

18.

19.

20.

21.

22.

23.

24.

25.

DON'T MAKE THIS HUGE MISTAKE

Congratulations. If you did the above assignment, you now have a list of twenty-five people that could potentially be customers and/or referral sources for your new career. Now stop right there! Don't start calling these people to tell them you are a real estate agent, and definitely don't send out twenty-five form letters telling them about your new position at so-and-so realty company. I didn't ask you to write down a list of people you want to *sell* or who you think may be buying or selling. That is what every other real estate program teaches you. It doesn't work. It usually goes down something like this: First, you make this great big list of everyone you know. Second, you call all these people to tell them you just got licensed, and third, CLICK! They hang up on your, never take your call again, and avoid you for six months. You are not going to make this huge mistake. You now know better.

I asked you to write down a list of people that you are grateful to and grateful for. There is an enormous difference between this and writing down a list of everyone you think will buy or sell. You're starting your journey with a mindset of gratitude, as opposed to traditional training which starts with, "Who can I sell?"

Take this list and call all these people to tell them how much you appreciate them and how they were there for you. If you prefer to write them a letter telling them this, that's OK too. Whatever you do, however, don't even *think* of mentioning that you are in real estate or asking them if they need help buying or selling a house. This is old school training hoopla that simply does not work. It has ruined more relationships and careers than you can imagine. Have you ever had that one friend who disappeared for three years, then all of a sudden out of the blue you get some fancy letter in the mail telling you they just got their real estate license and the letter asks you to call them with all your referrals? What did you do with that letter? Exactly. Straight to the trash.

Don't make this huge mistake of calling everyone you ever met and telling them you are now in real estate. You may not have talked to some of these people for months or years, so you have to develop, or should I say *re*-develop the relationships first. As you contact these people on your list, come from the spirit of gratitude and appreciation. Be genuine, speak from the heart, thank them for how they have helped you in the past, and be on your way. (NO SELLING!)

Your main mission is to thank them for all they have done for you. Period. I don't care if they live in NYC and you live in Omaha, you are not going to try to sell them anything, so where they live does not matter. It also doesn't matter if they don't live in your town or your area or your *"farm"* either. (By the way, you will never again hear that term in **Selling on the Edge**.) We do not "farm" people or areas. I always loathed that term. Your objective moving forward is not to *farm* anyone, it is simply to call them and thank them authentically, genuinely, expecting zero in return. Got it? The point of this exercise is to get you back to truly developing relationships authentically before you even think of trying to "sell" someone.

This may be a challenging exercise for many people. The world has forgotten how to say thank you and a lot of you may be struggling in other areas of your lives and may not feel in the best of moods to show your appreciation at this moment. Ever heard that it is hard to love someone else if you don't love yourself? I understand, I have been there. But let's put how you feel on hold right now and just see how you feel *after* you have spoken to all the people on your list. Take not, moving forward, that what you *do* will often change the way you feel. That's a gem, so you may want to go back and reread that last sentence. When people tell me they are in terrible moods, having a bad month, or feel down in the dumps and like they have nothing left to give, I say to them, "Try giving thanks and then tell me how you feel."

Edge Rule: When you have nothing left to give, give thanks.

PART III

(The System)

The Six Steps

CHAPTER 11

DANGER! WARNING: DO NOT ENTER

DANGER! WARNING: DO NOT ENTER PART III unless you are ready for something amazing. Do not even think of reading Part III unless you are ready to have your life changed and make more money selling houses than you ever imagined! Also it is critical that you follow this instruction:

Do not read Part III until you have read Parts I and II.

If you are like me when I was new, you want to jump to the end, skip this part or that part, and let me tell you it will hurt you in the end. To get to the right foundation and start your career the right way, it is essential that you fully read Parts I and II *before* you move ahead to Part III. If you have not yet read Parts I and II, then do not attempt to move forward until you have. I am serious. I will come to your house! It is your career that is at stake and you cannot afford to move ahead until you have laid the foundation that Parts I and II will help you build.

Foundation first. System second. Then the sky's the limit!

Selling on the Edge is first and foremost a selling *system*. In addition to the Four Cornerstones, it is six simple steps as the core of the program that you can use to sell houses. The foundational Four Cornerstones are critical to keep you on solid ground as you begin. If you lose sight of the Cornerstones, I promise you, no matter how good you are at following these Six Steps, you will eventually crumble. At the same time, if you don't use the *system* (Six Steps) that is built upon the Four Cornerstones, you will also end up struggling.

The Four Cornerstones (foundation) and the Six Steps (system) go hand in hand. (Think bread and butter, cheese and mac, ying and yang; you get the point.)

In typical, traditional real estate training school, they teach you how to pass the state test – and, if you're lucky, maybe some cool facts about real estate that you will never, ever use in the real world. The real title of this book could have been THINGS THEY DON'T TEACH YOU IN REAL ESTATE SCHOOL. The key question is, what SHOULD they teach? When you're new, you have to have a selling SYSTEM. If you don't have one, you will unknowingly default to a haphazard way of doing things, and this is why new agents fail. Popular ways of doing things by most agents include hope, pray, throw spaghetti on wall and see what sticks-type systems. This doesn't bring home the bacon. Without a system, agents will get slaughtered out there. If you just try and wing it, then be warned, because buyers, sellers, and all the other agents you compete against will eat your lunch!

In Part III you are going to learn a system. A system that is natural, organic, authentic, and one of a kind because you are going to help design it! The following Six Steps will be guidelines, but the final product will be custom-built by you. It will have your style, passion, and strengths at the forefront of each step. And since you are involved in designing it, it will be much easier to execute. Your uniqueness will be at the heart of every step and the more you bring out the you in you, the more you will succeed. You have the change to do something huge with your life and you have come across the keys to the kingdom. Some people are not so lucky. People like my good childhood friend, Doug.

IT'S NOT BECAUSE HE WASN'T GOOD ENOUGH

I grew up in Minnesota, where the winters were brutal but the icy ponds and seven-month winters helped foster some of the best ice hockey players in the world and in the NHL. I had a friend in high school named Doug, who ever since we were kids could skate circles around everyone. He had more ice hockey talent than anyone I had ever seen.

One cold winter day at the outdoor ice rink park when we were no older than thirteen, we were skating together, passing, shooting – had the whole rink to ourselves – when, boom! All of a sudden, some of the top older players from the Minnesota youth hockey team jumped the boards and onto the ice. They zipped around in circles, carving up the ice and giving us that look like, "Beat it, guys, it's time for the big boys to play" as they launched into a scrimmage. Well, I quickly jumped over the boards and headed for the warming house. I was no match for these guys and hockey is a rough sport; I didn't feel like getting smashed that day. I had no business even trying to skate with those elite players. I was halfway to the warming house when I realized that Doug was still on the ice.

"Come on, Doug, let's get outta here." Doug, however, had plans of his own. He didn't flinch, he held his ground and didn't even think about getting off the ice. I couldn't believe my eyes. It was an awesome sight to see. A smaller thirteen-year-old who wasn't backing down to what appeared like eighteen-year-old giants – bigger, meaner, stronger, and faster, but I knew Doug and guess what? Doug was badass! He had raw talent, strength, and speed like nothing I'd ever seen. Doug stood up to all of them, all five foot three inches of him, and I watched from the sidelines a sight I would never forget.

Doug was putting on a clinic. My buddy Doug, at thirteen years of age, was absolutely tearing it up, shooting, scoring, and skating circles around these bigger kids. He had amazing natural ability and he was lighting up the rink. He had more talent in his little finger than these guys had in their whole hand, and it was magical. He was destined for greatness.

Years went on. Doug and I were growing up in a modestly middle class neighborhood and hockey was very expensive, so our families never put us on the private youth teams, just the public leagues. We didn't much mind, as we didn't know what we didn't know and neither did our parents. We were just having fun skating at the parks playing a game we loved. To move a child into these traveling private teams, you needed two things. First, the talent – which Doug had easily – but, second, a clear understanding of the developmental system. An understanding of the steps, the paths, and the directions one must take to get in these youth programs to grow and get better. Otherwise, phenomenally talented kids would be left behind and eventually move on to other things with no one being the wiser.

You see, in hockey, in Minnesota, if you wanted to get really good, you absolutely had to know the system. And the system was something like this: Every year you needed new equipment, new skates, new coaches, and new tournaments. You had to travel to different cities to play the other top kids. As these kids grew and developed, they were getting tons of exposure, experience, and coaching, and by the time one was eighteen, he had played thousands of games in front of major college and pro scouts. This in a nutshell was "the system." At the time, neither my parents nor Doug's new much about the system. They never played hockey, so they just weren't that into it like us kids were and they just chalked it up to "Mark and Doug just love playing hockey, and boy oh boy is Doug better than everyone." And that's where it ended.

As the years went by, I noticed how other top kids began traveling to play in out-of-area tournaments. They would take buses to practice with new teams and better coaches. They played against top skaters from other parts of Minnesota. This was the system that one had to know in order to have any chance of making it. Everyone in it was getting better and faster – and learning what it took to make it in the big leagues and progress to the next level. Unfortunately, Doug never got that opportunity. It's not because he wasn't good enough. Many of the older kids who were fortunate enough to be in the system went on to play in top Division One colleges, and some even made it to the NHL. And my friend Doug was better than all of them.

I always wondered how different life might have been for Doug, had he simply had access to "the system." Or even just a mentor or guardian angel who could have pointed him in the right direction and given him some key advice back when he was a teen. Anything that would have helped him harness his talent and give him the opportunity he deserved to make it in the big leagues.

For your new future selling houses, let me tell you, my new friend, you are going to know the system. I am about to give it to you in Six simple Steps.

YOU NOW HAVE A SYSTEM

Your system is called **The Edge** and there are 6 Steps.

1. Be Yourself
2. Get Out There
3. DIS-Qualify
4. Focus

5. Own It

6. Have Fun

The Six Steps of the **Edge**, my friend, *are* your system. Those Six Steps are not a magic pill or a quick fix or flashy sales tips that will help you "close" anyone. The Six Steps are the fundamentals. They are the basics. And the beauty of this system is that you will be helping to design it. Yes, there are certain things you MUST learn if you want a fighting chance to make it in the cutthroat world of real estate. But **Selling on the Edge** provides a way for you to set the system that is best for you, using your unique strengths and characteristics. Only you know what is best for you. You'll have an instant **Edge** because no one can do YOU better than you.

Now, it will take some time, but anything worthwhile does. Building the right foundation is what most realtors never do. I see the same thing all the time: I see new realtors fail because they look for quick fixes, easy ways to make a quick buck – and these kinds of selling programs may work in the short term, but they don't give you the foundation to make it long-term. My passion is to help you build that solid foundation the right way, learn a system that puts you and your unique differences at the center, and ultimately enjoy a lucrative and FUN long, healthy career selling houses. Over the years I've seen real estate agents with amazing talent, ability, and passion – like Doug on the hockey rink – who didn't learn "The System." You are learning it now, and by the time you finish this book, you will know it.

If you have made it this far, I want to congratulate you. You have taken the time to learn the Four Cornerstones before jumping ahead. My hope is that by now you see the absolute necessity of having a foundation before you advance, but if not, I'll reiterate it one last time because it is paramount to your success.

No matter what you learn from the following Six Steps of **Selling on the Edge**, you won't be able to put the system to its full use if your foundation – meaning the Four Cornerstones – is weak. Gratitude, Service, Humility, and Forgiveness combine to give you the limitless thinking that will let you bring out the greatest YOU in you. Imagine having the belief that you can do anything, the belief that you can't fail. Keeping the Four Cornerstones in your life will ensure this mindset.

As we move forward, if you ever find yourself stuck, check your Four Cornerstones. See if they are solid. Are you being Grateful, of Service, Humble, and Forgiving? Are you? No one can do all of these perfectly all the time, but you now have a compass to get yourself back on track when things seem off. We all have issues and baggage and some days will be better than others. It's OK. Don't go off the deep end. Just focus on the foundation (the Four Cornerstones) first, and the System (the Six Steps that you are about to learn) second.

Steps One, Two, and Three are the *outer game steps*. They require action out in the field. Steps Four, Five, and Six are the *inner game*. They deal with what's going on inside your head. They could be called mental training, which is vitally important for success. Action plus mental toughness is tough to beat. To become great in any field you need to develop your outer game AND your inner game.

MAIN MISSION AND MAIN MOVES

As we proceed with Part III, you will see that each of the Six Steps has a "main mission" that is your goal and objective for that step. If you get confused, all you have to do is refocus on the main mission and you will get back on track.

Also note that each of the Six Steps has two key "main moves" that will get you producing and making money in that step.

Master the main mission and main moves for each step, and you will be well on your way to achieving things you never thought possible in real estate and in life. With that bold statement being said, I'd like to be the first to welcome you to Step One of **Selling on the Edge**. Be yourself. Ever hear the expression, "Be yourself, everyone else is taken"? Be yourself.

THE OUTER GAME: Steps 1, 2, 3

(Be Yourself, Get Out There, DIS-Qualify)

CHAPTER 12

STEP 1: BE YOURSELF

This above all: to thine own self be true, and it must follow as the night the day, thou canst not then be false to any man.

Shakespeare, *Hamlet*

Step 1 Main Mission: **Bring out the You in YOU!**

Step 2 Main Moves: **Know Thyself**

                                      Find Three Passion Arenas

William Shakespeare wasn't a real estate agent, but, boy oh boy, did he understand human behavior. Shakespeare understood that in order to really shine, you must be yourself "above all." This meant that, more important than anything else, you must be true to yourself, let the real you come out, and never pretend to be something or someone you are not. (Do not "be false to any man.")

Easier said than done, Will!

Be yourself. We've all heard it a million times, but do we really know or understand it? I didn't, and when I first got started in real estate I was anything but myself. I'd try to do what other top agents were doing and I found myself failing miserably because I was trying to be something I was not. I hated wearing suits or going to early morning network meetings, but that's what my first manager told me I HAD to do in order to make it big selling houses. I also hated scripts. What was even worse, I hated doing open houses. My first managers said that if you wanted to make money, you MUST sit an open house every single Sunday for the rest of your life.

I was becoming less and less interested in this career every time some manager who had never sold a day in his or her life told me what to do, what to wear, what to drive, where to work, where to sell, what type of clients to work with, and on and on and on . . . PUKE!

The typical manager or company or training program says, "OK, Mr. or Ms. New Agent, you are new so you must only work with buyers to start." Or, "You must only work with rentals – leases – to start, because sellers are too advanced for you at this point." I am here to tell you this is the biggest bunch of nonsense you will ever hear, and as a newbie you should work with whomever you want! Sellers, buyers, renters, lessors, whatever YOU are most passionate about.

Make sense? Let's talk about Step One. Being yourself is the biggest, most important step in all these Six Steps. What does it mean to Be Yourself, and how does it apply to selling houses? Most people think they act like themselves, but do they really? Let's find out. In order to bring out the YOU in you, it's important that you really learn who you are and what your passions really are. Being yourself starts with the following two Main Moves:

Main Move 1: Know Thyself
Main Move 2: Find Three Passion Arenas

Remember that each of the Six Steps has two Main Moves and one Main Mission. The Main Mission in Step One is to bring out the YOU in you. Notice it is not to bring out the "someone else" in you.

In real estate it is common for the new agent to think he or she has to mirror the top agent in the office. New agents are taught to do whatever the successful people are doing. This way, they are told, they too will be successful. I am here to tell you this is a recipe for disaster. If you try to act like someone else, your clients or potential prospects will sniff out your fakeness in two seconds and you'll be toast. This is why fancy scripts and closing dialogues will not work. They force you to be someone you are not and it's like putting a square peg in a round hole. **Selling on the Edge** means NO SCRIPTS EVER! You say what you feel and you say what is on your mind. If you're talking to a client that you feel is being evasive or shady, or you can see by their body language that they aren't interested – you simply call out the obvious and say it. You are learning many of the **Edge Rules** and here is an important one. You might want to write this one down in a place where you can see it often.

Edge Rule: If you feel it, say it.

If you are paying attention to your client and listening, as opposed to trying to spout off some bogus non-award-winning script, then you are truly hearing what your client is saying. You're now focusing on the client instead of on yourself, and this is the beginning of something good.

No, throttle back a bit here, because we are not selling yet. We're not even close. We are in Step One, which is about knowing thyself, being yourself, and learning how to bring out the YOU in you. Once you get comfortable with yourself and find out what you like and don't like, you can start to engage naturally with others – which is what we will talk about in Step Two. Right now I need you to figure out who *you* are. So I ask you, my friend. Who are you? What do you like? Go ahead, write it down. What don't you like? Write that down too.

You got your real estate license for a reason, yes? Why was that? To set your own schedule? To be your own boss? To work with whoever you want to work with? To sell houses? Condos? High end? Low end? Buyers? Sellers?

In this first step of **Selling on the Edge**, you have to figure out what you like and don't like and who you are exactly, and then stick to that! Say, for example, you hate wearing suits. Well then, stop wearing them. Or if you don't like attending the office meeting even if everyone else is doing it, then STOP doing it! You have to figure out your game plan, what you love, how you like to do things and then start doing things your way. I am here to tell you that the sooner you follow your own heart and stop looking to outside sources for answers, the faster you will succeed in real estate.

When you are new, everyone will try to tell you what to do and how to do things. I will not. I will say the following: Be yourself, bring out the you in you, and then you'll shine. BEWARE: your initial temptation will be to disregard or ignore your own great ideas and impulses. Your managers and others, even close relatives, will all tell you that you don't know anything yet about real estate, so your own unique ideas are no good at this point. Don't listen to these naysayers!

"Swing your swing. I know I did."

-Arnold Palmer, four-time Masters Champion

It will go something like this: you'll have some great new idea and you'll bounce it off a few other agents or your new manager and they will tell you, "Ya know, you are fairly new and that might not be a good idea; what you should try is this . . . " They steer you away from being you and this is the beginning of the end. You must follow your own heart and instinct and NEVER let anyone sway you. They will try. The reality is that people get uncomfortable when someone has new ideas and could easily just be themselves. But this is a sign that you're on the right track toward knowing yourself and BEING yourself in all areas.

As you continue to master the art of being yourself, your own brand will emerge. People will see that you are unique, that you are different, and they'll be drawn to you for this reason alone. The positive vibe of your ability to be yourself will attract people into your life. In sales, the first step is about developing trust, which you will gain by being authentic. Being who you really are is the first crucial step toward attracting potential clients.

THE HOUSE WAS A-ROCKIN'

I had been licensed for almost three years and I had yet to sell a single house. I had done everything my manager told me, I had mastered every script, I was dressing nice and doing open houses every Sunday, yet no one would ever work with me long enough to close a deal. I was about to give up when I said to myself, "Ya know what, Mark? F**k this sh*t!" I was living in Beverly Hills, trying to sell houses like all the other stuffy agents in town, sporting a suit, using these bogus scripts, printing out the same old boring set-up sheets, having people sign in at my open houses, only to call them the following day and find out they left me a fake number. I was sick and tired of the nonsense, I was eating at Taco Bell and pretty much broke and I said to myself, "This isn't me." If I walked into an open house and this guy started talking to me, I wouldn't want to work with him either. So I said This is it and from now on, I am going to be me, say what I want, and do what I want.

First thing I did was give my two suits away to Goodwill. Next thing I did was get rid of the stupid almighty "sign in" sheet. Then I said, next weekend I'm going to sit an open house on a Saturday because I like Sundays off. That is exactly what I did.

Why do open houses have to always be on Sundays? I hated working Sundays. I grew up Catholic. My family liked having Sundays off. Because the whole real estate industry says you have to sit open houses on Sundays as a realtor, does that mean I have to do it? "NO! NO I DON'T!" was my thinking. This was refreshing, so I said to myself, "OK, instead of Sunday, I am going to try open houses on Saturdays!" I take full credit for inventing the Saturday open house in Los Angeles. No one had ever opened up homes before on Saturday, but shortly after I did, they began popping up everywhere.

I also decided that at my open houses I was going to wear what I liked, which was a t-shirt, jeans, and tennis shoes. No more suits. And from now on, I was going to somehow make them fun, because I liked having fun. To me, fun was rock and roll music, so instead of lighting candles and serving cookies, I said screw that, I'm going to bring in my new Led Zeppelin box set and rock out for three or four hours and see what happens. So now I'm wearing my comfortable outfit, my tunes are cranking, and I'm actually enjoying things because it is also a Saturday and I'm happy because I don't have to sit an open house on Sunday!

For the first half-hour no one walked in, and I couldn't have cared less because I had great music playing and I was just so happy not to be stuck in a hot suit looking like every other realtor in town. All of a sudden this guy comes walking up the driveway, and it was on! He walked in the door and smiled instantly because Led Zeppelin was cranking loud and he seemed to like the song. First thing he said was, "Oh, sorry, I thought this was an open house." I said it was and welcomed him in. Then he asked me where to sign in. Me being in my new spirits, instead of spouting the old script I had been taught, it hit me, just say what you feel and what you feel is true. I said to the guy, "I don't use sign in sheets, because you will probably put a fake name anyway and you're probably not going to like this house either – it's pretty beat up – so just go ahead and walk around on your own."

OH SNAP! Did I really just say that? Yes, I did. There was about a three-second pause as the guy looked at me as if frozen to the floor . . . and then BOOM! He broke out laughing. "That is the funniest thing I ever heard!" He introduced himself and said, "Hi, I am Zeev, nice to meet you. I really appreciate your honesty. I take it you are not the realtor?"

HOLD! THE! PHONE! This is where I had my a-ha breakthrough moment. I was now a guy in a house, wearing a t-shirt, jeans, and tennis shoes, playing Led Zeppelin, with no sign in sheets, no fancy marketing materials – and most importantly I was telling the truth, speaking freely, using no scripts. And for the first time in three years, a person who walked into the open house was not running away from me. Zeev became my first client ever and my first sale ever and he ended up buying a house for $1.2million and BOOM! Just like that, my three-year drought had ended.

What was different? For the first time ever, I didn't try to jam a square peg into a round hole and act like all the other realtors out there. I was being myself. I loved rock and roll, so I started playing rock and roll at all my open houses. I would jam air guitar when clients were walking around and they'd laugh at me, but I didn't care! I liked pizza, so I started bringing pizza to my open houses. If I felt it, I did it. I didn't ask for anyone else's input. In your first year, if you have an idea, don't bounce it off anyone. They will talk you out of it. It's human nature. Being yourself means not giving a sh*t what others think, not asking for their input – and then just doing things *your* way.

One thing I learned quickly that no one ever taught me in RE school was about owners. I did NOT like having owners there when I did open houses because they made the people who were looking feel very uncomfortable. I would tell the owner, "You have to get the hell outta here or this is not going to work! You will scare off all the buyers just like a big fish scares off all the little ones. You have to beat it!" I would kick my sellers out of their own houses. I was doing what I felt was right. What was in my heart. Now, it is true that what worked for me might not work for you. I am not telling you what to do here. I am telling you that YOU have to figure out what you like – and you get to do that all on your own. This is what

Step One is all about. You can work on Step One for the rest of your life, but it starts with two key elements. What do you like? What don't you like? By the way, I still air guitar every day! In case you wondered what I was doing on that rock on the cover of the book? You guessed it! Rock on, **Edge** lovers!

KNOW THYSELF

If you are going to become a master at being yourself, you'd better get to *know* yourself. This is your time, my friend. You got into this business because you are tired of other people telling you WTF to do. You probably got into this business because you are tired of workin' for the man. So guess what? This is your time to do what you want to do! Get excited! You're one of the proud, the free! Free to *do* and *be* however you want because no one can do you like you. But first we have to figure out who the real you is, and then reset your clock, so to speak. A lot of people getting into real estate are so wound up from years of working for others that they are still stuck in the rut of thinking they have to act a certain way or say things a certain way. Maybe you come from a corporate background where you felt censored, or maybe you came from a blue-collar background where everyone had to toe the line and do exactly what they were told. Whatever the case, this is the step where we have to get to know the real you.

The simplest way to do this is to write down a list of what you *like* and what you *don't like*. Let's start with some examples, shall we? I always suggest starting with things you don't like. That one is fun. For instance, what didn't you like to wear at your old job? What didn't you like to say at your old job? Who didn't you like working with? And so on, etc., etc. . . .

When it comes to selling houses, make a list of everything you don't like and then stop doing that stuff. Just stop doing it. STOP! No mas! You got it? Yes, it's that simple. Make a list now of everything that you don't like in your real estate career – and stop doing it. You now have permission to stop right now and never do those things again.

How good do you feel right now? Better, right? My friend Sharon used to complain all the time about working with first-time buyers and how they were a pain and she didn't have patience for them and they drove her crazy. I asked her who she did like working with and she told me she love, love, loved working with investors. When I asked her why, she lit up like a different person. "Because they are not emotional, they are decisive, they always seem to have money, and they don't waste my time or their own just looking." I suggested that from this point on, when a new first-time buyer comes to her and asks for help, she should say, "No, I'm sorry, I only work with investors." BAM! KABLAM!! How empowering is that story?

Edge Rule: Only work with people you like working with.

When you work with people you don't like, it's like working at a job you don't like. You didn't get into real estate to do things you don't like doing, but I see it all the time. New realtors tell me, "I hate open houses, but I do them anyway." Stop doing things you don't like doing, or you will forever be miserable or resentful and you are not going to attract business that way. Another thing to think about is this: when people are new in real estate, there are so many areas to potentially get involved in: Condos, Houses, Leases, working in certain areas, in certain neighborhoods, and more. You have to figure out what you like and stick to that.

I hated condos. You had to deal with HOA fees and homeowners' dues and there was all that extra paperwork and I personally didn't believe in living in a condo, so I didn't want anything to do with them. I was attracted to a high-end market. Stuff over a million or two million. My goal was to someday sell a house over $5million! So when someone came to me to buy or sell a condo, I told him or her, "Sorry, I don't sell condos." Their reactions were unbelievable, because apparently I was the first realtor they had ever encountered who turned down business. But you see, ME BEING THE REAL ME started to cause a stir. I may not have sold that condo, but then later on I'd get a call from that person's friend saying "Hey, I heard you specialize in selling houses as opposed to condos" – and I realized that sticking to my guns was paying off.

It's a common myth for newbies to try doing catch-all (sell everything and anything) when they first start. Managers teach them to do whatever comes up. Leases, condos houses, apartment buildings, any area. What I suggest is that you pick the one you like the most.

When I got started, the $5million house was like the Holy Grail. Now, of course, it's $10million. Either way, when I was new the high-end arena attracted me and I always had this goal to sell a five million dollar house. I got juiced over the high-end houses. I was passionate about the high-end market. I stayed that course even when bankruptcies and foreclosures became the "hot new thing." Everyone urged me to get involved in that new scene. "Mark, you should go after foreclosures, short sales, and blah blah blah!" I personally had zero interest in short sales. Zero. In fact, one of my things was that if anyone called me as a potential client and said, "I'm looking for a *deal* or a short sale opportunity," I would quickly end the conversation. It just wasn't me. Period. I didn't want to get pulled off-track or waste time on these bottom feeders.

True, many agents were killing it in short sales, but just as many were getting killed, chasing deals for bogus buyers who could never seem to offer enough to take anything over the finish line. That's what bottom feeders do. I had a friend who spent eighteen months working with one couple who wanted a short sale. They spent twelve months looking and then were in escrow for over six months, only for the original owner to somehow sue the bank and get their house back. My friend's commission was $0.00 on that one. Eighteen months of work and doughnut hole.

During those eighteen months, I also had many buyers wanting me to help them "find deals," but that wasn't my bag. I liked high-end buyers and sellers so I kept my focus, kept my eyes on the prize, and continued to spend my two or three hours a week learning about the high-end area, walking the areas I liked, and steering clear of the short sale hype.

My intuition – my gut – said that if I would find just two or three areas I was passionate about in real estate and stick to those, then in the long term I'd be OK. I soon came to understand that I really liked actual houses. If someone called about a condo, I would tell them that condos were not my specialty, I only do houses. I was rejecting customers and developing specialties without fully realizing that I was doing it. But guess what, it was working!

The more I focused on doing only residential *houses*, the more I sold. Someone would call me, looking to sell an apartment building, and I would tell them, "Sorry, it's not my bag, man," and refer them to another agent. I sensed that getting stuck spending time on something or someone I was not passionate about would pull my focus and hurt me more than help.

How does this apply to you? My point is that you have to find out what you like and stick to it. Stay the course. Don't get caught up in the hype if some big shot says he wants to buy a hotel and asks for your help. If hotels are your thing, then go for it, but if not, then tell them no and get back to doing what you do best. Being you. When you stay true to what you like, your future customers will see your passion and joy in your eyes and will naturally want to work with you.

Agents fail when they work with people they don't want to work with and they work in areas they don't want to work in. You don't have to wait five years to work with people you like in a specialized area that you love. Start now!

KNOW THYSELF SO YOU CAN BE YOURSELF

No one can do you better than you, my friend. No one knows what you're passionate about more than you. In this Step One, you'll be figuring out who you are, bringing out and sharing that person with the world. That's the person who will shine and soar and sell more houses than me, more than the top agent in your office, more than anyone could have imagined. *Who are you and what are you passionate about?* Let's talk about your passions and what I call "passion arenas."

FIND YOUR PASSION ARENAS

What is a PASSION ARENA? It is an activity, hobby, or even that you love being involved in, where there are other people around. It could be a weekly event like a book or cooking club, a team sport, a bike club, a group, an organization – but it has to be one that you truly love and you have to be able to attend it at least once a week. You love everything about this event/hobby/club and you don't go to it because there's an opportunity to make money there, you go to this passion arena because you love it. It's an environment with three or more people that you love being in more than anything else on the planet. Ultimately your goal here is to find at least three passion arenas that you will regularly attend.

Find 3 Passion Arenas:
One Personal
One Charitable
One Professional

You have to find three passion arenas. One that is a personal hobby, like a cooking club or a basketball league. One that is some type of charitable/volunteer group – it might be a church cleanup crew, a boys and/or girls club, a homeless shelter that you're passionate about. The third will be a professional arena: your specialization, like house-only, the high-end market, short sales, or a particular neighborhood that you love more than any other area. As you identify these three arenas, you criteria should be that they bring you joy when you participate in them and you're excited to be there, no matter what. You want to be there. You like being there. The only requirement for a passion arena is that there must be more than three people there and you have to attend it once a week, minimum. Through your passion arenas you will eventually meet new clients!

Traditional real estate training tells you to go do an open house or go to the Realtor Expo or go join a network group that meets at 7:30 a.m. every Tuesday morning at the local Denny's. This can really suck, especially if you're not a morning person. I know, I tried them all. For example, I tried this supposedly amazing business network that met at 7:00 a.m., but I have never been a morning person, so needless to say I wasn't in the best of moods to talk to anyone. That bombed. I hated going to these formalized so-called network groups trying to give referrals to people I barely knew. The groups were made up of people from different industries, like a dentist, a carpenter, and a stockbroker, and I was supposed to refer them and they were going to refer me. Yeah right, I barely knew these people and they sure as hell didn't know me. How was I supposed to refer them?

Then one day after four months of these morning get-togethers, another person joins the group, and guess what? It's a realtor from my same area. Now what? Who gets the referral, him or me? I said enough of this nonsense, I'm going to volunteer at the boys and girls club because I like kids and I'd just had it with all these salesy people begging for referrals and whining when I didn't give them any.

I figured volunteering at the boys and girls club would get my mind off trying to make money selling houses. One day each week I would go to the Boys and Girls Club for two or three hours. I wasn't there to sell anything or even look for customers or get a single referral. I went because I loved kids, wanted to help out, and, if you want to know the truth, figured maybe I would meet a cute single girl.

Anyway, cut to a couple months later. Now I know the kids by name, I am meeting a lot of their parents, and I'm becoming known as "Mr. Mark from Minnesota" to all the kids. Well, one day one of the parents asked me what I did for a living, and because I hate the word "realtor," I said "I said houses." And that was that! The next thing I knew, Mr. Guerra was telling me how he and his wife were looking for a house, and boom! I just picked up my next customer without even trying.

What I was doing, however, was being myself in an environment I loved being in, coming from a position of service. This attracted the right type of clients and the right type of people into my life.

Then it hit me. "What else am I passionate about?" Well, as I've already told you, I love hockey as I grew up in Minnesota. I wanted to play more, so I joined a pick-up hockey team in a league that played once a week for two or three hours. So now I had Boys and Girls Club once a week for a few hours and my hockey league once a week for a few hours. Hockey was a personal hobby of mine and volunteering with the kids was a nice charitable organization to be involved in, but I felt like I needed one more passion arena to round everything off. I was very passionate about the high-end world of real estate, so I asked myself what I could do to learn more about the high end – or where could I go where there might be others who were passionate about high-end real estate. I didn't know, so one day a week I just drove around the zillion-dollar neighborhoods, saying hello to people and asking them about the area. This became my third passion arena, my professional arena as I called it.

I now had three viable weekly events that I loved attending and, though I didn't realize it, provided great opportunities for me to meet future clients. None of this felt like work because these were all things I wanted to do, not something someone else told me I should do. I was developing my own prospecting plan and didn't even know it! That is what I want you to do! I cannot tell you where to make your passion arenas, but let's figure it out together!

Your passion arenas are activities you love to do and places you love to go, where it isn't work, it doesn't feel like work, and you can't wait to get there. For a couple or three hours each week, you will find one personal passion arena, one professional passion arena, and one charitable/non-profit/volunteer passion arena. For me it was hockey league (Personal), the high-end housing market (Professional), and the Boys and Girls Club (Charitable/Volunteer). Instead of doing the traditional BS of going to meetings I didn't want to be at or doing open houses that I didn't like, I spent my valuable time at my three passion arenas. It was so easy, and I felt free because I never had to attend another silly office meeting again, except to collect my commission checks.

Does this make sense? If it doesn't, then call me now! You cannot go to Step Two until you've begun to see who you are and can start bringing out the you in you. That is how you will make a ton of money in residential real estate. By being yourself and prospecting and specializing quickly in areas that YOU are passionate about. Your passion arenas.

What worked for my passion arenas will not work for you. That's the beauty of this system. You get to pick your own. Step One is basically designed by you and that's why it will work best for you. I have seen too many talented agents bomb out of this business because they try to work in areas that they think will make them money, or where their sales managers told them to work, instead of just working in areas that they are passionate about. There are so many flavors of the month and newbies get sucked into this format because they do not know better. You now do know better. Only you can decide what your passion arenas will be. Start with three minimum. Over time you may have six, seven or more. Whatever they are, the number one rule is that you must love these arenas. For me, I loved hockey and kids and was fascinated by big homes, so I didn't need any motivation to go each week and spend a few hours a week at each. I liked it so it was easy.

Edge Rule: If you don't like doing it, stop doing it!

The more you become your own person, the more clients and others will pay attention to you because you seem focused and confident. Watch what happens when you start dressing or driving to suit yourself or say no to someone or something because it's "not your bag." People will be attracted to you. Why? Two reasons. One: you don't look desperate. Two: you're coming from a position of strength. The stereotype for real estate agents is that they'll do anything for money – and guess what? YOU just shattered that stereotype by turning down some business. You're now automatically elevated to a higher status, and this effect will snowball if you hold your ground.

Another reason people will be attracted to you is that you are being authentic. You're being honest. You are not salesy; you are not trying to "sell" them. You are being yourself, in environments you love being in and working with people you like working with. You can't help but succeed. Someone would ask me for help with condos and I would tell them, "I don't believe in buying condos, so I can't help you." BOOM! I was being honest. This would offend some buyers but it couldn't be helped. To me it was just like someone going to a food doctor and asking that doctor to fix his or her neck ache. You see how stupid it sounds with doctors, with realtors do it all the time, especially new ones. They just got their license and Mr. Bigshot Billy comes along saying, "Hey, Ms. Naïve Newbie, can you help me? I'm looking to invest in apartment buildings all over the area." Ms. Naïve Newbie says, "Um, OK, I can try, even though I don't know much about apartment buildings. Happy to help."

Ms. Naïve Newbie helps Bigshot Billy because she thinks, "I don't have anything else going on, so I'll just work with this person until I get busier and find some real home buyers." Naïve Newbie never ends up finding REAL clients that she is excited about because Bigshot Billy is wasting all her time. She gets resentful and miserable and one day soon says, "Ughh, I hate this business, I never wanted to sell apartment buildings anyway." And another one bites the dust.

We will learn in Step Four how to avoid these career killers like Billy Bigshot. In the meantime, focus on what you like and do more of that – and stop doing what you don't like.

NO MORE SQUARE PEGS IN ROUND HOLES

I have seen more realtors fail because they try to be that square peg in a round hole – trying to do it the way someone told them it should be done, or working in neighborhoods they "hear" are good to work in. The way to make a lot of money in real estate is to ask one person what gets you fired up, and that one person to ask is yourself! Period. The best area is the one YOU are most passionate about. Your third passion arena. What I call your PROFESSIONAL passion arena.

THE MAGICAL LEAD-GENERATING WEBSITE

My good friend Pat was failing miserably in his first year and was almost wiped out. One of the reasons he was failing was that he was spending five hours a day building this magical website that someone convinced him would capture leads and have the fish jumping into the boat! The website was linked to his Facebook and Twitter accounts and supposedly was even linked to the moon. According to the person who sold it, everyone who was anyone was using this new magical lead-generation tool. Pat was new and this was the only thing his company was teaching, so it's fair to say that Pat didn't know any better. After all, his company was promoting this and he figured they knew best.

It was the huge tech era. Social media companies were cleaning up on realtors. They would promote packages and programs to us, making all sorts of promises about how we would generate tons of business. I personally hated anything techy and stayed away. Pat, however, being new and not knowing any better, was all over this because it seemed like a quick fix, easy money, everyone was doing it so it had to be good, right?

The reality was that after almost a year of wasting time on this tech craze, it turned out to be just "Lookie-Lous" and time-wasters wanting free info. Pat spent over a year tweaking his site, hoping he'd get more or better leads, and it never amounted to jack squat! Finally he told me he'd given up. He was going to quit real estate and go back to his J.O.B. (Journey of the Broke, I call it.) Pat had been chasing these tech marketing plans because that is what everybody else was doing. It was the flavor of the month for realtors. I am not saying you should never have a website or that websites never generate leads, I am saying that if tech is not your passion arena, then in the beginning don't worry about it. *Capisce*? If you're a closet engineer, however, that loves everything tech/web/internet, then by all means find a tech group or a weekly nerd fest where you can meet others who are passionate about technology and, guess what, you have your first passion arena.

SIDENOTE – TRUE STORY: When I was selling houses, I NEVER HAD A WEBSITE. And I sold for 20 years thru 2021.... Let me reiterate that. I never used or had a website as a realtor. Shocking to many, I know. Why didn't I? Because I didn't like anything techy, it wasn't me. I put up a website for two weeks in 2008 and immediately closed it aw I knew it would only distract me. I called it a "weapon of mass distraction." Avoiding this and others like it would become my secret weapon, as well as the Main Mission of Step Four. Avoid Weapons of Mass Distraction.

So now back to Pat, who was now quitting real estate for good. This was a guy I knew could smoke anyone on the golf course and he loved golfing, but he'd given it up to spend time trying to sell houses. I ran into Pat right before he was going to hang it up and I said, "Pat, before you quit, why don't you forget about real estate, selling, and the magic bullsh*t website for now. Play golf once a week to keep your mind off real estate. Just go have fun." Pat said he would love to, but golf had gotten so expensive he no longer had money to afford such a luxury. "Then why don't you just go to the public course and practice your putting on the putting green where it is FREE and you will be some peace of mind before you make a rash decision to quit real estate." Pat agreed. "OK, I'll go a couple times a week and just putt, and maybe get some clarity."

I knew Pat loved everything about golf and he would find his answers there. "After a few weeks hanging out at the putting green," I said, "if you come to the conclusion you want to quit real estate, then OK, I'll believe you."

Pat went once a week to practice his putting and I even joined him a couple times. After a few times, some regulars saw how good he was and asked him for pointers. He would strike up conversations with other players. I saw it all happening and Pat didn't have a clue. Next thing you know, everyone wanted free putting lessons from Pat and it was almost comical how people would walk up to him and ask him how he was doing. Well, sure enough, one gentleman said he'd heard Pat was a realtor and asked Pat to help him sell his house. BOOM! Pat was back. He called me that day and said he just picked up an $800,000 listing because he was helping some guy with his putting.

This is how it works, my friends. That listing turned into two more deals. Pat stepped up his golfing to every day at the golf course and the snowball took off. It was all because he was doing what he loved and not what others told him would work.

It's not about your website, it is not about a script, it is not about some special closing technique. It's about you being you, in an environment you love being in, coming from a spirit of service (Cornerstone), and doing it on a regular basis. For Pat it was the free putting green. For me it was The Boys and Girls Club. For you it may be as simple as the dog park each week. I don't know, you get to decide.

The sooner you identify your three weekly passion arenas, the sooner you can get going developing relationships. It will take some searching and some faith, but you will get there. Keep it simple: One personal, one professional, one charitable.

More examples of personal passion arenas: favorite hobbies, book, cooking, painting or other clubs, a hockey team, group golf lessons, church groups. Find a personal passion and, at least once a week, spend two or three hours with it like Pat did with the golf course.

Examples of professional passion arenas: pick a particular area of real estate that you love, then – two or three hours a week – eat, live and breathe this passion arena. The high-end market, leases, listings only, buyers only, condos only, houses only, certain neighborhoods or areas that you're most passionate about (The Hills, the flats, the city, the country). One agent I know specialized in horse properties only. Everyone thought he was nuts, but who do you think every seller calls when they want to sell a horse property? You could be an expert in whatever type of property you are passionate about. If you choose condos, then get to know every condo building within a one-mile area, become the condo master, make condos your passion arena, and go knock on every condo door and introduce yourself. People ask me all the time if they should door-knock or not and my answer is always, "Do you like door-knocking?" If you do, then by all means knock yourself out! If you don't, then never do it again. Got it? Making sense?

I loved the high-end market, so I would go to high-end hotels, hang out in the lobbies and bars and have a salad once a week to see how the rich roll. I got to know the bellmen, the concierges. Celebs would come in regularly for drinks, and, well, the rest is history. If you want to catch a big fish, you have to go where the big fish are. I didn't know where they'd be, but I knew where they weren't: they weren't in my apartment! So a few hours every week, I would go and "whale hunt" (as I called it). Whale hunting became my passion arena. Yours may be different, but you get the idea.

Examples of a charitable/volunteer arena could be: Boys and Girls Clubs, church groups, volunteering events, find a charity you're passionate about and get involved once a week. This one is easiest and quickest for most people to grasp. I liked kids, so I volunteered at the Boys and Girls Club. Another realtor friend of mine plays the piano every Sunday at church because her passion outside of real estate is music. She volunteers at a church she doesn't even attend, because they need a piano player. She gets to know the other members in the music group and in the church and she cleans house, as everyone now knows she's a realtor. Hopefully you are seeing how this works and why passion arenas trump traditional lead-generating tools all day long.

BEWARE/CAUTION:

If you attend passion arenas because you think they are going to make you money in real estate, you are not choosing the right passion arenas.

Your passion arenas, first and foremost, must be events and environments that you love, love, love. You love being there, you love being around the people there, and you get inspired and fired up just thinking about going there. Have I drilled this point into your head? You go because you love being there, not because you think it will make you a lot of money. Don't make the huge and common newbie mistake of doing something because you think that is where the money is.

Also don't make the mistake of spending tons of money on market in your first year or two. You will be targeted by marketing people offering to "brand" you and you'll be tempted to spend money on websites, signs, and fancy logos that are supposed to bring business pouring in. It won't. You will just have a cool business card and a cool website and no business. If you do not build the right foundation early and learn how to incorporate your passions into selling homes, you will be in for a rough and rocky road. Learning how to be yourself will separate you from the pack. You are developing a system with consistency and this is what champions do. A passion arena is generally something you know a little about and enjoy a lot, so when you begin meeting people you will not be talking about houses, you will be talking about things you already share common interests in. This bond, this rapport, this natural connection will make selling seamless as you are beginning with developing a relationship and not trying to sell anyone anything. If it sounds simple, it's because it is.

Edge Rule: Keep it simple.

Don't overcomplicate any of this. Another good friend of mine, Steve, said he had no passion arenas and he was miserable and he hated everyone at most social events. This was a challenge, but we talked for a bit and I asked him, "What is one thing you like that is your favorite thing in the world?" He said, "Coffee." Boom! "Perfect," I said. "Every week, once a week for two hours go sit at the Starbucks on Ventura Boulevard. Steve did that and became one of the San Fernando Valley's biggest real estate agents by going to Starbucks every week for two hours, planting his butt in the seat and sipping his favorite cup of Joe. His passion arena was coffee. Don't overcomplicate this stuff. Keep it simple, pal!

PASSION ARENAS ARE ENDLESS BUT START WITH THREE

As you get passionate about finding your passion arenas, you may discover that four or five or six passion arenas surface. That is OK. I suggest keeping it at about three, tops, your first six months. The goal in your first thirty to sixty days is to really find your passion and interests and stick to them. Get to know thyself and really tune into whether you are doing things because you love them or because someone else is pushing you down that road. If it is someone else suggesting it, it is probably not *your* passion arena.

WRITE IT DOWN

You can figure out who you are initially by simply writing down your likes and dislikes and then staying the course. Write down what neighborhoods you like, what type of homes you like, do you like working with couples with kids or couples without kids, do you like working with single people.

I was single when I got started and tried working with couples with kids. I just didn't seem to connect, so guess what? I QUIT DOING IT! If something is not working, stop doing it now! Remember the Cornerstone of Humility and how being coachable is a necessary part of survival in your first year? Agents fail because they're stubborn or think they have to do things a certain way because everyone else is. You have to do things your way in your first year, meaning follow your passion and your heart and you can then follow the road to the bank.

All my friends would tell me that I needed to work with families if I wanted to make money. They told me I needed to get to know people with kids because they were the ones buying houses. I could not talk to married couples with kids in my first year or two or even three! I had nothing in common with them. They looked at me like I was toast from the beginning. And this is no big shocker, I didn't have any success working with couples with kids, so I quit doing it. I wish someone had told me sooner. I liked working with people that were single and later I eased my way into couples. Over time this evolved, I became more comfortable working with families, and as I grew my clientele grew.

Selling on the Edge is about listening to your soul and your gut and if something feels off, or the person is shady, or you just don't click, then move on, my friends. Follow that first impression, it is rarely wrong. You will learn all about gutcheck in Step Three. Learning how to say no will save you time, money and heartache.

Are you starting to know thyself? Going to start doing more of what you like? Going to stop doing things you don't like (no matter who told you to do them)? Going to bring out the YOU in you? Congratulations, you are now ready for Step Two. It's time to get out there.

CHAPTER 13

STEP 2: GET OUT THERE

"It is not the critic who counts; not the man who points out how the strong man stumbles, or where the doer of deeds could have done them better. The credit belongs to the man who is actually in the arena, whose face is marred by dust and sweat and blood; who strives valiantly; who errs, who comes short again and again, because there is no effort without error and shortcoming; but who does actually strive to do the deeds; who knows great enthusiasms, the great devotions; who spends himself in a worthy cause; who at the best knows in the end the triumph of high achievement, and who at the worst, if he fails, at least fails while daring greatly, so that his place shall never be with those cold and timid souls who neither know victory nor defeat."

-Theodore Roosevelt, 26th President of the United States

Step 2 Main Mission: **Get your FAIL on!**

Step 2 Main Moves: **Engage, Crash, and Burn**

                                           Develop Relationships

Step Two is all about action. As you learned from our twenty-sixth president, it is also about getting into the ring and getting your fail on. Getting your fail on means falling on your face, taking chances, making mistakes, crashing and burning, falling down, only to pick yourself up and try again. Many new realtors and even experienced ones suffer from perfectionism and what I call "analysis paralysis." They get ready to get ready and they study and they listen and they take classes and they get more funky letters behind their name – like GRI and GDD and PTA and CBS and BROKER and SUPER AGENT GED, LMNOP!! But guess what? Until you can understand the two most important things in selling, which are GETTING OUT THERE and DEVELOPING RELATIONSHIPS, you're not going to make a red nickel.

Becoming the best in sales and in real estate is not about being the best closer or best salesman or saleswoman or most perfectly dressed or equipped with the right script. It is about being the best at FINDING real clients. Getting out there means you have to get out of your house, your office, your car, and TALK to people.

I go back and forth about what is more important, Step One or Step Two in these Six Steps of **Selling on the Edge** and I have come to the conclusion that they are tied – but if it came to a decision I would say Step Two wins the tie breaker because no matter how much you are capable of being yourself and bringing out the you in you, if you don't *get out there* and consistently attend your passion arenas and do your best at developing relationships, you will be as our 26th president said, *"among those cold and timid souls who neither know victory nor defeat."*

What does it mean to "get out there"? It means you have to go out and build relationships. And to do this well you have to get good at doing it 90 percent of your time. This is what your real career is. You are a relationship developer! While doing this, you will come across people that need your help. You make money when you FIND the winners. Everything is easy after this. We call real buyers and real sellers WINNERS. Winners close themselves. You just have to find them and that is what Step Two will help you do – better than anyone else out there. I could care less what you call yourself. You may call yourself a real estate agent or salesman or area expert or broker or Dr. Viddiboombah, it's what you DO that matters. I know some of the smoothest-talking salespeople who are dressed to kill and drive the perfect car and have the most amazing website and marketing materials, but each week if you ask them how many new people they talked to or said hello to, the answer is ZERO. ZERO!

It's only a short, short time before these agents return the car, cancel the marketing campaign, hang up the skates and go back to their old J-O-Bs. If you are new, you need to listen to me now. I have lasted fifteen years in this business and I have shockingly NEVER had a website and I don't use Facebook. I'm not saying you won't need these things someday, but we have to teach you first things first. The number one most important thing you can take away from this program is that if you master the art of getting out there on a regular basis and never, never, ever stop, you will ALWAYS have more business than you know what to do with. The scary part is when I see real estate agents fail, lose a deal or have a bad day – and pack their bags and give up. They are scared to get back out there. They are scared to even try again and they are usually right around the corner from a huge success story if they would just hang on.

HOMELESS GUY IN THE PARKING LOT

So I was sitting in my car in the Walgreens parking lot on Robertson Boulevard, just about to leave but finishing a phone call. As I looked across the parking lot, I was watching this homeless person ask people for money. He kept getting turned down. Car after car he went to, and nothing. People kept coming out and he would ask, and unfortunately no one was giving him a penny. I was about to get out of my car and walk over and hand the guy a ten dollar bill. I had it in my pocket and, oh well, what did I need it for anyway? I was only about twenty feet from the guy and he never approached me. He saw me sitting in my car, but he never came over and asked. Who knows why and who cares, but I thought, "Wow, this guy is thirty feet away from someone who is going to give him ten dollars and all he has to do is ask." So instead of getting out of my car, I wanted to see if he would ask.

I said I would give it ten minutes and if he didn't ask, I was leaving and keeping my ten dollars. Three minutes went by: nothing. Five minutes went by, he glanced over at me, but nothing. At the eight minute mark I was reaching for my keys figuring this guy was not going to ask me for money.

But why not? Did I not look like I had money? Was my Jetta turning him off? Did I look stingy? This homeless guy was literally now less than ten feet away from me and he was about to lose out on ten dollars simply because he didn't ask. The ten minutes was up. I looked down to start my car, adjusted my seat slightly, and just as I was about to reverse, I looked back up and KNOCK! KNOCK! This made me jump and sure enough, he was knocking on my window. I happily gave him the ten bucks and was on my way.

My point in all this is what? You just never know who you are around, so if you can learn to engage and be the person who initiates "hello," you never know where it may go from there. Engaging is the key. Forget about what happens next, just be yourself and say what you feel. Some people you will click with, some you won't.

Do you know how refreshing it is to have someone say hello to you? You know that feeling when someone says something to you that is genuine and you didn't expect it? That is what engaging is. Being the person who starts the ball rolling. The two Main Moves in Step Two will help you do this.

Step Two Main Moves:
Engage, Crash, and Burn
Develop Relationships

If you recall, the Main Mission for Step Two is to get your FAIL on! That means go out there, open your mouth, be yourself, say hello and speak from your heart. And yes, screw up! Fail! Get beat up! Get rejected! Make mistakes! Say something stupid! BE YOURSELF! The only way to find out what works is to ENGAGE! The more you engage, the more you will crash and burn – and it's important to understand that if you're crashing and burning, meaning getting rejected, then you are in the game! You have to be in the game to win.

Let's use dating as another example. Most people want to have someone special in their life, but they are afraid to put themselves out there and open up to someone. We're afraid we may be shot down. Ever had that experience? We all have. You are not alone. In real estate you have to put yourself out there. Just as in dating, isn't it amazing when you do put yourself out there and someone responds positively? Yes, it is! There is nothing better.

In real estate you have to learn to make the first move. Period. If you never take a shot, you will never know.

> *"You miss one hundred percent of the shots you never take."*
> -Wayne Gretzky

I was at a grocery store once and saw Dwight Howard in line two rows down. I couldn't talk, he was a sight to see. The most amazing athlete I've ever seen in person. I thought to myself, I should go up to him, say hi and be myself. Maybe welcome him to L.A. and tell him I'm a fan. What's the worst that can happen? Well, I chickened out. He walked past me, smiled, and I didn't take a shot. Three later, I read in the *L.A. Times* that Dwight Howard was looking for property in L.A., as he was about to be traded to the Lakers.

You miss one hundred percent of the shots you never take. Engaging is simply about putting yourself out there and making the introduction. The rest will take care of itself. Think of some of your best friends right now. How did you meet them? One of you had to say hello first. When you are new, if you learn to be the one who engages, you will reap the rewards and sell many, many houses.

We're not selling anything yet, and as you say hello to people or attempt to get to know them, they may happen to be in a bad mood and not respond. This is OK. You can't control other people or how they interact. This is the crash and burn part. Know that it is all part of the journey and the more you crash and burn, the closer you are to developing that one relationship where everything could change. You can't control people's response to you, but you can control your attending your passion arenas each week, being yourself and having fun getting to know people.

I came up with this Step because as a new realtor you have to understand that rejection and getting lots of NOs is a good thing. You will get a lot more people telling you NO and not wanting to open up to you than you will get YESs. This Step is about embracing that this is OK. Do you remember being a little kid, say from around age 4 to 7? Children are not afraid to engage. They don't know the word "rejection." As we grow up, we get more fearful of approaching people because we don't want to get hurt. Get over this, start living like a kid again, not being afraid to say hello. You will be surprised how others will respond and before you know it you will have many new friends and you'll be off and running! Getting out there is not about selling anything yet, it's about developing relationships and this is what you are doing in Step Two.

DEVELOP RELATIONSHIPS

Edge Rule: Relationship first. Sell second.

When I first joined my pickup hockey league, I did it because I love hockey and figured it would be a great way to hang with the guys in a healthy environment where we all would have fun. I had no idea that months down the road, my teammates would be asking me for real estate help. The main reason was that I was never trying to sell anyone anything. I was there becoming friends with other adults and we were all passionate about the same thing: hockey. I was in an environment where I could be myself, that I liked being in, so I would go every week. Over time I realized that this was a better place to meet potential new clients than any cold-calling list or networking group that I could ever attend. So that was that, I made it my mission to be there every week.

It was great because doing this did not seem like work, yet I was technically building relationships. It was something I didn't have to force myself to do, because I loved playing hockey. It was my passion, so I made it my first passion arena!

Then I added another passion arena and another and another. I was prospecting without even realizing it. And yes, the sales started pouring in. Teammates were referring me, calling me to buy and sell and Kablam blam blam!! Life was bueno. I have not sat an open house in years. Why? Because they are not for me. I don't like them. Not my passion. They may be for you. If you like them, then by all means, do them. You have to figure out what you like and do more of it, and trust that it will work. New sales people bomb and end up leaving the business in their first year because they prospect at functions or events they hate attending. They do what they think is the right thing to do and don't follow their heart. They do what everyone else seems to be doing, like open houses, business network groups, or office meetings.

My friend Sandra loved books more than air so she attended book clubs and helping people write books – and when they found out she was a realtor, she started getting business. It is that simple. She didn't go to book club meetings to find new clients, but clients ended up finding her.

YOUR SUCCESS TREE

Be yourself, bring out the you in you, figure out your three passion arenas (Personal, Professional, Charitable), get out there and get your fail on! Do it each week. If you stop attending your passion arenas, your success tree will die. Prospecting is like water for your success tree, and if the tree dries up you are in trouble. As you water the tree regularly, sometimes nothing changes, and the next week you water it again, and nothing changes, but then that third week you notice a new branch or a new bud starts to flower, and week four or five all of a sudden you have flowers, buds, and new branches. Soon birds are building nests, butterflies come to fly around, and one day an eagle even lands there! These are all the fruits of your regular watering. Consistency is the key. New realtors fail because they don't consistently water their success tree.

Salespeople get one or two sales and then guess what they do? They stop attending their passion arenas. Which means they've stopped watering their success tree. Not good. I've been there. Yes, I've done it. You may think, "Oh, I can skip it this week, look at all the branches and buds and leaves." Soon enough, the tree starts to dry up, a leaf falls off, the green turns to brown, some of the branches are sagging, and all of a sudden, no birds are flying in it anymore. You find out your tree is dying.

I hope you see the analogy here to how important getting out there each week and *consistently* watering your success tree will be for you. Water and sunlight are lifeblood to a tree. Consistently getting out there and developing relationships is the lifeblood to your success in selling houses.

THE BEST FRIEND EXERCISE

Many people have asked me for help with talking to people without using any type of script. The **Selling on the Edge** system has absolutely no scripts, so if you are attending a passion arena or anywhere, for that matter, and you want to speak to someone, what can you do? How can you start an authentic conversation without sounding like every other salesperson and real estate agent on the planet? I have two solutions for you. I call them the *best friend exercise* and the *5-to-1 drill*.

Before I explain these two concepts, I want to remind you of the Main Mission of Step Two, which is to get your fail on. Get out there and make mistakes, say the wrong thing, get yelled at or hung up on or, yes, even rejected! This is normal for a successful realtor. You have to remember not to take it personally. If you are going out fishing and you take 40 casts and don't get any bites, do you say to yourself, "I am such a bad person and such a loser"? No. You say, "Fishing sucks!" OK, kidding. The top fishermen don't say any of that, they simply move to a different fishing area until they find an area that works for them. You have to do the same when deciding on your passion arenas, getting out there and selling houses. In Step Two I want you to understand before you move on to Step Three that FAILING IS OK and you are going to make mistakes and screw up and even fall down. This is part of honing what works for you and what doesn't. I told you in Step One that I hated wearing suits and one day decided I was going to wear whatever the hell I wanted, which was t-shirts, jeans, and tennis shoes, because this was me! I was more comfortable, didn't feel like a salesman, and I felt more like me. Translation: I felt good and genuine so the result was that I came across as authentic and it worked.

Cut to many years later (as I still was criticized for dressing the way I wanted to dress) and I had managed to develop a relationship with a very, very big client. He was a very famous person and when I first met him, everyone (like they always do) was giving me advice. They told me that if I was going to sell him a house, I needed to wear a suit, or drive a better car, or blah, blah, blah – they all had their two cents' worth. Many laughed and said, "We understand you love your t-shirt and jeans, but to bag this whale you need to step up your wardrobe." I said, "Nonsense!" For years my style was working and I was sticking to it. You see, only I knew this client personally, so in the end no one knew better than I did what the situation was. What I wore or drove didn't matter one bit.

It is true that as we began working together, I was a little worried because initially I thought he looked at me funny, maybe thinking, "Hmm, this guy Mark seems a bit off." Were he and his entourage looking at me suspiciously, thinking "This guy isn't wearing two-thousand-dollar suits, snazzy lizard-skin shoes, or driving a fancy luxury vehicle . . . so how good could he be?" Kind of like, "If you're so smart, why ain't you rich?" I was rockin' the t-shirt, the haggard jeans, and driving a beat-up Jetta. The ironic part, though, was that this client was actually well known for wearing a t-shirt and jeans almost everywhere he went. So by magic or miracle or the bond of a simple t-shirt, we clicked and I started helping him. Somehow things were working out. He liked me. He seemed to really trust me. I would later learn that it was because I was being myself and not your typical "let's make a deal" stereotype real estate agent. I was a little insecure at the time about not driving a fancy luxury vehicle like most real estate agents in L.A. However, at one point, one of his associates told me they were happy to be working with a down-to-earth agent who didn't drive a fancy high-dollar ride. My theory had now been validated.

Edge Rule: Drive a low-profile car.

Every time this client came to look at a property, I would pinch myself. "Is this really happening?" It was. Yes, it was surreal to be working with this man. This gentleman had a net worth of over $500million and every agent in town was trying to show him property, yet somehow I was holding court with him. When I called, he picked up. I was working a major celebrity and all of the biggest agents in all of Los Angeles were also trying to get his business. The word got out that he was on the hunt for a property, so all the sharks were doing anything and everything to get his attention. Somehow, he was responding to me. Me, the kid who – what seemed like yesterday – was living in a garage with Ricky Raccoon.

When I first met this person, I was nervous. He had a huge entourage. I knew I didn't want to sound like a salesperson or look like everyone else, but I froze when I saw him pull up or if I was going to talk to him. What I came up with was this: I said to myself, "How can I calm down and just be myself, speak from my heart and make it natural?" I was sitting in my car and here he came rolling up in his Bentley and it hit me! "I'm going to pretend I am talking to my best friend, Dave. I have known Dave since I was zero, we grew up together and we've been like brothers since we met." I knew that if I just pretended this client was Dave, I would be myself, I would be loose and totally at ease, and everything would be OK. The *best friend exercise* was born.

The client stepped out of his car and boom, I looked at him as if he was my best friend Dave. I smiled and said hello, was totally relaxed, he smiled and it was on! When you're with your best friend, you are totally yourself. Your best friend doesn't judge you. You're not afraid to look stupid in front of your best friend and you certainly don't censor what you want to say. You know your best friend gets you, no matter what. As I was speaking to this man, all my insecurities were gone because I kept reminding myself, "You're talking to Dave, you're talking to Dave." If you use this concept when talking to any client and feel nervous or unsure about what to say, this technique is magical. It's lightning in a bottle. I promise you, you will always know what to say if you imagine that you're talking to your best friend instead of some client.

For starters, you speak from your heart and you never sound scripted or unnatural – and this authenticity, my friends, will start your new relationship off on the right foot. If you hadn't seen your best friend in three years and you were meeting him or her to look at a house they were thinking of buying or selling, what would you say? How would you say it? I don't know, only you do. Only you know who your best friend is and how you would act. I act like a complete goofball and extremely blunt in front of my friend Dave, and this is how I acted in front of this client. Turns out this particular client was a giant goofball himself, probably the most blunt man on television today, and he appreciated my bluntness.

The moment that changed my life forever was when we had found a house that he liked and we were all sitting around in the back yard discussing the best way to make the deal happen. He looked at me in front of his entourage and flat out asked me, "OK, Mark, so what's the deal? What do you think we should offer on this house?" The asking price was sixteen point five million and the reality was that I had never sold a house even close to that price point. I didn't know what the value was. I really had no clue. That very moment I froze up like the proverbial deer in the headlights. The jig was up. I had no idea what to say to him. Scouring my brain for the perfect script, I was panicking as everyone stared at me in silence, waiting for an answer. Then it hit me! What would I say to my best friend Dave if he asked me what he should offer? And instead of some bullsh*t script or bogus sales line, what came out of my mouth when the client asked me what to offer was the line of my career. I snapped out of my deer-in-headlights freeze, visualized Dave right there in front of me, and said to this man, "How bad do you want it?" They all broke out in laughter and the rest is history.

The lesson here, in case you missed it, is to say what you feel, not what you think the client wants to hear. I had no clue what that house was worth, and if I had recited a bogus script or given him a number that I didn't know was good advice, I would have gone against my own integrity, and that would have done me or the client no good. When you don't know what to say, say "I don't know." The moment you tell a client something that is not true or not authentic, they will see it and you will lose that client. If you don't know, don't pretend you do. The script that you use in **Selling on the Edge** is called the truth. And the truth shall set you free.

This wonderful gentleman went on to work with me and purchase the home for fifteen million dollars for one reason. He trusted me. Because I was myself around him and spoke to him honestly and directly like I would with my best friend Dave. This allowed authenticity to come out with a genuineness that no script or fancy sales move could ever provide, and the *best friend exercise* was forever etched in stone. Thanks, Dave.

When the sale finally closed, the buyer and his top business associate were leaving the property and getting into their cars. The buyer was a man of very few words, so I didn't expect him to say much. It was all good, I was grateful to have closed the sale and wished them well. As they were about to depart, the associate stopped and said to me something I would never forget. "Ya know, Mark, you are the first person we have ever worked with who didn't seem like a realtor, and we very much appreciate that." They closed the doors and began driving off. The buyer, at the wheel of his Bentley, drove about twenty feet, then stopped the car. I was walking away higher than a kite, having just closed a fifteen million dollar sale, but turned to see if there was a problem. The buyer rolled down his window, looked back at me and said in his famous British accent, "Mark . . . well done!"

I felt like I just won Wimbledon. Game. Set. Match. It was the greatest moment of my career. Unfortunately, due to confidentiality I cannot disclose who this wonderful gentleman was, but I can tell you that if I were to describe him, he definitely has the X factor and you don't want to be on his bad side. Thank you, Mr. X Factor! If you are reading this, I wish to personally thank you and your entire team from the bottom of my heart.

Now, if you are new, I understand that you may not have a moment like this tomorrow or next month, or even next year. However, if you keep the Four Cornerstones at the forefront of your mind, follow these steps, and most importantly, stay true to yourself, I promised you, you will have your Wimbledon moment.

> *"This above all: To thine own self be true."*
> -William Shakespeare

THE 5-to-1 DRILL

The five-to-one drill is another technique I discovered because as a new agent I would get nervous and talk too much. Yep, that was me! I would babble about nothing and always be talking about my company or myself, the way I was originally taught. Not good. The 5-to-1 drill means you are not allowed to say anything about yourself until you have learned five things about the other person. Try it. It is magical. It's harder than it sounds. But one thing that never changes is that people love talking about themselves. It's OK if you are the customer, but if you are the realtor and doing too much talking, I can assure you the end is near. In real estate sales or any type of sales, if you are talking too much about yourself, you're toast.

Edge Rule: If you're talking, you're losing.

Traditional training says you should do your dog and pony show, do a huge presentation, tell people how you are number one and your office is the biggest in the area, blah blah blah puke. This will kill any chances of developing authenticity and rapport with your new friends in your passion arenas. By remembering to find out five things about someone before you say one thing about yourself, you will learn a key skill that will make you lots of money: *How to listen*. Understand, you have to find out five things about the other person for every one thing you share about yourself. Got it? Once you learn five things and tell them one thing about yourself, you have to find out five MORE things about them before you start yappin' again. It may seem difficult at first, but this is the **Edge**. With the **Edge**, we don't do what other salespeople or realtors do. Just take a day to observe other real estate agents or salespeople and see how many talk too much. Remember, if you're talking, you're toast!

You have learned a lot in this Step so I am going to recap it for you. I want to make sure you have it all before you move to Step Three, which will be your selling system once you find a live prospect. In other words, Step Three is what you do when you find someone who actually wants your help in buying or selling.

IMPORTANT NOTE: Keep in mind that in Step Two we are NOT selling anyone anything. Not yet. This is vitally important. The goal is to get your fail on, engage, crash, burn – and ultimately develop relationships. PERIOD! If you try to sell before you have developed something real, something genuine, you are done. You will turn off your new friend and they will think you are "just another realtor." Not what you're looking for. Remember the rule?

Edge Rule: Relationship first, sell second (or not at all).

Why would you NOT try to sell someone? Answer: many reasons. One could be that you just don't like them. They might seem shady to you. They could seem mean. Another reason could just be that your gut said this was not someone you wanted to work with. So you "DIS-qualify" them. I will get to this more in Step Three but for now it's important to remember, we are not selling anyone anything yet. Step Two teaches one of the most important elements in building a long-term wonderfully lucrative real estate business. You're learning how to develop relationships the right way: *From your heart and with zero agenda in mind.*

New realtors blow so many possible deals because they jump to selling way too soon. It's not their fault, this is the training that's out there. "Go for the close." "Sell, sell, sell!" "Sell everyone!" Not with the **Edge**. **Selling on the Edge** is about authentically building relationships first and foremost and then, and only then, making a decision about whether you can truly help this person. Let's recap Step Two: Getting out there.

Step 2 Main Mission: **Get your FAIL on!**

Step 2 Main Moves: **Engage, Crash, Burn**
                                            Develop Relationships

Step 2 Techniques: **The Best Friend Exercise**
                                            The 5-to-1 Drill

As you begin to develop relationships, you will soon have people coming to you with real estate questions and wanting your help. With the **Edge** you will always be ATTRACTING future clients. As opposed to old-school training where you're constantly trying to promote yourself and "sell" people. This next sentence will be very long and may seem like a run-on, but it's the only way I know how to say this: When you are yourself, speak from your heart, consistently get out there by attending your passion arenas and are looking ONLY to develop relationships and NEVER SELL, you will be well on your way to having more customers and more business than you will ever know what to do with!

I told you it's long, but read it again, it's bad ass!

Now the fun begins! Let's say you finally meet someone in one of your passion arenas who is dying for your help to buy or sell a house, what do you do? Simple, you're going to try to DIS-Qualify them. Congratulations, you are ready for Step Three. DQ Time!

CHAPTER 14

STEP 3: DIS-QUALIFY

"Learn how to say NO."

-William B. Malevich (1933-2015)

Dean of Students, University of St. Thomas, St. Paul MN

Step 3 Main Mission: Quickly Determine a Reason NOT to Work with Someone

Step 3 Main Moves: Gut Check

                                      Sales Triage™

I was twenty-two years old and I had just finished my college graduation ceremony. I still had my cap and gown on, friends and family were jumping and celebrating, it was a perfect day outside, and for some reason I had this urge to run back into the main hall by myself and say goodbye to the empty halls. I looked around, saw all the smiles and tears, and my heart and gut were telling me to run back into this particular building, the main area where I had spent a lot of time as a student. I told my parents and friends there was something I had to do before we headed off to the parties and celebration festivities. I took off running, bolted through the quad, and came to the building. The door was locked. It was graduation day and most of the student areas were shut off and closed. However, I knew of a back door where the maintenance crews went in and out. I walked in through that back door, found my special area and sat down for just a moment to take it all in. It was a quiet, peaceful spot where I used to study, rest, recharge, and even sleep. It was a special place that I knew I would always remember, and I wanted to go there one last time and say goodbye. I wanted to have one last moment there alone. I had often found strength in taking some time alone, as this helped me recharge. I didn't know it at the time, but recharging would ultimately become one of the key ingredients in the **Edge** selling system.

This was four years of hard work, all coming down to this one moment in my special place. It was pretty exciting. If you have ever committed to something for that long, whether it be college or anything else, you know the feeling of joy, gratitude, and even some vulnerability, as to *what now?* I sat there in this quiet place that for me was unlike any other, thanked God and everyone that had helped me make it through the last four years. I even said a prayer asking for the knowledge to carry on after graduation into the "real world," as everyone used to call it.

It was still the best place on campus. With all the commotion going on outside, it was as silent as a church, and so I sat there and contemplated some of my biggest lessons in college. My first failures, first heartbreak, first scary situation with being on my own, meeting my best friends, learning about loyalty, success, growth, life, discovering disappointment doesn't always equal disaster, and many more memorable moments flashed before my eyes. Too many to list here. Grateful, flooded with emotions, at the same time I found myself being recharged by the second – almost like plugging in a cell phone. I could feel my whole body filling with energy as I sat there smiling over all the unforgettable moments I was blessed to have and all the wonderful lessons I had learned. What I didn't know was that the biggest lesson that I would ever get in college was just about to come to me.

There was not another soul in sight. As I stood up to walk out again, I heard someone say, "Well, Mr. Williams, it has been quite the journey." I turned around to see the Dean of Students of the entire College, Mr. William B. Malevich, walking toward me.

Dean Malevich was my mentor and savior during the four years I attended the University of St. Thomas in St. Paul, Minnesota. Dean Malevich gave me my first work-study job, he got me out of my first bind, he helped me with insight and advice and was always there for me when I needed help, muscle, permission, guidance, and on and on and on.

In my second week of college, I nearly got kicked out of the dorms for an irresponsible thing I did that jeopardized the safety of all the students living there. I lit fireworks off in the hallway. Yes, I was an idiot, I get it. You don't have to tell me. I was 18, immature, and a ham who thought it was my duty to entertain the new students and make sure we were all having fun. Think Justin Timberlake with the troops or something similar. Was it reckless and self-centered for me not to think of the consequences of my actions? Absolutely. I had only been at St. Thomas for two weeks and already I was getting kicked out of the dorms. Not good. Not good at all.

The fireworks caused the fire alarm in the entire dorm to go off. Thousands of students had to be evacuated at one in the morning. The fire department came and it cost the school a serious amount of money to deal with this situation. Turned out one of the Resident Assistants had seen me with the fireworks just before the fire alarm went off, and I didn't know whether I would get caught or not. I just evacuated with the rest of the students and kept my head down. After the fire department left, I tiptoed back to my dorm and found the friends I had been entertaining were all gone. I realized what I had done. Oh boy, was I in trouble. I could have burned the whole building down. I knew I had screwed up big time. Yes, I was young, but I was about to grow up real fast.

I sat in my dorm room with the door locked, hoping I'd wake up the morning and no one would know it was me who caused it all. All of a sudden, a heavy knock hit my door. Boom boom boom! I shot up to hear, "Hello, Mark, this is the St. Paul Police Department."

Eighteen years old. First time ever, living away from home. Two weeks into college and I have the St. Paul PD knocking at my door. The jig was up. Turned out the Resident Assistant had called me out, turned me in, and I was busted . . . but I was actually grateful. I was about to go and tell them anyway – OK, no I wasn't. Bottom line, I was way up the creek without a paddle. The St. Paul PD asked me if I was shooting fireworks inside the dorm and I told them yes. The next morning I was asked to leave the dorms until further notice. Those were the exact words of Campus Security and the Board of Safety Advisors. It was the school's right to do as they thought best, and for the time being, they wanted me to live outside the dorms until they determined I was not a threat to the other students or some kind of pyro. What I had thought was just some college fun had now turned into a full-on disaster and I was in real trouble.

I didn't want to call my parents and tell them I was just kicked out of the dorms with no place to sleep, so I called my best friend's older brother, who lived off-campus. "Hello, Mike, mind if I crash on your floor?" And there I would stay for three long weeks, waiting for the verdict on whether I could move back into the dorms or be banned forever. During those three weeks, I was a trainwreck. It was possible that I'd even be completely kicked out of college. I knew this was getting out of control. I screwed up and I needed someone to help me before it was too late.

I remembered a giant of a man welcoming everyone during orientation, a sincere, honest, kind man. This man claimed to be some kind of representative of the students and I remembered his saying that his door was always open to anyone, especially the students. I remembered having a good gut feeling about him. If I could find that guy, maybe he could help. I found out he was the Dean of Students, William B. Malevich. The following morning I marched into his office, told him I was the kid who almost burned down Ireland Hall, and said I needed his help. I told him I had not told my parents and that I was living on the floor of a friend's older brother's basement and I was about to get kicked out of college for a mistake. In hindsight I should have told my parents and asked them for help, but sometimes we have to learn the hard way. I told the Dean my situation, and after I'd spent some time with him, he made the executive decision that I was an "OK kid." He decided that I was not a pyromaniac trying to set the dorm on fire, but simply a typical college freshman moron who made a mistake. He understood that the administrative types had turned this into something very grave, and unless I had some serious support I was going to be out on the tiles.

Dean Malevich called the disciplinary board and insisted I be allowed to move back into the dorms immediately. He also urged that any discussion of my being kicked out of the college be dropped at once. The only condition would be one semester of probation and two fire safety classes. Let me explain, I was not to attend these fire safety classes. I was to give them! Dean Malevich was a wise one. Within thirty days, I was to give two one-hour presentations on student fire safety to everyone in the dorm. That was over 500 people. "Oh boy," I thought. Whether I liked it or not, my career as "the guy in the front of the room" was officially launched.

The Dean was a much bigger shot than I realized at the time. He saved my ass with one phone call and he based it all on his heart and his gut. He righted the entire situation based on his first impression of me, and, just like that, I was in the clear.

Was it a bad move to shoot fireworks off in the dorm? Of course. Was the Dean going to make sure I made amends and learned from my mistake? Absolutely. I went on to do the two safety presentations to all the students, went quietly back to living in the dorms, kept going to my classes with no issues, and life was back to normal. Phew! What a way to start college.

Later, while I was still a student, I asked Dean Malevich how he was able to assess the situation and me so fast. He replied, "My gut." He went on, "With people, Mark, you have to go with your gut." The Dean's philosophy and his grasp of listening to his instinct – his awareness of this magical ability we all have to do a "gut check" – in time would become paramount and integral to **The Edge**.

After those first few weeks of madness, Dean Malevich and I became great friends. I'd pop into his office to say hi and make him laugh. I kept myself on the straight and narrow, and in return he taught me many life lessons along the way. He got me my first work/study job at the information booth, as he figured I liked the attention, so why not put me in a booth – which, I might add, became my first college passion arena. He had the gift of seeing people's gifts.

So four years later, on graduation day, here I was. Many lessons later, ups and downs, strikers and gutters, I now stood by myself in my favorite hall, remembering it all. A little in shock and a little scared, but very proud. I closed my eyes, thanked the University of St. Thomas for an amazing journey, and was on my feet heading out the door when I heard that greeting from Dean Malevich. "Well, Mr. Williams . . . " We hugged, said goodbye, and as I started to walk away the Dean said, "Hey Williams, one last thing before you venture off into the next chapter of your life." He chuckled. "I know you like to learn things the hard way, but I have one last piece of advice before you go, since we'll probably never see each other again . . ."

I thought it was odd for him to say that, as I knew I would be back to see the Dean in the years to come. He got very serious all of a sudden and put his head down as if to emphasize the significance of what he was about to say. He looked me in the eye and said one of the most pivotal things anyone to this day has ever said to me:

"Mark . . . Learn how to say NO."

He paused, looking into my eyes and branding that message and lesson into my soul and being. Confused, I wasn't really sure of the point at the time, but he continued to gaze at me in silence, imprinting his words deep on my soul so I would never forget them. Then all of a sudden, poof! He lifted his head, smiled, and as he turned around and walked off as he cheerfully said over his shoulder, "Take care, pal, it's been fun." Wow. I stood there almost in shock. Something powerful was imprinted on me and I knew there was a deeper message there and that someday I would understand.

Unfortunately the Dean was right, we never would see each again after that fateful goodbye. He passed away in 2015 and I still regret never going back to visit him after I wrote this book. I would never forget him or his words of wisdom. "Learn how to say no." This mantra, combined with the Dean's "gut check" technique, laid the groundwork for what would become Step Three of the **Edge**.

Your Main Mission here is to quickly determine a reason *not* to work with someone. This may come as a shock to many of you, as most training programs encourage you to "keep an open mind: and "everyone is a potential client." Well, sorry, but not in this program! Time to learn how to say no. You are going to learn how to turn down business.

With **Selling on the Edge** you are going to say no to a lot of people. This Step is where for the first time, you, as a salesperson/realtor, are turning the tables and you are going to decide whether you want to work with someone, as opposed to the other way around. You're going to decide if you like this person. You're going to decide if they fit your criteria for taking them on as a client. In this system it is you who are essentially interviewing the potential client to see if you will make the time to work with them and invest in helping them. Just like the Dean decided whether he would let me stay in school as a student, YOU are going to decide who gets to work with you!

YOU DECIDE WHO GETS TO WORK WITH YOU

Edge Rule: You decide who is IN and who is OUT.

Traditional selling says go and work with anyone you can, keep prospecting hard enough and it is a numbers game, give everyone your card, put everyone on your drip campaign and sell, sell, sell. In this system you now have the **Edge**. Your clients will have to sell you on the idea of working with them. This is a 180 degree spin from traditional selling. In essence the concept is this: "Why, Mr. or Ms. Buyer or Seller, should I work with you? Prove to me why you are worthy of my investing my time and energy to sell your home." Do you see the power in that? It's very empowering. Very.

Let me set the record straight, this is not a script or some technique. This is a mindset, a state-of-mind, and a new way for real estate agents to think. This new way of thinking will make you rich. It is a paradigm shift from beggar, peddler, pest, and salesy-sales guy – to respected advisor, trusted representative, decisive leader. You are not a real estate agent, remember? You sell houses and you are the CEO of YOU, Inc. Got it? this is a new belief system that I want you to develop. I want you to understand the concept of DIS-qualifying someone versus trying to "sell" them on you. Ninety-nine percent of all real estate agents "sell." You, my new friend, are never going to sell again. You are going to *dis*-qualify.

Part of this whole dis-qualifying process is developing your conviction and your instinct: your gut. Then, following this intuition, say no to, and turn down, people that may *look* like buyers, but in reality, you feel they are not. To say no to someone in this context means you are going to tell him or her that you are unable and/or not interested in helping him or her. You dis-qualified them. DQ'd. What is the first test for whether someone gets DQ'd or not? Your own gut.

GUT CHECK

As you now know, dis-qualify means to figure out as soon as possible whether there's a reason NOT to work with someone. If your gut says "no go," then move on. You have been wired with the ability to tell whether someone is legit or not. Most agents disregard these feelings and that will always lead to trouble. We all meet people all the time, at events, at parties, wherever. Some you may like instantly and some just rub you the wrong way. When it comes to selling houses, if you meet someone and you don't like them, you think they are shady, you just have a bad gut feeling, then guess what? Pass! It is that simple. This is the gut check. If you have a bad feeling about them from the get-go, it's the real estate gods telling you to move on. This Main Move gives you the power to decide who you will work with. I don't know what your criteria will be, that is up to you. **Selling on the Edge** means you decide WHO you work with, WHEN you work with them, HOW you work with them, and it all starts with your gut check.

To be dis-qualified or not to be dis-qualified, that is the question.

OK, that is not Shakespeare, that is the **Edgespeare!** It's not nearly as complicated as Shakespeare, it is simple. This is a relationship business and if something tells your gut that someone could be trouble or not a good fit, then listen to that little voice and move on. I want you to start developing this intuition muscle and practicing the gut check, because it will develop your instinct. A strong instinct is key to long-term success in this business.

I know you are saying, "Mark, I can't just blow off these people if I don't like them, that is not good business." Well, aren't you here to find out how to get real buyers and sellers fast? You do that by not getting your time wasted by the ones that will drag you down. The ones that are left may just end up being real clients. Making sense yet?

So what if your gut check tells you someone is good to go? Great, then maybe they do qualify, but let's make a few attempts to dis-qualify them first. How does that work? What would you do? If you are struggling with understanding how dis-qualifying works, it's OK, I understand. This is a complete about-face from typical behavior for most salespeople. If you are questioning this or feeling confused, don't worry, that is not unusual. I understand that this way of thinking and the idea of turning someone down is probably unlike anything you've ever heard before, especially if you have had some previous sales training. To simplify the dis-qualifying process further, I will break the concept down to seven words: *Try to talk them out of it.*

You are now saying to yourself that this might be the dumbest selling technique ever, and if you are new, again, I understand. You're probably also thinking that when you are new, you will hardly have any clients so when you finally get one, why on God's green earth would I suggest that you try to talk them out of buying or selling? I will explain shortly, but first, let me share something before we move forward.

If you are adamantly opposed to trying this and disagree with me, I have to say one thing. You may be uncoachable. My gut is telling me to be honest with you this very moment. I don't think you should get into real estate. I am telling you, my friend, that this business is not all it is cracked up to be and maybe you should try something else. I have met thousands of new agents and my experience is that most new agents (including you) are not very open to suggestions and are simply not coachable. This will hinder you from making serious money, so maybe it's best you hang up the skates sooner than later. Do you really want to sell houses? Why? The money? Let's look closely at how much agents really make per sale.

HOW MUCH AGENTS REALLY MAKE

Let me tell you, the money is really not what you think it is. It is important that you know the facts before you start selling houses. Most of our friends think we get these huge commissions, but the reality is that it is a lot of work and at the end of the day we are lucky to take home one to two percent of every sale we make. Did you know that? One to two percent! That is it. If you are like me, when I was new I thought realtors got seven percent commissions. I figured on a $100,000 sale, I would make $7000 and that seemed pretty cool to me. I could do one per month and be making close to six figures. Then I learned the reality. You see, that seven percent is actually six percent. And that six percent is five percent on eighty percent of the listings. Then that five percent is actually split between me and the agent representing the other party. But wait, there's more! Then my broker got almost half of my piece. Ugh. It was falling like a rock. In the end I was barely making 1.5% per sale. Not 7%. The reality was 1.5% and that was what I call a dizasty! A disaster.

Here I was thinking I would make seven or eight thousand on the sale of a hundred thousand dollar house, but in reality, I was making less than two thousand dollars per sale. One sale a month was not going to pay the bills. YIKES! Had someone told me this in the beginning, I never would have got into this business.

So here you are now, brand new, and you have a chance to get out. I am suggesting that maybe you go do something else. Do you really want to sell houses? It is cutthroat and stressful. This business really is not for everyone. Are you sure there is not something else you'd rather do? Like work at the bank or at the park or just go back to your old job? In fact, I suggest maybe you should return this book now if you are feeling doubtful and get your money back. It's OK, I would totally understand.

Do you see what I just did? I was trying to DIS-Qualify you. OK, sorry, but sometimes showing it to you is more effective than telling you. I hope you are still here, because if you are, then you may have what it takes. I would rather be straightforward with you right out of the gate than have you feel deceived down the road. So, yes, I was trying to DIS-Qualify you from becoming a realtor and if you are still here, I am excited! You may just make it.

TALK THEM *OUT* OF IT INSTEAD OF INTO IT

DIS-Qualify simply means *talk them out of it*. Got it? Talk them out of it. All realtors out there today try to talk people **Into** buying or Into selling. With the **Edge**, we talk them OUT of it. If they are still standing after your every attempt to try to talk them out of it, then you probably have a live one. If you have a buyer, try initially to talk them out of buying. See what happens. If you have a seller, try at first to talk them out of selling. If you can't, then you may just have a real client on your hands.

I discovered this out of frustration after so many failed, overpriced listings and dragging around deadbeat (no money) buyers that I finally snapped one day. I was well into my third year in the business and I met someone who claimed to be interested in selling. "Yes, yeah, whatever," was my first thought. After three years of feeling used and abused by buyers and sellers out there, I just didn't believe anyone anymore. I was tired of sellers just calling me to see what their house was worth so they could refinance or, even worse, end up selling the house with someone else. I'd do all the work and then the owners usually ended up selling with their cousin's brother's wife's friend who they had known for twenty years. Either way, they'd use me to get all the information they needed and then I'd never hear from them again. What I was doing was not working. I'd had enough of this sh*t. I had seen this program before and I had had it. This guy was not getting sh*t from me! Not today.

I was at the end of my rope. I was so upset with sellers always wanting free information, free suggestions, more money than their house was worth and all for free. Then, when I couldn't get them their unrealistic price, they would blame me and go try and sell it with someone else at the price I originally told them was correct! Always the same ol' same ol'. Buyers were always complaining about overpaying and sellers were always complaining that agents never got them enough. That was it, I was quitting. Rather than being bitter, unhappy, and resentful, it was time to try something else. This would be my last meeting with anyone regarding anything to do with real estate. I was fired up and Thank God, because it was time to give this up. I wasn't making a penny, nothing was working, I was officially quitting this business and would soon be off doing something more fun.

So here I was at my last appointment ever as I rolled up to this guy's fine Hollywood house. Nothing intimidated me at this point. I didn't care, and I was going to be in and out. Let's just say, I was feeling no pain. I wasn't drunk, I just had zero attachment to what was about to happen. For the first time ever, I really, truly, honestly DID NOT CARE. In other words, I didn't give a rip! I thought, "This is going to be fun." I walked into the house without any marketing materials and sat down with the owner, intending to make it my mission to convince him not to sell the property.

First thing the owner said was, "How much is my house worth?" Not hello, not thanks for coming. All these sellers want is free info and then they kick you out. I was tired of being a public service agent so I looked the guy in the eye and said, "Not much." He was taken aback. I went in for the kill and said, "In fact, from the looks of it, I would even sell this house right now." His jaw hit the ground. I could see three marketing brochures from the last three agents he had met were lying on his piano. I said, "Ya know what? You clearly have plenty of agents you are working with, so I am sure you can find out what you want to know from them. This is not a listing I would even want to take and I need to get going." I stood up and started to walk out.

The seller jumped up. "Whoa, whoa, whoa, wait a second, that's it? You don't even want to see the house?" My response would be the turning point in my career and a moment I would never forget as I said:

"Well, for starters, Mr. Seller, your wife isn't even here so I am guessing this whole idea of selling is not very important to her, otherwise she would be here. Since she is not, it's crystal clear that she wants to keep the place. Second, by the looks of those cute kids in the picture, I'm guessing they don't want to leave their schools and I sure as hell don't want to be the agent that pisses off your wife and displaces children from schools and their great friends. So to answer your question pal, yes, that is it. My advice is you should keep the house or use those other agents when the time comes to sell."

The guy's jaw was on the ground and I felt like superman all of a sudden. I finally told the truth and wasn't reading some nonsense script. I was literally trying to talk the guy out of selling just so I could get out of the house and off to the beach because I was over and done with real estate. Then came the final blow. He stood up, literally blocked me as I was about to exit and said, "Wait, I like your honesty – so how much should I price my house at with these other agents?" He still wanted free info! And I was not about to give it to him. I was feeling confident and this was getting to be fun. "Sir, if I told you what your house was really worth, you would have a heart attack and would never use me anyway, so I really must be on my way."

He ended up listing his house with me at the price I told him and I knew I was onto something. From that point on, I would never "sell" again. I would try to talk people out of what they thought they wanted to do. If I couldn't do it, I knew they might be worth having a further conversation with. This is the process I named DIS-Qualifying. For me, DIS-Qualifying – trying to talk people OUT of buying or selling instead of INTO buying and selling would be the new gameplan. I had a new life. Could I really be a realtor and not have to "sell"? YES! I made it my mission never to look like realtor again. DIS-Qualify would help me do this.

What else did this do for me? A lot! For starters, it helped me blow through all the timewasters fast. And what did that do? It allowed me to get to the winners faster. By a winner I mean someone who was going to buy or sell and literally make a move within the next 30 – 60 days with or without me. These people needed help, they meant business, they were hurting, they were motivated, and they needed to make a move fast. I found that many of these people didn't know a real estate agent. Finding these winners faster than anyone else would become my new mission. Avoid time wasters. Find winners. The rest would take care of itself. I was flying high, feeling really good, and I knew I was onto something big. I was developing a system.

THEY WILL SELL YOU

We are going to break down DIS-Qualify, but in essence you are trying to talk your clients out of making a move. You want to turn the tables and this move does it. Try it out. The result is that – if they are a real client – they will try to well YOU. And that will make you different. The client is now trying to sell you on why you should help them! It's much easier this way. So go ahead, get out there and DIS-Qualify!

DENIAL ISLE AND ONEITIS (prncd. ONE-itis) like a disease

Do you really grasp the power of this Step yet? And what it will do for you? I want you to understand this, because this is the secret sauce. This is it. this is why you bought this book and if you can start using this Step and see the power of Step Three, your life and selling career will change forever. New real estate agents get destroyed and toast out in their first year because they get stuck with time wasters and bogus buyers. People that think they are going to guy and deep down may really want to, but for whatever reason, they just don't. New agents spend months with the same person, which makes them feel "vested" and like they have to stick with this person, no matter what. Figuratively speaking, they send good money after bad instead of facing the fact that this person is never, ever, going to make a move. I call this place in an agent's career *Denial Isle*. Somewhere you do not want to be. If you are stuck on *Denial Isle*, get out fast! GET OUT! SHOOT UP A FLARE FOR HELP! S.O.S.! Escape, or the end is near. The end of your career. Next stop after Denial Isle is Death Valley.

I can hear what you are saying right now. I understand, you don't want to be a quitter. Whatever training program you just took urged you to "stay on them" and to "follow up" because "they will buy someday." NO THEY WON'T! Most newbies don't listen to this advice for two reasons. One: they have no other clients. So firing their one and only client makes no sense to them. Two: traditional training programs have taught them not to give up on a lead or prospect. Traditional training says, "Don't quit, hang in there, you will close them one day, keep on them, follow up, stick with it, put them on the drip campaign, Facebook them, trying calling again, and again, and again blah blah blah!!!

And what do you end up looking like? Besides a pest? You guessed it, an annoying salesperson. Game. Set. Match. You lost. The **Edge** teaches you to find clients, assess whether you want to work with them, and if not, then you DQ and get rid of them before they drag you down. Which system do you think is better for you?

If you could take only one thing with you out of this entire system, my wish would be that it was an understanding of Step Three. This is the Golden Rule of *The Edge*: A! B! D! Always Be Dis-qualifying. DIS-Qualifying will save you years of heartache and wasted time and I guarantee one other thing. By following this philosophy, you will never, ever look or sound like a salesperson. Your clients will appreciate that. This is a core concept of **Selling on the Edge**. Instead of working with everyone, you will now DIS-Qualify some, because ultimately it is best for them as well as for you. Buckle in, this is where the real fun begins.

When you get your license, everyone is going to want free information from you, free consulting, free appointment setting, free *everything*, because that is the norm. I can't blame them, it is just what they have been taught. That is what other agents do. Buyers and sellers walk all over these types of agents. It is your job to stop the madness, put the brakes on, and turn the tables. I will see new agents even write offer after offer for people like "Kenny No Dough" only to find out three weeks into the escrow that "Kenny" is broke, he was wasting the new agent's time trying to impress his new girlfriend. (Yep, I did that one too.) If your gut-check didn't catch "Kenny" or others like him, how do we figure this out? The answer is by running *Sales Triage*™, which we will get to right after I remind you not to get "One-itis."

One-itis is a disease that new and even experienced realtors get when they are convinced they have a client who is real and really going to guy or sell someday. Instead of continuing to put in time each week on their passion arenas and trying to meet more people, they put all their eggs in that one basket. That one basket being the one client that they *think* will buy or sell. They keep chasing and chasing and investing more and more time in that one potential, maybe, prospect – until in the end they realize they have stopped everything else completely. No more weekly passion arenas, no more developing relationships. It is only a matter of time before you find out your supposed client was never, ever going to buy with you anyway when they tell you, "Sorry, I just found out I can't buy for a few years because I may move to another state, but thanks, it's been so much fun seeing houses with you over the last year and a half and here's a Chipotle gift card for $50." (True story!) Now this person has left you high and dry and won't even return your phone calls. Another one bites the dust. On the other hand . . .

BUYERS ARE NOT LIARS

Buyers are NOT liars. They are just not Buyers.

There is a phrase in real estate that "Buyers are Liars." I disagree with that statement. It's brainbaggage. It is your job as a realtor to assess the buyer or seller and determine whether they are real or not. New realtors take on weak clientele and then get upset when they find out the client is never going to buy. Well, my friend, I say that is your fault. As an agent with the **Edge**, you will learn in Step Five that everything is your responsibility. That means you cannot get upset at clients (or anyone) for doing things you never told them they could *not* do. (Reread that sentence.) If you take on a broke client and spend all your time with them, it is your fault. This means it's your responsibility to ask them about money *before* you invest a lot of your time. You will have a system and a formula on how to proceed with the potential winners and turn those people into sales. **Sales Triage™** will be your process for clients that make it past the gutcheck.

CHAPTER 15

INTRO TO **SALES TRIAGE**™

You are now learning that not everyone is a client or even a potential client. The reality is that most people are not and never will be. The reason gut check and **Sales Triage**™ is that they help you blow through the bogus bullsh*tters as quickly as possible so you can get to the real deals faster. While most agents are busy trying to sell themselves to everyone, you will be different. The reason realtors crash and burn s that in their first few years they are afraid to say NO to anyone. They meet someone who appears wealthy and seems to be interested in buying, but the newbie doesn't dig deep enough and never finds out the buyer's true motives or what is really going on. Instead the newbie wants to trust everyone and be helpful. They do what they've been trained to do, which is show the prospect houses and HOPE they find a good one. Once we find a good one, the newbie thinks, then we can ask about money and all that stuff that most people are uncomfortable talking about.

Well, with this step you are going to make a lot of people VERY uncomfortable, but that is a sign you're on the right track. The only reason prospects get uncomfortable in sales is that you are getting to the truth and they don't want you to know that, so they try to convince you that it's none of your business. For example, some people will get upset if you ask how much money they make or why they want a house in the first place. Do you get upset when your doctor asks for your insurance card? No. So, moving forward, put yourself in the mindset of the doctor again.

Let me explain to you the stereotype most prospects see in you as a realtor. It's certainly not that of a doctor. But it will be your job to change that stereotype and break the mold. Most people will initially see you as similar to a waiter in a restaurant, a car salesman, or somewhere in between. This is the stereotype, it will not be you. You will have the **Edge**. The **Edge** will dramatically and quickly change that perception, leading clients to take you more seriously. A lot more seriously.

In order to understand, though, we have to be aware of what clients will think of you initially. Most people think you get a salary from your broker and you are hanging around waiting to bring someone their meal like a waiter who is there to attend to their every need. Or the perception is that you are one level up from a used car salesman, just there to make a quick commission. Go ahead and test this out. Ask anyone what their first impression is when they hear the word, "realtor." They have been led to believe that realtors will do anything for a commission and they think they ring the bell and you show up. If you are trained with **Selling on the Edge**, I promise you, they have another think coming. How do we do it? How do we use **Selling on the Edge** to DIS-Qualify someone? First step is GUT CHECK and second step is RUN **SALES TRIAGE™**.

First move: does your gut say this is OK? Do you like the person? Do they seem like good people? If your gut says NO, then do not work with them. Your gut is NEVER wrong. That is Step One. Remember Dean Malevich and the art of learning to say NO? Remember the Main Mission of Step Three is to quickly determine a reason NOT to work with someone? That is your mission. If your gut says no, they are out! Period. No one can set the criteria but you and only you. If you don't feel right about someone, then boom! They are gone. You have to understand that this is not only OK, it is more than OK. You're passing on the ones you don't feel right about so you can immediately get to the ones you *do* feel good about. Making sense? You have to fully ingest the concept that you do not have to work with everyone and I do not want you to.

Edge Rule: Always follow your instinct, your heart, and your gut.

Assuming a prospective client makes it past round one of the gutcheck, you proceed to **Sales Triage™**. This is a filter system. "Triage" originated as a medical term during wars. If they had a number of wounded soldiers, they would prioritize who should get attention first. Triage is still used to describe this process of deciding who goes to the head of the line, both in medical situations and in other contexts. If you're seeing how this relates to dealing with clients, you are a fast learner. In **Sales Triage™**, you're going to prioritize the clients who are the most motivated in the same way that the emergency room doctor prioritizes the patient who needs most immediate attention.

Sales Triage™ will help you master the art of finding and identifying the "emergency cases" of the real estate world. Once you identify them, you can devote your time and energy to these people – the buyers and sellers who *must* make a move quickly. These are the types of people you will be looking for. Find those people and you will be a rich real estate agent!

TRIAGE definition:

The determination of priorities for action in an emergency.

Sales Triage™ is your process, formula, and system for *sorting* the real clients from the ones that will waste your time, your energy, your money, and your career. And what are "real" clients again? Clients who are prepared to do whatever it takes to get their house sold, or do whatever it takes to buy a house, with or without you, within the next ninety days. When someone has a gunshot wound in the head, they don't stop in the middle of the ambulance ride and ask to interview three doctors! They don't ask for marketing materials to see if you've ever operated before. They don't care, they're just crying "HELP ME!!" It is the same in real estate. Real clients are out there and they're begging for immediate help. **Sales Triage™** will help you find these real clients quickly, and this is critical in your first year if you want any chance of making it. I don't want to sound harsh, but if you don't have a system or plan in your first year, you are in big trouble.

Most new agents understand that they have to find buyers and sellers, but they have no system for figuring out how to find them, where to find them, who is real, and who is a waste of time.

You now have a system and it can be simplified like this: DQ, Gut-check, and **Sales Triage™**. But watch out, because you are not the only one with a system.

BUYERS AND SELLERS ALSO HAVE A SYSTEM

For years I foundered around trying to do whatever buyers and sellers wanted, thinking it was a numbers game and if I had enough open houses and cold calls and mailers, emails, magnets and calendars sent out, eventually I would catch a fish! Instead, all I got was people wanting free information, free service, and no sales. I got worked over, wasted tons of time, and found myself broke and selling cell phones on the side to try and make money. I had no strategy to find REAL buyers and sellers. I was throwing spaghetti at the wall, hoping something would stick.

I would meet a client and just start showing them property blindly. I would meet a seller and just list their house at whatever price they wanted. I felt like a waiter, a bellboy. I certainly didn't feel like a licensed professional. I had no system and I was getting slaughtered . . . to the point that I was only days away from the poor house once again.

Then one day it hit me. All these buyers and sellers seemed to have a system that they were using on me. They had a plan that looked like this: Step 1 – Get a real estate agent to do everything for free. Step 2 – Get all the information we can from the real estate agent for free. Step 3 – Buy or sell the house ourselves OR use someone else. Buyers and sellers had a system, and it was kicking my ass every time. I knew I had to have a system, or like my friend Dave from the hockey story, I would soon fade away in the real estate world. I realized I had to come up with my own system. **Selling on the Edge** was in its embryo stage and my instinct was telling me that things were about to get good if I could just grow it to its full potential. Think of the Scarecrow in *The Wizard of Oz* when he realized, "If I only had a brain!" This system was like getting a brain in real estate. Let's slow down and recap:

In Step One of **Selling on the Edge**, you have mastered the art of being yourself. Step Two is Getting Out There with the main objective of developing relationships. You are, more than likely, beginning to develop trust between your new friends and potential clients. Now you can go to the next level, if you choose, with anyone who wants your help or expresses interest in real estate. After that, if they pass the gut check, is to run them through **Sales Triage™** and see whether they are serious or just another lookie-lou. Getting this?

The first three steps of the Edge (Outer game) can be simplified and summarized as follows:

1. Be you and attend your passion arenas.
2. Get Out There and develop relationships.
3. Run **Sales Triage™** on any potential new customers.

So many new agents get hung up on phrases like "buyers are liars" and "sellers are criers," but don't buy into this brainbaggage. Simply use the system to see if they are real or not. After your assessment, you can either take them on as a client or not. It's your call. Look, deep down, these buyers may really want to buy, but maybe they can't, due to lack of a down payment, or it's not the right time, or the husband wants to move but the wife doesn't. Many sellers really do want to move, but because of circumstances they cannot, and it's OK. That doesn't make them liars.

The number one reason people don't go through with buying or selling is that they are comfortable where they are, and there is no compelling or emotional reason to make a move. They are not "hurting" enough to change. People will NEVER change, meaning take action, unless they are hurting -- there is trauma -- where they are. Period. This applied in real estate and in life.

Edge Rule: Your job is to find trauma victims.

Make sense? You're looking for the ones who are hurting the most. In other words, the ones that will be the most motivated. We are going to refer to them as TRAUMA VICTIMS. These clients are the ones that will want your help the most. Trauma victims are the real deal. They are real clients. A "real" buyer or seller, remember, is one who is going to make a move (buy or sell) in the next ninety days with or without you. I will repeat this over and over until you can recite it in your sleep! What's the definition of a "real" buyer or seller?

You will spot these people because they will be willing to do whatever it takes to get it done, whether it's buying or selling. **Sales Triage™** is your selling system that you will use to identify real clients vs time wasters. Ever heard stories about how your friends went and looked at houses all day? Or how the neighbors across the hall have been talking about buying a house for ten years? Everyone loves to talk to realtors, and it's FREE! You have to learn to move quickly past the time wasters. You have to remove them or they can be lethal to your selling career.

"**Selling on the Edge** is the cure for sales cancer."
-Bill Perry, 15-year top selling agent,
First Team Realty, Newport Beach, CA

New realtors lose big money by getting stuck with people who are a waste of time. If I have learned one thing, it's that real deals happen fast and smooth and easily. If people get upset with you or accuse you of prying too much into their world, or say things like, "It's none of your business," or my favorite, "You're being aggressive," or blah blah blah, these are signs that they are hiding things from you and they're not real. Buyers and sellers have learned that if they say these things to an agent, the agent will back off and throttle back. The truth is that when this happens, it means you are doing a great job. You are getting to the truth and you'll hear these condescending statements when you have hit a nerve and called them out. If someone gets uncomfortable, don't worry, they are the ones who should be uncomfortable, not you. Keep your cool and don't get emotionally involved. I learned this lesson the hard way. If you blow your top, it's over. If they are blowing their top, it could mean they need your help, they may be going through some difficult stuff and it's usually a sign of trauma. You are eventually going to save them, so keep your cool. If you both lose your head, that won't end well, I promise you.

Edge Rule: If you lose your sh*t, you will lose the deal.

When someone gets a bit upset with you, don't take it personally. It just means you hit the "I am not a real buyer and you might find out and stop helping me for free: nerve. Buyers don't want us to know the truth because, guess what? If we find out they are just using us, we might stop the free service. You still with me? **Sales Triage™** will help you find out who is real and who is not, only if you use it. You're going to learn the five steps of **Sales Triage™** and if you don't use it, you will lose.

What is the point in quickly determining a reason NOT to work with someone? Answer: If you can blow through these bloodsuckers quickly, you can get to the real deals faster.

#1 REASON AGENTS FAIL: They waste valuable time with people that have no intention of ever buying or selling, and miss out on the ones who do wish to actually buy or sell.

The whole residential real estate world is out of whack because salespeople and realtors since the beginning of time have been programmed to do whatever anyone asks of them. Not in this system. In this system, your clients will have to convince YOU to take them on. Do you see the power in that? You are no longer a desperate used car salesman, or a waiter, or a bellboy, or people pleaser, you are an empowered badass agent! You are not in this business to please people and do whatever they ask, you are here to sell houses.

Let me repeat that. You are not in this business to please people and do whatever they ask! You are here to sell houses. You do that by finding trauma victims (highly motivated buyers and sellers) and saving their lives! (By assisting them in buying or selling their house.) In order to make it huge in real estate, you have to understand your real value and why you are so important to this industry. I need you to be crystal clear before we move forward. You are going to piss off a lot of people initially as you disqualify them. If this is happening, I want you to know you are on the absolute right path, so stay the course and don't waver. If people are accusing you of being abrupt, or dismissive, or short, or too fast, then send me an email because AMEN, brothers and sisters, I can tell you that is the number one sign you are getting this! Over time, you will smooth out your DIS-Qualifying style and it won't come off as harshly as it might at first. If you ever feel bad about disqualifying someone, don't! Understand that you can't help everyone and besides, it was really the buyers and sellers who initially taught me this process. Let me explain.

DON'T FEEL BAD, THEY'VE BEEN DOING IT TO US FOREVER

When I was new and showing houses, buyers would walk up to a house and before I could even open the front door they would tell me, "Nope, it's not going to work." Then on to the next house, and one look at the back yard or kitchen and boom, "No chance on this one, let's go." I couldn't understand how buyers could so quickly see a reason they would not buy this house. Then it hit me. The real buyers were looking at every house in order to disqualify the house as fast as possible because REAL buyers hated wasting time, especially the very real ones. They were "hurting" big time and needed to buy quickly, so the last thing they wanted to do was hang around and see the whole house if they knew it was never going to work.

I started to spot this as the true sign of real buyers. The ones that always wanted to stay and see the whole house and "make a day of it" were the clowns that never had any intention of buying. They just wanted to get ideas for their own home or enjoyed talking to realtors and wasting time looking at nice homes with no intention of ever buying.

Real buyers were DIS-Qualifying houses quickly, and on to the next! So never feel bad for buyers that you need to DQ. They have been doing it to us for years and I'd like to thank them now for teaching me this wonderful concept.

OK, so let's break all this down. Step 3 of **Selling on the Edge** is DIS-Qualify – which is a two-part process:

Main Moves for Step 3

1. **Gut check**
2. **Sales Triage™**

REPETITION, REPETITION, REPETITION!!!

Remember this motto from earlier? Getting good at Step Three will take practice and the more you use it, the better you will get at it. You will be tempted to disregard your gut because you have no other clients, but DON'T DO IT. Go against your gut and it will cost you down the road, I promise you. It's time to develop this skill. The more you practice and repeat, the better you will get at it.

DEVELOP YOUR DQ, NOT YOUR IQ

Edge Rule: Develop your DQ, not your IQ

What are some ways you can develop your ability to DIS-Qualify and use your gut? Number one is, if you feel something is not a good fit, tell your client that and dump them! Try it, it feels great. If I met a client that I simply didn't like, guess what, I told them we were not a fit and I couldn't help them. (See how learning to say NO is very valuable in this Step?) You're going to shoot down a lot of people that want your help. This is why I want you to learn how to say NO. It's like a muscle, you'll get better at it.

Another way to get good at this and develop your DQ muscle is to practice on your friends and co-workers. For example, when a friend invites you to a silly even that you really don't want to go to, tell them "no." Or if that one annoying co-worker keeps calling you to go to lunch, instead of avoiding them or postponing, practice by telling them "no." All these things will make you a better realtor. How? It will save you years of wasted time. Two of my best friends, Hawk and Aaron, are experts at this, but in a slightly different way that you will find helpful in understanding the art of disqualifying.

HAWK AND AARON

My two great friends, Hawk and Aaron, love to fish for muskie, one of the largest freshwater fish in America. And these guys know how to catch them. They do two things very well that lead to their success. One, they go out every week and spend three or four hours fishing. (Interesting! Sound like a passion arena, perhaps? YES!) Two, when they are in a bad part of the lake that is not doing anything for them or producing any fish, they move the boat! In essence, they have disqualified that particular area of the lake. After a few casts in a certain area, if they are getting no action, they move the boat to another area with better weeds or more shade or what looks like a drop-off or whatever they feel is better.

It seems obvious in fishing why you would quickly dismiss a particular area, but in real estate I see new agents spending weeks and months casting in the same spot and working with the same unmotivated or abusive clients over and over and over. The result is that they never catch a thing, but they don't move the boat! Are you with me? Moving the boat in sales means: cut your losses, dump that irritating client, the one that is driving you nuts, for whom it seems like nothing is ever good enough. The one that never makes a high enough offer to get the deal accepted. DIS-QUALIFY THEM, MY FRIENDS! MOVE YOUR BOAT BEFORE YOU SINK OR STARVE!! DQ 'em! This program gives you DQ people. This will empower you, give you confidence, and help you move on and get to the winners quicker, and that is what I need you to do.

We have discussed gut check and the concept of **Sales Triage™**, but let's now share the five specific stages of **Sales Triage™** and see what that would look like.

Sales Triage™ Overview:

1. Hurt level
2. Pre-op
3. Insurance
4. Operate

5. Post-op

These are the five stages of **Sales Triage™**. These five stages will be your selling formula for when you think you have a live one on the hook. Meaning someone you, your gut, and every fiber of your being believes is sincere and real. A buyer or seller that claims they are willing to do whatever it takes to find a home or sell their home, and you want to help them. But before you run out and show this buyer twenty houses, or tell this seller what you think their house is worth and start "selling," you hit the brakes and first run **Sales Triage™** on them. You will run them through the five stages of **Sales Triage™**. Got it?

This will help you get to the truth. If you can slow down the selling process at this point and meet one-on-one with your client and go through the first three steps of **Sales Triage™** -- HURT LEVEL, PRE-OP, and INSURANCE – and they meet all three of the necessary criteria, then boom! Jump on this client, you have a live one! Let's look more specifically at each of the five stages of **Sales Triage™**.

1. Hurt Level (Injured, Severely Injured, Trauma)
2. Pre-Op (Who, When, Consent)
3. Insurance (SEE proof that they have the money)
4. Operate (SAVE SAVE SAVE, not SELL SELL SELL!)
5. Post-Op (Prevent Buyer/Seller Remorse & cancellations)

HURT LEVEL

What you are looking for as a real estate agent is not whether someone is buying or selling, but whether they are hurting.

Step One of **Sales Triage™** is to determine someone's hurt level. Let me introduce you to Shawn and his family so you can understand the difference between injured, severely injured, and trauma when it comes to buyers and sellers.

Hurt Level Example 1: SHAWN <u>INJURED</u>

If someone in real estate is "injured," it means they would like to buy but the reality is that they are never going to, mainly because there is no real cost involved in staying in the same situation. My friend

Shawn, who had an apartment, came to me one day and said, "Mark, my girlfriend is giving me grief because I don't own a place, so I want to go look at properties ASAP." I told him, "Shawn, that is no reason to buy a place, because you had a little tiff with your gal." He said, "You're right. I'm probably going to break up with her anyway." BOOM! I disqualified Shawn in two seconds and he agreed. A new agent takes a client like Shawn, sees this as an opportunity and runs with it. They get busy working with Shawn, putting time and effort into helping him – all the way up to the point where the buyer himself realizes he doesn't need to buy. One day Shawn disappears and doesn't bother to tell the agent he is no longer interested. Shawn has no qualms about wasting the new realtor's time, and another realtor bites the dust wondering what went wrong. The fact is that NOTHING went wrong, they were just working with someone who never had any intention of buying in the first place. It is your job to figure that out BEFORE YOU spend time running around with people.

"Injured" means that, however these people are living now, it is OK with them so they will never change. It may be a crappy situation, but it's not that crappy. It's not COSTING them anything financially, emotionally, or physically, so they will never change. No matter what you do or how great a home you show them, they will never buy it and never change their current situation.

Edge Rule: No Trauma, no change.

Shawn's ego was a little bruised from his girlfriend's comment, but the reality is that a little ego bump is no reason to go and buy a house. Bruises go away, injuries go away. Injured Shawn will never change his situation. Therefore, he is DQ'd!

Hurt Level Example 2: SHAWN SEVERELY INJURED

"Severely injured" means there is now some kind of *cost* involved if they continue to live as they are living. My friend Shawn calls and says, "Mark, I really need to look at moving. My wife Sara is pregnant and we cannot all fit in our one-bedroom apartment anymore. Sara is really getting anxious about this, she's in her fifth month, and I am getting nervous. I spoke to my accountant and he says I'm wasting money on rent each month and I need to buy a house ASAP before the rates go up." Now we have someone who seems severely injured. The difference between injured and severely injured is that their current situation is COSTING them something. It's costing them money, or long-term trouble like embarrassment, or major anxiety stress putting a marriage in jeopardy. Severely injured people are losing something by not changing. In other words, their current situation is COSTING them something. The question is, what is it costing them? It's up to you to assess that.

In this hypothetical with Shawn, we can't DQ him yet. We have to explore this further and ask more questions. After talking to Shawn and his wife together and asking them if they were OK living there maybe one or two more years, would it be that bad, they agree that staying put was the best idea. They agreed to have the baby and then wait until the baby was one or two before they really needed more space. So Shawn and Sara were once again DQ'd!

Now, don't get me wrong, someone who is severely injured is worth putting on your watch list and checking in with them occasionally, because most people who are severely injured will almost always end up in trauma down the road. This is someone you could stay in touch with, possibly start to work on CONSENT and INSURANCE, but spend minimal time with them until you determine they are in TRAUMA or you'll be wasting your time. In this example, when I tried to talking Shawn and his wife out of it, I did. You can't talk trauma victims out of wanting your help or wanting to make a move. They will do it with or without you, as we will see in our last example.

Hurt Level Example 3: SHAWN IN <u>TRAUMA</u>

My friend Shawn calls because his wife just had their second kid, they are living in a one-bedroom apartment, and they are bursting at the seams. Shawn's wife Sara is threatening divorce if they don't move into a house soon and she is embarrassed in front of all her girlfriends because they haven't bought a place yet when they could easily afford it. Shawn tells me, "Mark, I'm losing sleep because of the stress, my wife is threatening to leave me, and I have been drinking too much. I need your help to find a house RIGHT NOW or all hell is going to break loose. The stress and lack of sleep is affecting me at work and I may get fired if I don't fix this." This person is suffering trauma. Trauma is the highest hurt level you can find. It means that the current situation is costing them a lot *and* they are freaking out mentally, physically, and emotionally. In this example, Shawn may lose his wife and that is trauma! Trauma victims are hurting so much that they will take action and change. Meaning they will buy or sell to deal with their trauma and they want help right now. When Shawn and his wife got to this point, they did end up buying a house. True story.

The lesson here is that you have to find out what people's situation is, and you do that by going back to Step Two and coming from the position of developing relationships. You focus on developing relationships and if you encounter someone in trauma, then it's up to you as to whether you want to help them buy or sell a house. Trauma victims will do whatever it takes to solve their problem. You will spot this by getting to know them better. It is up to you to determine their hurt level. Ask more questions. Dig deeper by suggesting they wait, or ask them what would happen if they didn't make a move. Trying to talk them out of it, playing devil's advocate. The more you do that, the more real trauma victims will try to convince YOU to help them. Use the best friend exercise to really find out what's going on and determine whether you could help. If you like this person and genuinely feel that they are sincere, then by all means help them! Get to know them and their situation, help them, save them, and go cash your commission check!

Sales Triage™ is your formula for quickly finding out who is worth spending time with and who is not. However, **CAUTION: Sales Triage™** is a game plan, a roadmap to keep you on track so you can get to the real clients faster and avoid the ones who are not, but it is not the Ten Commandments. Use it to the best of your ability to guide you toward developing your own system for disqualifying. Yes, I want you to follow your gut and use these tools to blow through the lookie-lous ASAP. Just make sure you stop, really listen to your gut and run **Sales Triage™** before you cut someone loose. This is a powerful tool and like any powerful training program you don't want to abuse or misuse it. I've seen agents mistakenly pass on real clients because they rushed the **Sales Triage™** process.

Edge Rule: Don't abuse the system.

If you recall, in the first example I told Shawn I didn't think he had a good enough reason to buy a place and he quickly agree with me. In Example Two, if you recall, I got to meet both decision-makers; one was in trauma but the other was not, so they were DQ'd for the time being. In Example Three, ALL decision-makers were freaking out and their current situation was costing them a lot. Trauma!

Trauma victims will always want your help . . . even if you are a bad real estate agent.

Think about that statement above. You may have laughed when you read it, but imagine that you were lying on a park bench and you just got shot. Would you care what kind of doctor was walking by? Would you care whether he was the number one gunshot expert in the area, a completely no-name doctor, or someone who just got out of medical school? Would you care if he was good, bad, or ugly? No. Trauma victims will ask for, and appreciate, your help. (For example, if you call them because you found an amazing house that you really want them to see, they will come see it ASAP.) I want you to get good at finding trauma victims in the real estate world. In your first few years you need to find people who need help immediately so you can make money immediately. If someone passes your gut check and they have trauma, you can take it to Step Two of **Sales Triage™**, Pre-Op. Think of pre-operation procedures in the hospital as we move through this stage.

PRE-OP

What you are looking for here is to see WHO all the decision-makers area, WHEN they want to make a move, and that you and all the decision-makers have agreed to a list of expectations or what we will call "CONSENT."

A completed Pre-Op means you know three things: (1) WHO is involved in decision-making, (2) WHEN they intend to buy or sell and that it is sooner rather than later, and (3) CONSENT is in place, meaning that they like you, you like them, and you all agree on how you will work together, everyone's expectations have been discussed and are realistic. (In the hospital the patient must sign a consent form that explains how the proposed procedure will go down and states that the patient fully agrees to the steps of the procedure before the doctor will operate. Making any connections here?)

Simplified: In the Pre-Op step you must determine WHO, WHEN, CONSENT!

In real estate, if the client doesn't agree to your terms, it is up to you whether you want to help them or not. Or you might discuss it further with them and figure out what *would* work. This is where you let your clients know what works best for you and you ask what works for them. Maybe they have kids and don't want you to call after 6:00 p.m. No problem. Whatever it is, it is best you find out their wish list up front. Then you won't upset them later and this makes life better for not only them, but you as well. I call this process "Consent." Having a talk about CONSENT will truly separate you from the pack, making clients respect you and see that you're not a typical realtor. Consent in a medical context means the patient agrees to let you, the doctor, operate, all parties are aware of how the surgery will be performed and all have signed off – a parent or guardian signing, if the patient is a minor. In real estate the analogous "consent" step is similar. All the decision-makers are at the table. We know WHO is involved, WHEN they want to make a move, that they agree to your way of doing things and you agree to theirs. We call this setting a list of expectations. Just as the doctor informs the patient exactly how things are going to happen and obtains the patient's consent before proceeding, new realtors need to get a comparable kind of CONSENT from their buyers and sellers before moving forward. If the client is in Trauma, you have a complete Pre-Op step and you can't DIS-Qualify them, you then progress to the Insurance step.

INSURANCE

What you are looking for here is that they have proof of the money and you have SEEN IT, and secondly, that they understand the 90 percent rule.

Insurance Step = You must SEE the money and get the client to agree to the 90 percent rule.

"Show me the money!"
-Rod Tidwell (Jerry McGuire's only client)
From the Movie, *Jerry McGuire*

So before you run a buyer all over town, you are going to ask him or her in your own kind way to show you the money. Period. End of story. And if they don't want to do that, then guess what, they are DIS-Qualified. Making sense?

Secondly, you have to make sure they understand the 90 percent rule, which is the following: The 90 percent rule for a buyer looks like this and it is your job to explain it to them. If a property is listed for X amount – let's say $100,000 to make it easy to understand – if you find your buyer a property in this price range, they will agree to offer AT LEAST 90 percent of the asking price or more in their first offer. You set this expectation up front in order to week out the "bargain hunters." In fifteen years of residential real estate, I have never sold a house to a buyer for less than 90 percent of the asking price, and I wasted years with unmotivated buyers that would want to write offer after offer for 60, 70, and 80 percent of asking price in hopes they would get some kind of deal.

Edge Rule: Apply the 90 percent rule.

Let me ask you a question. If you put up your property for sale for a million dollars and someone offered you $700,000, what would you tell that person making the offer? Exactly. You'd tell them to go fly a kite. And that is exactly what will happen to your bargain hunters. New agents will be preyed upon by these bargain hunters because experienced agents will not waste time writing offers that are low-ball. If you write low-ball offers, you will look like an idiot to other sellers and agents and you will be wasting your time. DQ these low-ballers if they do not agree to the 90 percent rule. Period!

If you have a seller, it works the same way. If you have their house listed for X amount, let's say $100,000, someone offers $90,000 and your seller's ego says, "That is ridiculous, I am not even going to counter them," you have not explained the 90 percent rule. To a seller the 90 percent rule tells them that if someone brings them an offer that is 90 percent or more of the asking price, then they are to understand that this is a REAL buyer and they must counter or take it seriously. If your seller doesn't counter a 90 percent offer, it means you didn't properly run the insurance step.

The 90 percent rule for a seller also looks like this. If you're going to list their house and you have shown them the comps in the area that put their property at $100,000 and they want to list their house for more than $110,000, you MUST DIS-Qualify them. Let's say your seller wants to list his house for $130,000 and you know it is only worth $100,000. What do you do? You DIS-Qualify them. Period. Follow the 90 percent rule. It will save you time and money.

OPERATE

Operate means go for it! You have a 100 percent real client if you have made it this far, so give them your full attention and do whatever it takes to help them find their house or sell their house.

What you are looking for here is someone who has successfully passed the first three stages of **Sales Triage™**. They are in TRAUMA. You have full CONSENT (who, when, list). And you have INSURANCE (seen the money, 90 percent rule).

If clients have trauma, consent, and insurance, then you go full steam ahead, spend all the time you can with these people and do whatever it takes to help them buy or sell. Disregard what others say. Only you know their real situation. They have passed your gut check, you have run them through **Sales Triage™** and they pass on all levels. It's time to operate. OPERATE means to show them houses whenever you can, work with them, give them your full attention, get the house listed, and go for it! These are people that will turn into sales and you are on your way to the bank if you stay focused. And FOCUS, for those of you ready for the next step, is Step four of the **Edge**, but not before doing your Post-Op phase of **Sales Triage™**.

POST-OP

This is to ensure that there are no surprises to the buyer or seller AFTER they have successfully put their home in escrow or under contract. This step will protect from back-outs and prevent buyer's and seller's remorse from causing problems.

Post-Op stands for Post Operation. After a patient has been operated on, the medical team informs them of what will happen next, so that they are comforted as they leave the hospital. Think of the last time you left the hospital or ever had some kind of surgery. The good crews/doctors/nurses always gave you some kind of Post-Op advice and talk. As a realtor you are going to do this as well.

Remember when I wanted you to think of yourself as a doctor rather than a realtor? I did this because I wanted you to look at your business from a professional standpoint, to dispel any limiting beliefs you may have had or stereotypes you might have in mind about what or how a realtor is "supposed to be."

You are not typical, my friend, and you are not going to be a typical realtor. These steps may take some time to grasp, but don't beat yourself up. You bought this program to make it big and worthwhile things will take some time. Repetition! Repetition! Repetition!

Sales Triage™ SUMMARY

HURT LEVEL - Injured (Not serious). Severely injured (Costing them, more serious). Trauma (Costing a lot and emotionally freaking out, very serious).

PRE-OP – Find out WHO the decision-makers are, WHEN they want to make a move, do they agree to your way of working and you to theirs (expectations from both sides). If everyone agrees to expectations, we call this CONSENT.

INSURANCE – Do they really have the money? Proof! Meaning you must physically SEE PROOF. Also, are they aware of the 90 percent rule and do they agree to it?

OPERATE – Go for it! Give them your full attention. Congratulations, this is a real client if they have made it this far. Do whatever it takes to sell them. (SAVE THEM!)

POST-OP – After they are in escrow, you make sure they know what to expect. Teach them what is normal and address your BIGGEST CONCERN. Result = Prevents back-outs and cancellations.

Edge Rule: Trauma + Pre-Op + Insurance = Real Client

The hard part is disqualifying them when we don't want to. Maybe you really feel compassionate towards them or really want to help them. What do you do if you know they simply can't afford a house right now? A doctor has a patient come for help with a backache and the doctor determines that the patient doesn't have any insurance. Does the doctor operate anyway? NO! Imagine going to a doctor for a nose job and saying, "Hey Doc, I want a new nose, I can't breathe too well with this one, please fix it and after you are done if it heals and if I like it, I'll pay you. Sound good, Doc?" This is what real estate agents do every single day, they operate for free.

Edge Rule: No Free Surgery.

The point is that you must DIS-Qualify people if they don't have the money and are unwilling to show it to you. Period. New agents and even experienced ones are afraid to discuss money. The majority of all agents avoid the subject, only to find out later that their client is broke. New agents waste time running "uninsured" people around town, hoping they will buy one day, only to find out eventually that this person thought they had enough money, but after further investigation found they did not. And YOU, my newly licensed realtor friend, just wasted four months with this person before you found out they were broke. I want you to learn how to do this in four minutes. Four seconds! However, **Sales Triage™** has five stages and we don't go to the next one until we have completed the ones before. If you skip Trauma and Pre-Op and ask for Insurance first, you'll lose clients and lose business.

Talking to someone about their finances before you have developed a relationship would be inappropriate. If you go for too much, too soon, it kills the relationship. The **Sales Triage™** steps are designed in a certain order for a very specific reason.

Edge Rule: Sales Triage™ steps must be done in order.

With **Sales Triage™** you're going to weed out the lookie-lous and the brokey-brokes very quickly. This is what you want to get good at in your first year: finding <u>real</u> clients. You are *muskie hunting*, you are a *doctor looking to save lives,* you are looking for trauma victims, you are not trying to sell anyone anything. The real buyers and sellers will close themselves because they will want your help. If you make it to Operate stage, then yes, you can finally start selling and going bananas and doing whatever it takes. But until you have determined that they are in trauma and you've done a proper pre-op and have confirmed that they are fully insured (they have the money), you do not operate. Ever wonder why they call it *real* estate?

Selling on the Edge *puts the real in real estate.*

CHAPTER 16

ADVANCED SALES TRIAGE™

DEATH VALLEY

A lot of people ask me, "Why not run **Sales Triage™** on everyone? Maybe my gut check is wrong." For example, you meet someone and your gut says, "This person seems mean," or "I don't feel comfortable around them," but you think, "Ya know what? I don't really think this person is someone I want to work with and I feel they aren't sincere about really buying or selling, but since they drive a Maserati and are sharply dressed, I'm going to proceed." Bad move, McTavish! If you go against your own inner belief and initial feeling, then you, my friend, are on your own. You just went against your gut instinct and that puts you on a road I don't want you to go down. You are now acting against your own integrity and what happens next is you find out this particular buyer (let's refer to him as "Abusive Billy") is indeed mean or dishonest or whatever your initial impression was. You are on the fast track to Death Valley

Edge Definition of Death Valley:

Final resting place of all failed realtors.

Factoid: Average lifespan of a newly licensed residential real estate agent is 12-18 months before they quit, go broke, or end up where I like to call Death Valley. This is the final stop for many talented people that never learned what really mattered in real estate. They unfortunately failed, never to return to the real estate ring again. They now smoke cigarettes, look for water coolers, and roam aimlessly as they rot in the depths of Death Valley with no escape or hope in sight for a commission ever again.

Say "Abusive Billy" asks you to make an offer, but refuses to show you his proof of funds. (No Insurance.) Another point where you should be DIS-Qualifying him, but you decide to let it slide. He then gets upset at you for even asking to see his finances. (Big Red Flag!) He bullies you into making an offer for him and says, "Just tell the sellers I have the money and we can deal with that later. Money is not an issue!" (Famous last words of a time-waster.) You didn't listen to your gut in the first place and now you think, well, this person really seems to want to buy and I don't want to upset him any further, so what's one little compromise . . . and boom! You are now building a different kind of muscle. You are building the muscle that says DON'T follow your instinct, and this is trouble. You justify it by saying to yourself, "Well, I don't have any other clients, so what difference does it make? I might as well work with this abusive and annoying person until something better comes along." This is the typical journey of a new realtor. At this point you either recognize your initial gut check was correct and DIS-Qualify this guy immediately, or you go against that gut feeling, ignore your own instinct, and face what follows. And what follows is wasting time you don't have.

The one thing you do have in this business is your gut instinct and if you go against it, I promise you, you will fast-track yourself to Death Valley – where lie millions of stereotypical failed real estate agents who have gone before you. These are the Death Valley agents who helped create the public view to begin with that we are shady, we're crooks, commission whores, slick, do-anything-for-a-buck agents. This is the prospect's initial view of you. They expect you to do whatever they want and not ask any questions.

Not you, my friend. The buck stops here. This is where you cut your teeth and earn your stripes. Step Three will once and for all allow you to break that mold, shatter that stereotype that real estate agents do anything for money, and you will be on your way to great heights. You will have changed their perception. This is why they will want to work with you. You are different.

THE POINT OF NO RETURN

The point you come to, where you realize you either go against your instinct and the system and head toward DEATH VALLEY or you stick to your guns, follow your gut, and use the system to head toward the **Edge** is the critical point you will face with many potential clients. I call this all-important moment and turning point the point of no return.

The Point of No Return: Critical crossroads where you choose to head toward
Death Valley **OR toward the** *Edge.*

The Point of No Return

[sign graphic insert here]

DEATH VALLEY>>>>>>>>>>>>>

[arrow that way]

<<<<<<<<<<<<<<<<<<<<<<<<THE EDGE

[arrow the other way]

Death Valley deals will attempt to appear sexy, real and lucrative, but: know that you are being fooled. If your gut is telling you otherwise, then head toward the **Edge**, my friends. How do you do that if you are already too far along with Abusive Billy or Linda-Lookie-Lou and you feel it's too late? Simple solution: TURN AROUND! Put your foot down, slam on the brakes and DQ!

You are going to turn down Abusive Billy's business! You are DIS-Qualifying him for many reasons. You're going to politely tell Linda-Lookie-Lou that you are not a good fit and move along. These clients will be shocked because you're no longer behaving the way they expect traditional real estate agents to behave. Turning down business is vintage **Edge**! This will do two very important things for you. One, your confidence level will go through the roof. And two, you will have more time to focus on what is more important, like finding the real clients, like attending your passion arenas and finding people that you DO feel good about. Abusive Billy and Linda-Lookie-Lou are DIS-QUALIFIED! Get rid of them! NEXT!

Your job as a realtor who is now **Selling on the Edge** and with an edge is to wipe out that typical stereotype that you will do anything for anybody. No doctors do whatever a patient asks. You are a professional. You have standards and before you OPERATE, you have to make sure the client is for real.

You wouldn't tolerate an abusive personal relationship, so why would you do so in real estate? Because no one ever told you not to? Well, I am here to tell you! If someone is abusive to you in any way whatsoever, then dump their ass! Period.

GUTCHECK TRUMPS ALL

You now have a system to help you do this. If you stick to it, you follow your gut and if your gut says move on, you listen to your heart and gut and MOVE ON! Everything starts with a gut check. What's next if they pass the gut check? We then run them through **Sales Triage™**. Keep in mind, however, that if your gut says NO, you don't even need to go on to **Sales Triage™**. Gut check trumps all. If you DO like the prospective client, you run **Sales Triage™** on them and if they make it through that, then sell them a house! Regardless of price range or area or whatever, if your gut says work with this person, you like them, they seem like a fit, then boom, we check their hurt level and if they are in trauma, we proceed to the next step of **Sales Triage™**, called Pre-Op. Don't worry, the more you practice and study this, the easier it will get. Repetition! Repetition! Repetition! Use the rules if you get lost.

Edge Rule: Gut check first, then run Sales Triage™.

PRE-OP: THREE IMPORTANT ASPECTS

You know that Pre-Op stands for *Pre-Operation*, the process in the medical world that you go through *before* they will operate on you. The medical team gets the patient's legal consent to do the procedure. In addition, they find out who the interested parties are in case of emergency, and they set a clear date for the surgery. They also discuss what the patient should do beforehand and they outline how the surgical procedure will be done. Similarly, before you show a client houses or give them a listing presentation, you will find out three very important things:

- WHO is involved with making the decision.
- WHEN do these people want to move.
- Do the parties CONSENT to each other's expectation list?

Remember, we do not advance to Pre-Op if we have determined that there is no Trauma. If there is no trauma there is no need for a pre-op step. You put them on the back burner until they really need your help. A lot of new real estate agents will be tempted to start operating – showing houses – right away. The minute they find someone who seems extremely motivated or claims they are ready to go, the newbie kicks into "sell" mode. Hold your horses, pal! Beware, you must advance to PRE-OP FIRST and then to INSURANCE or you could be on the road to Death Valley.

Edge Rule: Never Operate without Trauma, Pre-Op, and Insurance.

IF YOU DON'T DO A PRE-OP STEP YOU WILL REGRET IT

Once I was showing a property to a single gentleman, we had looked for almost six months and we found a winner. He said, "I want it." I said, "Great, I will get the offer ready and send it to you in the morning." He held up a hand. "Mark, before we do that, my mom has to see the house." What? This was the first time I had ever heard about his mother's being part of the decision-making team.

However, I knew it was my fault because I never asked. I never performed a Pre-Op! Buyers and sellers will often claim that they make all the decisions independently, with no one else involved. You will hear things like:

"Oh, you better believe I make all the decisions around here, my wife will do whatever I decide." (Husband in denial)

"Yep, no one but me is involved – my girlfriend is thinking about moving in, but she really won't care what I do." (Clueless single guy)

"My husband has assured me that he wants to sell as well, but he can't be at the meeting and told me to handle it." (Wishful wife)

If you move forward without meeting the other decision-makers, you are heading to Death Valley. You have to find out everyone involved and meet with all of them before you proceed. If you can't get in front of all the decision-makers, then you must put everything on hold until you can meet with *all* the interested parties. Like, in my case, the client's mother, who was playing a big role in the decision-making process. This was a 45-year-old man and I knew he wasn't married, so I assumed it was just him who was the sole decision-maker. Don't ever assume. Pre-Op is getting all the cards on the table, early in the game. I didn't do that. So I told him, "OK, no problem, let's have your mom come see it tomorrow and she can give her thumbs up and we can make the offer then." He said, "I'd love to have her come see it, but she is currently living in Greece." I was so mad I could've almost jumped off a cliff. Here was a guy who was actively looking at houses all over town with me, and not once did he ever mention that his mom had to bless the house before he bought it!

Oy vey! It was completely my fault, though. I never asked the guy who else had to be involved in the buying decision, so it's not like he lied to me. It was my fault. I was operating without doing a Pre-Op. Not good. But wait, it gets better. I said, "OK, so she is in Greece, that's cool, when is she coming to visit?" With a completely straight face he said, "In about six or seven months." I wanted to strangle the guy. But I couldn't because I never took the time to ask who else needed to help him make a decision. Sure enough, the mother shows up in six months and I get the call to go see the hose, but by now, as you have probably figured out, the house was long gone, sold to someone else. I literally could not get out of bed for a week. I was paralyzed with agony from wasting so much time. I knew if I didn't start doing things differently, I would soon be rolling down the side of the cliff, bouncing all the way down to the bottom of Death Valley.

From that moment on, I vowed never to work with anyone until I knew all the decision-makers involved (WHO) and specifically WHEN they saw themselves moving. PRE-OP was born! If anyone wanted to see houses now, but had no intention of moving for twelve months, I would not help them. I told them I'd call them in ten months. If a seller wanted me to tell them what their home was worth, but they had no intention of selling until their kids, who were now sophomores, finished high school, I'd put their information in my calendar to call them closer to the time when they wanted to make a move. People like these, who are not in trauma, will waste your time. They may appear like real clients, but don't be fooled! Dig deeper, find out their hurt level, do a Pre-Op, and get to the truth before Death Valley gobbles you up.

Finally, in Pre-Op, I would make sure that potential clients agreed to my list of expectations and that I agreed with theirs. (As you now know, this is called Consent.) Do you have an understanding of how things work between you and your loved ones? It's the same concept with your relationship between you and your buyers and sellers. My Mom was a nurse, and the more I heard of her stories from the hospital, the more I saw how I could use the systems and processes in the medical world as a model for making my life a lot easier and more manageable. One day I was complaining to my Mom about all my lookie-lou clients and time-wasters and she said, "Too bad you can't use triage like we do at the hospital, or get them to sign a pre-op form, hahaha!" She walked off laughing at me, not realizing how pivotal that remark was. Thanks to my Mom – a Registered Nurse for 35 years – the seeds of what would eventually become my trademarked formula, **Sales Triage™**, were planted. As I explored the concept and tried it out while selling houses, the good news was that I was getting rid of the time-wasters fast because I could see right through them with this new "triage" mindset of mine. Prior to that moment of revelation based on my Mom's suggestion, I had nothing, no plan of attack besides the traditional training methods, and those were not helping. Buyers and sellers had been eating me for breakfast. I just thought this must be how real estate goes. I knew that if I didn't make some changes, the end of my career was near. From that point on, I learned my lesson. I would not show anyone property, not even one house, unless I had met and knew exactly who all the players were. Was there a wife, a mother, a father, a girlfriend, boyfriend, contractor, or a psychic that has to help make the decision? Yes, it's true. One client said she could not buy until her psychic said the house was a winner. I was OK with that. I simply told the client that I would not show her homes unless she brought her psychic with us. **The Edge** was starting to work! Eventually we found her – and her psychic – the winning house!

ACTIONS NEVER LIE

New realtors struggle the most with identifying motivated new clients because they are vulnerable in the beginning, naïve, fresh, green. New real estate agents will believe what they want to believe, as this will give them hope. HOPE, however, does not pay your bills. So how can you come up with a foolproof way to make sure you are not being fooled or having your time wasted by someone who just likes looking at houses or wants free information? Answer: Pay attention to their actions.

Real buyers will respect your time. They will call you back when you call them. They will pick up when you call them. When you say a house for them to see, they will schedule the time. They will DO what is necessary to find a home with you. For buyers, the critical action to look for is that they will make time to see houses, they will tell you who all the decision-makers are, and you will have met them. You will also have no problem getting their proof that they have the funds that make them qualified to buy. Real Buyers happily show you this information and are not hiding anything.

Real Sellers will also behave in a way that lets you know they are serious. Real Sellers will happily let you in their home. They will make time for you to show it whenever you need to. Real Sellers will give you an actual key to their house and even give you the alarm code. Real Sellers will introduce you to all the people that are on the title and actually own the house.

You must find these things out by asking, and in addition to giving you answers, Real Buyers and Sellers will provide you with whatever you need. If they don't and they get upset when you try to run **Sales Triage™** on them, take special note here: they are not real.

Edge Rule: Actions trump words all day long.

Pop quiz: What are you looking for in the Pre-Op step?

Answer: WHO, WHEN, CONSENT.

WHO and WHEN are simple to understand, but what does *consent* mean? It means that both you and the buyer/seller agree as to how things are going to be done. You can ask them what they expect of you, and if you can't meet their expectations, then tell them you are not the right realtor and DIS-Qualify them. Or help them understand how things would work. If you all agree to each other's expectations, then you have CONSENT!

If a seller's house is worth $750,000 but he wants to list it for $999,000 to "test the market," guess what? He is DIS-QUALIFIED! Do not take an overpriced listing. It tells you two things. One, you are not dealing with a real seller, the seller has zero trauma and zero consent. If they did, they would know that listing their house for 25% over market was going to waste everyone's time. This is the point where you, as the realtor, have to decide: Do I take the overpriced listing or do I DQ this seller? POP QUIZ: What is this critical crossroads called? And where will you end up if you don't do the right thing?

OPTION 1: You take the listing. If you take the overpriced listing, now you have a house that sits on the market for months and months, you end up showing it to people only to have them tell you – rightly – that it's not worth the asking price. Low-ballers send in terrible offers, your seller gets upset with you, they blame you for not being able to sell it, and other agents talk about how you overprice properties and are upset with you so your reputation gets bad. Your initial thought was that having a sign in the front yard would be a good advertising for other listings, but now it's been so long that other sellers think you are a bad agent because you haven't been able to sell this house where you have your sign out in front. They don't care why you haven't sold it, they just make a mental note to never use you as their realtor. Your strategy has now backfired and you are on your way to Death Valley.

OPTION 2: Tell the seller he is wrong, you will NOT take an overpriced listing and either get him to list at market price or DQ him. By DQing this seller, you can spend your valuable time finding real sellers and trauma victims, and you will make a lot more money. The seller you just DQ'd will now have more respect for you, since you didn't allow him to overprice his home. Maybe he didn't know that overpricing was a bad idea and will now agree to price the home at what you think it's worth. Don't take this DQ stuff to a harsh extreme, it's true that you have to be nurturing to clients and help them understand their options, but if they insist on doing stupid things or you can't get consent, then you must DQ them and move on. The opportunity cost it too high and you either get consent from your clients on how you will work together or it's over until you can work it out.

My good friend Merrie was a new realtor who started when I did. She told me she was struggling with a particular client and asked me for some help. The client was a very successful businessman from England but he was also very abusive toward her, calling her late at night, demanding to see homes at the strangest of hours, ungrateful for her help, being sexually inappropriate, no-showing on appointments, and she didn't know how to handle it. I told her how to figure out her ideal client and make a list of what that would look like. Then, discuss with all her prospective clients that, if they wanted to work with her, they would have to agree to what was on the list. She came up with the following:

1. Clients must be nice to me.
2. Clients can only call me between 9:00 a.m. and 6:00 p.m., Monday through Friday.
3. I will only work with people who respect my time.
4. Clients are not allowed to cancel unless they give me at least 24 hours' notice.
5. Any disrespectful or inappropriate behavior or sexual suggestions will not be tolerated.

6. Clients will only be shown property between 10:00 a.m. and 2:00 p.m. (in other words, not during rush hour).
7. Clients will be appreciative of my hard work and will agree to be loyal to me if I am working hard for them.

From then on, Merrie gave this list to all her clients and it was a giant success. They had the upmost respect for her as a result of her setting these expectations and laying down the law in a way that no other realtors did. In return, she told her clients that she would deliver excellent customer service, help her clients find or sell their homes at great prices, and do it all faster than other agents. She has been flying ever since and is one of the top realtors, all because she no longer operates without a thorough Pre-Op.

Your list may be different. It can be whatever you want, but the point is to have one and make sure you use it in your Pre-Op step every time. With this in place, if clients don't abide by the rules, you can either give them a warning or DQ them. The important part is that you make your list, share it with your clients, and if they want to work with you, they must agree to it. Are you following this?

You can also have them make a list of what they expect of you, and you can either agree to it or not. This stimulates communication and you learn more about your client. Once you all agree, you have *CONSENT*. If you know all the decision-makers (WHO), you have determined that they are making a move within six months or less (WHEN), and you have identified trauma in ALL the decision-makers, then and only then you can move toward the INSURANCE step. If you don't have Trauma and a complete Pre-Op, you can't proceed to Insurance. Getting this?

Let's imagine that one of your Pre-Op consent requirements is that clients must call and cancel with at least 24 hours' notice. You have been working with someone who has repeatedly not only cancelled at the last minute, but has no-showed twice! You have a choice here to either disqualify the client or ask yourself, did you really run a clear Pre-Op step? Did you and your client sit down and discuss your expectations of each other? Did you get consent from the client that they would agree to this? If not, then you can't disqualify them just yet. You have to communicate with your clients before you run them all over town or spend time helping them sell their house. Understanding and managing expectations is the essence of the Pre-Op phase. Most agents never do anything like this and never will. They will end up in Death Valley selling pet rocks! Not you! You are learning how to sell on the **Edge**! This is your secret weapon that will help you quickly identify real clients or determine the reasons not to work with someone. The faster you find out someone is not serious, the less time you will waste. Once you have done a successful hurt level analysis, determined that they are in trauma, and have a clear understanding of Pre-Op with your client, you can proceed to the Insurance step.

INSURANCE: SHOW ME THE MONEY

Show me the money!

This is my favorite part of **Sales Triage™** because I love the movie *Jerry McGuire* and how he simplifies this step so beautifully. Show me the money! Yes, it's that simple. Remember I asked you at the beginning to put yourself in the mindset of a highly paid doctor and use that metaphor when you think of yourself as a Doctor of Real Estate. OK, keep that mindset, it will help guide you and keep you on track. So now that YOU, M.D., are back, let me ask you a question. What is the first thing the doctor's office asks you for when you walk in the door? Your insurance card! So how come in real estate, especially with newbies, no one ever talks about the money? Answer: Because we have been taught all our lives that it is inappropriate to ask someone about his or her finances. We have been brainwashed into thinking that you can't ask someone how much money they make. Even worse, new realtors tell me all the time that they had a feeling a certain client could not afford to buy, but the new realtor didn't want to bring it up because they were secretly hoping for a miracle. In real estate you cannot rely on hope. Hoping in real estate leads to Death Valley. You have to have concrete evidence that a buyer is financially qualified or you have no choice but to DIS-Qualify them. For a seller, Insurance means a *signed listing agreement*. No sig, no sell. Beware of sellers that refuse to sign a listing agreement. It usually means one thing. No trauma.

GET COMFY TALKING ABOUT MONEY OR QUIT NOW

In real estate you have to get out of your comfort zone and become very comfortable talking about money. Your first few times you may say the wrong thing, you may upset a few people, but this is OK! Better to ask and get to the truth than not to mention it, only to find out later that they can't afford it – after you have spent six months running them all over town. Remember the Main Mission of Step Two? Get your fail on! Well, you are going to fail a lot, trying to get people to show you the money, but the point is, just by discussing the subject you will separate yourself from thousands of other realtors who never do, and you will save yourself time by figuring out whether a client is real or not.

I can't tell you how many people *appear* to have money that actually do not. So why not just ask? You don't have any scripts in **Selling on the Edge**, so I ask you now: if you had to find out how much money someone had for a down payment, what would you say to them? Use the best friend exercise. Remember that? Go ahead, what would you say? Awesome! Whatever you just said is perfect. You see, when asking someone what their budget is, it doesn't matter how you ask it, it just matters that you ask. If you started your new job next Monday and the employer said, "After you've worked here for ninety days, we will tell you what we're paying you," what would you say? You would think they were nuts. Insurance is the third step of **Sales Triage™**. You're going to find out whether the client has the money, and you are going to need to see physical proof of that money. You could get a letter from their lender for starters, or my personal favorite, a checking account statement. Of neither of those works for them, ask for a copy of their tax return. In the Insurance step you must *see* documentary proof of the money or you cannot move forward. If you skip this, I will hunt you down. I will find you. I will come to your house and personally put you on the AMTRAK to Death Valley because that is your next stop if you don't ask buyers to show you the money or sellers to sign the listing agreement!

Edge Rule: Real buyers have no problem showing you the money.

Edge Rule: Real sellers have no problem signing listing agreements.

My experience has been that when people are in trauma, they will do whatever it takes to find a home or sell their home and that means show you their money or sign a contract. Buyers are happy to put you on the phone with their lender or banker and it is your job to see how much down payment they have and if it's enough. You have to get an actual hard copy of their financials like the following:

- *A letter from their lender stating their purchasing power.*
- *A copy of their checking/savings account statement.*

- *A copy of any account in their name that shows funds.*

If you get any or all of the above, you have done a successful insurance step. Use the best friend exercise here to hone in on difficult questions because most people will not want to discuss money, but if you don't, then you are on your own – and it's a slippery slope that leads to DEATH VALLEY every time.

CAUTION! Many new agents will accept verbal answers from their clients. This will look like, "Oh, don't worry, I have plenty of money." Or, "I will show you the money when we find a house we like." Or another favorite of mine is, "Money is no object." Don't believe the hype. Ask them to SHOW YOU THE MONEY or you will suffer later. Remember this ancient Chinese proverb, now one of the more famous **Edge** rules if you ever get lost:

Edge Rule: No ticky, no laundry.

In the Insurance step, remember: verbal financial statements mean nothing. And verbal agreements from sellers telling you they will pay you if you sell their house are nonsense. For sellers, you must get them to sign on the line which is dotted and then and only then you have successfully completed your Insurance step for your seller. For buyers, you must *see* the dough. "Show me the money, Jerry! SHOW! ME! The MONEY!!"

OPERATE (GO ALL IN)

If you have a client who is in trauma, combined with a complete Pre-Op, and you have confirmed that they have Insurance, then you are ready to Operate.

Trauma + Pre-Op + Insurance = Operate!

You operate when you have a real client, and this is the fun part. This is when you do whatever it takes to sell this person a house or sell their house for them, because they are the real deal and are going to buy or sell soon with or without you – so you'd better make sure it is you! Once you have run them through the first three steps of **Sales Triage™**, they are clear for takeoff and you must be all over these clients or they may use someone else. It will happen more than once in your career. However, don't worry about that now, just know that you have a real client on your hands. If it is a seller you are dealing with, at this point you list the house, get it on the market and sell that sucker. If it is a buyer, then show them houses, schedule time with them, and find them a house. *Real* buyers will quickly respond to your emails and phone calls when you find a house for them to see. *Real* sellers will sign the listing agreement, agree to price their home at market value, let you list it ASAP, keep their house clean and easily accessible for you, and, yes, they will even give you a key! Believe it or not, I have seen real agents take listings and not even get a key! Why? Because the seller said they wanted to be present at all the showings or came up with some other reason they didn't want the realtor to have a key. This is not a good sign. It indicates that the Pre-Op was not done properly.

Edge Rule: Always get the key.

Remember it's the *actions* you pay attention to, not what people say? If you've done a good Pre-Op and managed expectations, you will be fine. But be ready, because sometimes clients will forget what they agreed to and start to behave differently. You have to call them out on this if you see it happening. For example, buyers may start no-showing on appointments or cancelling at the last minute. This is not acceptable. Or a seller may let you list the house but then never let you show it. In that case, you have to remind them of the PRE-OP! Kind of like reminding kids of the rules. I have been doing this for fifteen years, yet buyers and sellers sometimes even fool me. You have to keep an eye out for this. The reality is that during the selling process, people's situations may change and they may not tell you. Their hurt level may change. They may no longer wish to sell or buy and that is OK. If you are a good agent, you will recognize this training coming long before they have to tell you.

Just as a doctor constantly monitors a patient, a great real estate agent must constantly gauge a customer's hurt level and pay close attention to the customer's behavior. If their vitals change, you have to be ready.

Customers may not want to tell you the whole story or what they are exactly up to all the time. It doesn't really matter why. That is just how it is, some of the time. Don't freak out, people change their minds. Keep your cool, remember your Cornerstones in these moments. It is your job to be aware of their behavior and watch for changes. Remember the **Edge** rule? Actions trump words every time. Actions never lie. Pay attention to their actions and you won't be misled. Clients will sometimes attempt to mislead you, as they're embarrassed or there is something personal that they don't want you to know, so it's important you watch for this or learn the hard way, like Joe did.

> *"You want the Truth? You can't handle the truth!"*
>
> -Colonel Jessup
> *A Few Good Men*

My partner Joe took a listing last year on a very expensive house in Malibu for $8million. The owners were a highly successful married couple who were starting a family and needed to move into a bigger home. Joe called me one day, extremely frustrated, saying that every time he had a showing request, the seller would NOT allow him access to the home. He would make some excuse about how no one could let Joe in, which was causing Joe a lot of stress and wasted time and money. I asked Joe question number one: "Why does the seller need to be there for the showings? Don't you have a key?" He replied, "The seller didn't want to give me one." (Red flag.) Secondly, I asked, "Why are they preventing you from getting in?" He said he didn't know. I told him to call the seller and either get some answers or disqualify them. Joe agreed a hundred percent. What follows is what Joe told me happened as a result.

Joe called the seller and said, "Mr. Seller, I appreciate you, but unless you give me a key and allow me to show the property when I have showing requests, I think it's best that you find another agent, or maybe just take your house off the market until you can give me access." The seller instantly got furious and said, "I don't want to show the house when it is inconvenient for me and I don't want to have to leave just because a buyer is coming." (Client getting upset, another Red Flag.) "How am I supposed to sell it if I can't show it?" Joe asked (disqualifying). The seller responded, "Figure it out!" Yikes! An unreasonable seller. (Big Red Flag.)

Joe waited a few days to let them cool down and finally said to the seller, "I think it is best if we cancel the listing agreement and you can find another agent." The seller's jaw dropped. Joe went on, "Because by not letting me show the house when the buyers want to see it, you are telling everyone out there that you are NOT a real seller and you are making me look bad. So if it's OK with you, let's just part ways."

The seller said, "Joe, listen, I'm very sorry, there is something you don't know. My wife and I are getting a divorce and she is trying to keep the house. The truth is, she doesn't want to sell, but I do, and that is why she never makes time to let you in. Our attorneys are saying we cannot sell at this point and I don't know what to do."

So there you go. Joe finally got to the truth. Although it was saying goodbye to an $8million listing and a $200,000 commission, Joe made the decision to disqualify and not waste any more time with this seller. He gave back the listing and that was that. Before you could even link, Joe was back to immediately finding real buyers and sellers, losing no more time on Mr. Malibu Seller. This is an excellent story illustrating how disqualifying can get to the truth. Joe has been doing this for twenty-five years, yet even he sometimes gets off-track. But the important thing is that he stepped up and did what he had to do when things didn't seem right. He went for the truth, as he knew something was wrong and his client's behavior was not acceptable. And he got to the truth. The most interesting part of this story is that because Joe was no longer wasting time on this house, he secured another listing in the area and ended up selling a different Malibu home, making well over $100,000. The original home is still sitting on the market to this day with another agent, and it is no surprise it has not sold. Joe made the right decision in cutting that seller loose and it paid off.

New realtors are scared to offend clients, or feel they are too inexperienced to be tough with someone. Sometimes when you are new, the fact is that you don't want to know the truth because it may mean losing a client or a commission, and, yes, maybe we can't always handle the truth. No realtor wants to admit they have a bogus buyer or seller on their hands after they have invested a lot of time with them. Nevertheless, be honest with yourself and with your clients. If something is off, address it immediately. Don't wait for it to blow up later or waste any more time. If your gut tells you something is wrong, it probably is, so bring it up. If doing this pisses off a few people, congratulate yourself, you are on the right track, my friend. Keep it up!

Edge Rule: If you feel it, say it.

It is better to address the obvious and get all the issues out on the table. Otherwise you can spend months and months wasting time with Lookie-Lous, Timmy Timewasters, Bill Bullsh*tter and Kenny NoDough! And I don't want that. I want you to work with Joey Easy Client and Mikey Moneybags and Tony Trauma. LOL, you get my point? Running the first three steps of **Sales Triage™** will, without a doubt, cover many of the issues. So make sure you USE **Sales Triage™** or I will happily book your reservation now for The Death Valley Hotel and Suites!

YOU RUN THE SHOW

Finding Trauma, doing Pre-Op, and getting Insurance is not something you're going to do in one thirty-minute meeting. It is possible, but not likely. These things take time and you have to go with what feels right with your clients. Some move faster than others. You have to be aware of this and work with them accordingly. Getting through the first three steps of **Sales Triage™** has taken me as long as three weeks and sometimes as fast as a few hours. The point is there is no set timeline here, and you are the one who sets the pace. No one else. Only you know the client. Only you know how to interact with them. Only you have been the one who has developed the relationship with them. So don't let anyone tell you whether your clients are real or not, or whether they are a waste of time or not. (Especially other agents.) Since most other agents will not have your best interests at heart, unless it's someone you trust completely or who is part of your dream team (you will learn about this in Step Five), be careful of discussing too much with other agents. In residential real estate, talking too much about your deals to other agents or with other customers can lead to your demise.

Edge Rule: Loose lips sink ships.

With this system, you work with who you want, how you want, when you want, and don't let anyone tell you otherwise. You've heard the phrase, "Live and let live"? In real estate I have an **Edge Rule** that a lot of know-it-all overzealous agents really should take note of:

Edge Rule: Sell and let sell.

Don't worry about other people's deals and never let them tell you how to work yours. Unless it is a member of your dream team or someone you trust implicitly, bottom line: it's none of their business. You run the show.

POST-OP: THREE IMPORTANT ASPECTS

Three important things to accomplish in this step:

1. Diffuse buyer/seller remorse.
2. Address any major concerns so there are no surprises.
3. Communicate what is "normal" from contract to close.

"Post-Op" stands for Post Operation and it is the fifth and final step of **Sales Triage™**. You have a real client on your hands, you have "operated" and found them a house or listed their house and you are now "in escrow." (In some states they refer to this as the house is "under contract.") Either way, it's the moment when you are very close to the end of the selling process. You are in the final phase and have thirty to forty-five days before the sale closes. Never assume the deal is closed at this point. In this "escrow" period, believe me, all hell can break loose and the sale may not close. It's never closed until it's closed.

Edge Rule: A sale is "final" when the commission check has been cashed and the check has cleared.

Many times buyers and sellers will start freaking out during this escrow period. Don't panic, this is normal. Think of a patient just waking up from surgery. They're vulnerable, scared, and a little concerned for their safety. A good doctor and medical staff will inform them about what just happened and what is going to happen moving forward. You will do the same thing with your clients at this point.

They have signed off on selling their house and they are now having regrets, second thoughts, or doubts. This is called Seller's Remorse and Buyer's Remorse. It is a normal psychological reaction everyone has whenever they make any kind of purchase or they sell something. Your job is to diffuse this psychological phenomenon or minimize it as much as possible. People get emotional at this point, as they just made a huge sale or purchase and they will begin to have some doubts. Preparing them for these doubts and letting them know that the feelings they are having are normal is all you have to do in this step. Let me repeat that, because I don't want you to overcomplicate this step. Your only objective at this point should be to let your buyer or seller know that they may have second thoughts about buying or selling and that this is normal. By telling them BEFORE they have these feelings that they are can expect to have them, you will deflect 99% of cancellations and back outs. How you tell them this is entirely up to you. Just make sure you tell them.

THE RUNAWAY BUYER AND THE NEVER-ENOUGH SELLER

I had just put a house under contract and we were in the escrow period. After the inspection, we found out the roof had a leak and the buyer immediately insisted on backing out of the deal. What was I to do at this point? How was I to stop them? It's very difficult at this point to change their minds. Even though a small roof leak and a little wear and tear can be a normal discovery in an inspection (especially it it's an older house, which this was), this buyer was not open to any further discussion. She was a first-time buyer and didn't realize that every house is going to have some issues. Even brand-new houses have minor issues. But this buyer didn't know that because I screwed up. I never told her what to expect during the escrow and inspection period. No magic script was going to save me here. The buyer was over it and the deal was canceled. I lost a sale that I should not have lost over an eight hundred dollar roof leak that was blown out of proportion. I knew there was something I had to learn from this. The POST-OP step was officially invented!

That lesson was only the beginning. This same client asked me to help her find another house and I did. I forgot how she canceled the previous deal like it never happened. After all, I was excited again! My one client was still looking and this gave me hope. (I was heading toward Death Valley and didn't have a clue.) We found another house she liked, went into escrow, and this time I said, "Remember, certain things may be wrong with the roof so be prepared this time." She said, "I understand, but on this house it won't matter, I LOVE it and will never back out." Sure enough, as we moved forward and got into escrow again, she decided to back out. I was crushed. This time it was because a friend of hers told her that crime was high in this particular neighborhood. The funny part was, this buyer had been living in that neighborhood for almost ten years. I still didn't learn my lesson. We proceeded to move on from that house and I ended up finding a third house for this person. Keep in mind, now, this has been almost a year of my life running this person all over town. We were now on our third escrow and it didn't matter because this time we had definitely found a winner! I really believed there was no chance she could back out from this one. I was wrong. We were close to closing and she wanted to bring her new boyfriend, her parents, and everyone to see this house one more time. This house was finally the perfect one, she told me. It was in brand-new condition, spotless, and everyone loved it. No roof leaks, no crime allegations, just a winner through and through. I was already planning how to spend my commission. This time I had no doubt in my mind we were finally going to close. Oh, how wrong I was. Enter the Runaway Buyer once again. Dizasty.

Two days before close, the buyer calls me once again and says, "I just found out that the people living on the street a few doors have three dogs and they seem to bark a lot. My boyfriend is a little concerned." I just started laughing. I knew she was backing out. I tried everything to stop them, I brought my manager in to try to save the deal, I had top agents talk to them. It didn't matter. They still backed out. This was a runaway buyer. To this day, this person *still* lives in the same apartment they have lived in for the last seventeen years and will never, ever, ever move! The good news is I no longer waste my time with this person or anyone similar. I learned the hard way. You will know better.

The runaway buyer is a buyer you should run away from. You can spot them because they keep trying to buy houses but they always back out for whatever reason. They are always complaining about something and nothing is ever good enough. Ya know what? DQ this sucker ASAP! You don't need the headache. The mistake I made with my runaway buyer was that in fact I knew this person was not a real buyer from day one. My gut told me that from the get-go, but I didn't listen. A simple gut check could have saved me a year of my life when I was new, but I didn't have a system for this situation. Thankfully you now do.

Another story you will hear from runaway buyers is that they know every house will have some issues. Even brand-new ones. But the truth is that certain buyers will always find a reason to back out or cancel at the last minute. Ever see the movie, *The Runaway Bride*, starring Julia Roberts? Same concept here. Sellers can be the same way. Sellers will often list their home with you and then complain that you aren't getting them enough money or they no longer wish to sell because they are too emotionally attached to the house.

I had a customer list their house with me and they were very happy about the price we agreed to list it at, $649,000. They even affirmed, "Mark, if you get us $649,000, we are out of here and will move ASAP." After a few weeks on the market, I brought them a full price offer. They refused to take it. WHAT?!? The seller now claimed they wanted more money, so they had me raise the price of their house to $679,000. Three months went by with no other offers, another two months went by, and finally a new offer came in for the same price as the original offer. After weeks of counter offers, we finally got this new buyer to go to $655,000. After six months of haggling, the seller squeezed only $6,000 more. The wife was furious, screaming, "Let's please just sell and get out of here!" But Mr. Never-Enough husband was not satisfied. The prospective buyers refused to pay any more than $655,000 and the wife was insisting on taking the deal, but the husband was adamant that he could get more money. I told them the buyer would not go a penny higher, period. Mr. Never-Enough Seller said, "Well, Mark, then why don't you kick in some of your commission to get us to the $679,000?" I told this guy that even if I kicked in ALL of my commission, we would still not be at $679,000. My commission was going to be approximately $15,000. Because I was new and didn't know any better, I said, "OK, what can I kick in to make this work?" He said, "If you do $5,000, I will sell the house." I agreed. Big mistake!

I said, "Great. I will get the paperwork ready." I brought it to him and his wife. The wife signed, but the husband hesitated – and then refused. I could not believe my eyes. I said, "But we got the buyer to $655K, I am giving you five grand of my commission, and you said you would do it!" He said, "Sorry, now you need to go ask the buyer's agent to kick in some of their commission." I exploded. I could never ask another agent to reduce their commission. It was not my nature and I refused. This guy was out of his mind and was never, ever going to sell his house because no matter what amount or terms he got, it would never be enough.

I was furious. Not only did I waste six months with this irrational seller, once I got him everything he wanted, he still didn't sell. It was nobody's fault but mine. I was terribly upset with myself because I felt like I had sold out. I felt cheap. This person got me to give up my commission and still didn't sell. I swore from that moment on that I would never let anyone haggle with me for my commission. In fact, I would put that in my Pre-Op step and tell people from the outset that if they even *asked* for a commission reduction, I would *double* my commission. I joked about it, but I let clients know early on that my commission was non-negotiable. You will encounter the runaway buyer and the never-enough seller as you put more and more deals in escrow. Beware and be aware of them, make sure you do a thorough Pre-Op and Post-Op on these characters, and you will be fine.

So what does a Post-Op look like in the real world of selling houses? Let's first take a look at what it looks like at the hospital. When a patient is being discharged, what do doctors typically tell them? Things like, "Be prepared, you may have some slight pain for the next few days and you may get a little queasy from the medicine, but don't worry, *that's normal*." The key words here are, "that's normal." The doctor tells the patient what to expect so that the patient doesn't freak out over the next few weeks. The same goes for real estate and your Pre-Op. I want you to tell your clients what to expect over the course of the escrow.

For example, I don't have a script, but what would you tell your clients who just bought a house and are currently in escrow? I don't know, it's up to you to figure out, but ask yourself, what is one reason they might get nervous and back out? You may answer, "Because they are first-time buyers and every first-time buyer gets scared the first time." So your Post-Op may look just like that: "Mr. Buyer, I know you are very scared and excited at the same time, but it's normal to feel a little nervous during the escrow period." That's a simple example, but it all depends on your client.

Another example might be that during the search for the perfect house, your clients said their most important criterion was that they wanted a "bright" house – and for whatever reason, this house to you seems dark but they are buying it anyway. So your Post-Op might look like this: "Mr. Buyer, I know you mentioned that you really wanted a bright house and this house seems dark to me, so I am just making sure that you are OK with that before we move forward with the offer."

You will know what to discuss in Post-Op if you think about it for each client. The important thing is to do a Post-Op step on *everyone*. It will keep them loose and it will prevent back outs and cancellations.

You are going to have some people back out and cancel and it will be tough on you, but understand it will happen even to the best of the best. It even happened to me recently as I was getting a little lazy and not doing a very good Post-Op – which was a mistake. I sell houses in California and I had a very great client who was purchasing a $2million home. This was a successful entrepreneur who had just moved here from the east coast. We found a great house and went into escrow and after the general inspection, it came back that the house had termites. Lovely. Approximately $3000 worth of termite repairs were needed. Now this was not a lot of money to my client, he as more just freaked out that the house had termites. You see, where he was from there was no such thing. However in California, I had neglected to tell him that every house has termites. That is the truth. I knew the house would have termites, it's a standard part of every sale. And in California, every house has termites that they must clear up before the home is transferred to a new owner. I assumed he knew this and it would not make a difference.

The problem was I never told him *prior* to receiving the news, which was really not so much news as confirmation of information I knew we would get. Had I told him once we found the house and were making the offer, "Listen, Mr. Buyer, just to give you a heads up, every house in California will have some termite work when the owners transfer to a new owner, so that is normal stuff and I just want you to be aware that this house, too, will probably have some termites too." This would have at least planted the seed and the buyer wouldn't have freaked out as much when he saw the report.

Unfortunately, that was not the case. I did not do a Post-Op and the buyer freaked out. He insisted we pull out of the deal. It was an unknown, from his point of view, it spooked him, and I was toast. No sale. Why? Answer: a very poor Post-Op step. Verdict: my fault. It was too late to try to explain and it was all my fault that this sale was lost. Four months later my buyer was still looking and had even moved to an apartment in L.A., and was now much more comfortable with California and aware of California things including termites. He said to me, "Mark, I wish I had not freaked out over the termites. I should have bought that house, I was just having typical buyer's remorse." The house was sold to someone else at that point – and I learned another huge and expensive lesson.

POST-OP SUMMARY

1. Diffuse buyer/seller remorse (Tell them what it is).
2. Red Flag (Bring one up. If there are none, find one.)
3. Share a story of what is "normal" moving forward.

The point of a Post-Op is to diffuse buyer or seller remorse as best you can. The key to a good POST-OP step is communication. You have to let your client know the process and what can happen as you move forward. Let them know the bad things that can happen, too. Pick one RED FLAG so this will get your client thinking. If there are no red flags, then find one! This is behavior contrary to "selling," but your client will appreciate your honesty and through your bringing up the Red Flag before it turns up as a surprise, you will look like a hero and it will diffuse your client's remorse as they had been made aware of it.

The Red Flag is the hard part, but the point is to tell them something. Something to get them thinking so that when the remorse feeling comes, they will be reminded that you told them about it and it won't be such a big deal. Sometimes buyers and sellers will cancel for completely valid reasons and that is OK. A Post-Op is a step to make sure they don't back out for reasons that are not valid and regret it later. Surprises freak clients out. By bringing up a red flag you are helping to minimize surprises. Your clients will appreciate your help with this matter, so do your best to communicate to them that buyer's remorse and seller's remorse are normal occurrences. If you want to make your own list of things you want them to be ready for, that's even better. Mine sounded like this:

"Every house has termites, traffic noise, and roof leaks, and your friends are always going to tell you that you overpaid. So be ready for these things."

I would tell buyers that these things were going to happen. They are part of living in California, so be ready because it is part of buying a house. Adding this critical Post-Op step was key to helping complete the sale.

Edge Rule: Post-Op diffuses remorse and prevents backouts.

If you are selling houses, you will have cancellations and backouts now and again. Understand it is part of the journey. No one closes every single one. When you're selling houses, if you are doing a good job, you will have a lot of deals in escrow. Some of them are going to fall out of escrow for reasons beyond your control. Clients will cancel, back out, and they will change their minds. This, my friends, is normal. Don't beat yourself up over it. It happens now and again and sometimes it can really crush you. Don't quit just because you had a few deals cancel on you. The busiest agents lose the most deals. Just understand you are on the right track and learn from every cancellation. Did you catch my Post-Op step I just did on YOU? ☺

Step Three of **Selling on the Edge** is your ultimate toolbox and you have to get familiar with these tools. It is loaded with powerful material for you to make your own. **Sales Triage™** is your actual selling formula within this program that will make you instantly different from any other realtor. It will make clients look at you differently and with respect, because you are NOT trying to "sell" them. You will actually spend more time trying to DIS-Qualify people than sell them. It will completely mesmerize your prospects. They will look at you like you are NOT a salesperson, and that is exactly what you want. For the first time ever, you, the realtor, are in control and the tables have turned. You are running the show because you have a system that allows you to really look like a professional. **Selling on the Edge** is your six steps to a successful long-term career selling houses, and **Sales Triage™** is your selling system-within-the-system for implementation when you have a live, viable potential buyer or seller and need to help them. **Sales Triage™** will help you identify the winners quicker than any other system out there. Once you master this step, you can pat yourself on the back because you are on your way. The key is to be totally honest with yourself and your clients. Sometimes you will feel things you don't want to say. You must put them out there or ask questions to get to the truth.

Be honest with yourself and with your clients and really focus on communicating the truth to your clients. You will find that DIS-Qualifying, saying NO, following your gut, and using **Sales Triage™** will make you hundreds of thousands of dollars over the years to come. I feel this step is so valuable that originally I didn't want to share it with anyone – but then I realized that would be a giant mistake. I came up with this program to help real estate agents and change lives everywhere, and to withhold something so powerful would be going against every fiber of my being.

The sad part (and I hope this is not the case with you) is that I can share this powerful system with millions of people and the reality is that most of them will not have the courage to use it. Most agents will not use it. They just won't. With every client you meet, you will always come to the Point of No Return. To the left you will have Death Valley and to the right you will have **The Edge**. If you use this system, it will get you to the **Edge** every time, and that means success!

Most agents, however, will default back to traditional training and run around like public service agents, jumping whenever the client rings the bell, which means Death Valley is right around the corner. Runaway Buyers, Never-Enough Sellers, Linda Lookie-Lous, Timmy Time-Wastes, Billy Bullsh*tters, and Kenny No-Doughs are out there looking for new realtors to prey on every day, so beware!

I hope I have equipped you with tools in Steps One, Two, and Three to protect you from these characters. As you head out there on your own, it can be rough. Being new will make it even scarier, but selling homes and working for yourself can be the most fulfilling thing you have ever done. Remember: Be Yourself, Get Out There, and DIS-Qualify! Steps One, Two, and Three of **Selling on the Edge** will give you super powers if you use them. The key is to *use the steps*. Don't try to do it perfectly or beat yourself up if things don't come off flawlessly; that is OK. We like flaws, we like differences, we like things a little rough around the edges. Your Main Mission in Step Two was to go out there and crash and burn and never be afraid to fail. If you are failing and crashing, I promise you, you are on the right track and getting close to the finish line. People out there want and need your help, but they need to trust you – and they will if you will simply be yourself and share your gifts with them. Don't worry if you make mistakes. Just know that the more you screw up, make a fool of yourself, and continue to engage, crash, and burn, people will appreciate your flaws and mistakes because this will let them know you are human, not some robotic salesperson.

I am here to tell you it is humanness and authenticity that will attract buyers and sellers to you. Your flaws and humanness are what will make you unique, so embrace failure, laugh at it, and get your fail on! People will appreciate your imperfections. These will show them that you're a real person and comfortable in your own skin. Your being at ease being YOU will *attract* more and more people to you because at some deep level, everyone wishes they could open up and be themselves a little more and be comfortable making mistakes. It's scary to show the world who you really are and that you are not perfect, but being perfect in your imperfections is what **Selling on the Edge** is all about.

I am getting excited for you, you have made some real progress, and this is not easy material. It is simple, but not easy. You stumbled across this program for a reason, and the reason is that it's time for you to share YOU with the world. You are the person I have been trying to reach. You are the one I want to take this system and make it your own. I love the individuality of everyone and how we are all different. It starts with my helping one person to be themselves just a little more today, and tomorrow they affect someone else and the whole thing perpetuates itself. So thank you in advance for helping me achieve something bigger than we both had planned. This is what happens when people start being themselves and it starts with you bringing out the YOU in you. You are on your way!

FORGET ABOUT REAL ESTATE FOR 48 HOURS

I have given you the road map. It's now up to you. HOW you want to get there: drive, fly, or take a bike for all I care. The beauty of the **Edge** is that you do things the way YOU want to. Just follow the steps and you will be selling more houses and finding more REAL clients than you ever could have imagined. Now it's important that you go take a mental nap. Yes, go take a nap, hit the beach, or grab an icy cold one. I know I said I would never tell you what to do, but one thing I do tell people to do is recharge, even though they think they don't need it.

You should take some time off from reading even if you are fired up and want to keep going. You need to let your subconscious catch up to you. I need you to ingest this and let it settle into your being. It is important to rest your brain and recharge your soul. If you don't, you can damage your mental engine with overload and overwork. If you have made it to this point in the book I commend you, but please go take a two-day time out now. You are no good to anyone if you are overcooked! Recharge, and I will see you soon. I am serious here. I need you to take a break. PUT THE BOOK DOWN! ☺ And while you are at it, shut your cell phone off! Just try it. Go take a walk, call your Mom, volunteer somewhere good and FORGET ABOUT REAL ESTATE. Are you being coachable or are you going to fight me on this? ☺ See you in two days for the second half of Park III – The Inner Game.

DO NOT TURN THE PAGE

UNTIL YOU HAVE

TAKEN AT LEAST A **48-HOUR BREAK** FROM THIS BOOK!

I'm serious!!! I'll come to your house!

(In real estate, so many new and even experienced agents make the mistake of never taking a break and never scheduling breaks. They think they can work, work, work, and what happens is they burn out. You have to force yourself to take breaks in this business. It can get very busy and most real estate agents have a tendency to overdo it, overwork, and this is trouble waiting to happen. Taking little breaks so you can recharge is essential for your wellbeing, not only physically but mentally as well. It's essential to performing at your best. So take breaks. You're not going to miss anything. It will all still be here when you get back. You may have noticed that I have several scheduled breaks, intermissions, and take-fives in this book. I do this in the hope that you carry this behavior with you as you embark on your new journey.)

Edge Rule: Take breaks.

☺

THE INNER GAME: STEPS 4, 5, 6

(Focus, Own It, Have Fun)

First say to yourself what you would be; and then do what you have to do.

-Epictetus

CHAPTER 17

THE INNER GAME

Steps One, Two, and Three require action and are what we call the *outer* game because you are on the court, in the field, you are IN the game, you are out there meeting people, developing relationships, sitting live in front of customers, it's on, it's game time. However, OFF the court, the best of the best also have work to do, like sharpening their skills, improving their mental game, or recharging their body and spirit. These steps are what I call the *inner* game because it's more about you and what's going on inside that mind and body of yours. The Inner Game is all about your honing yourself and making sure you are the best you can be on the inside. Inside your mind, your body, and your spirit. To win at selling houses, you have to know you are great and know that you deserve to win just as much as the next guy. Winners win long before they ever set foot on the court. They have seen victory long before the game ever started or the puck ever dropped.

"I have failed many times, but I have never gone into a game expecting myself to fail."

-Michael Jordan

As you may have already figured out, this is not a book on how to fill out contracts or how to schedule inspections or what to do when a client wants to ask you about interest rates. It's not a litany of manufactured scripts that are going to "wow" buyers and sellers so you can "close" them. It's not a bunch of technology tips that are going to deliver thousands of leads to your doorstep. That stuff never happens. It's all a big lie. If you don't believe me, try some quick-fix real estate seminars out for yourself. Subscribe to an online lead-generating marketing program for six months and see how it works for you.

"Give a man a fish and feed him for a day. Teach him how to fish . . . and feed him for a lifetime."

I'm not here to give you leads and bogus scripts that may get you one or two lucky sales. I am here to teach you how to fish. **The Edge** is about the fundamentals. It's about building a foundation of the right fundamentals – what really matters – in your first year, so you can fish on your own without my help and without anyone else. Once you master these fundamentals, if you want to add internet and social marketing and websites and techy-tech to the nines, then by all means that is your choice. Without a doubt, these can support your fundamentals, but they can never replace them. New agents want the quick fix so they disregard the fundamentals and fall prey to these marketing companies that make big claims for "quick and easy" leads. Beware of this when you are new. In the beginning, you must put all these WMDs (Weapons of Mass Distraction) on hold or you will get quickly derailed and be out of this business before you can say "Linda Lookie-Lou."

The Edge is the raw, real stuff that will help you embrace and develop these fundamentals. What really matters is how to genuinely develop relationships, how to quickly find REAL clients, and how to continue being of service to your exclusive group of clients so that you can enjoy a great quality of life and do the things that are most important to you. In the Inner Game, we will explore what to focus on, how to live life with "no excuses," and how to completely detach from the outcome so you can enjoy the journey along the way.

The reality is that most realtors will be gone by the end of their first year because they are never taught what really matters. No one ever teaches them HOW to fish. They get their license with excitement and great anticipation. They have great hopes of instantly making tons of money. It's so exciting, having the newfound freedom of running their own business. However, ever a few months of getting their teeth kicked in, another six months of skating around the wrong neighborhoods with the wrong people and no system, they start to question whether this is for them. Then another few months go by and someone suggests a terrific training course that "the top guy" in the office is taking, so everyone piles into a car to go see a "seminar." After two days, the "sizzle" and the "fast-cash-hard-sell-closing-tips" have worn off and you're back in your basement, sitting in your underwear watching Ellen, wondering if there is anything else you can do. AHA! You think to yourself, "I will go to work for some top agent and learn the business from him or her and find out what they do." Then you realize you got into this business to work for yourself, not to work for someone else. Now you are right back where you started and you begin to question your life and everything in it. The reasons you got into this business are now the reasons you are getting out of it.

What's even worse is that now all your friends and family know you still haven't sold squat in almost a year and when they finally ask you, "Hey, have you sold anything yet?" to cover your tracks you simply lie and say, "Oh yeah, I'm doing great!" (Lie #1) "I got a bunch of deals cooking!" (Lie #2) The truth is you haven't even met anyone who wanted your help, let alone sold a house. It's not much longer until you will be back at your temp job Monday morning, head down, happy to be getting that small but steady paycheck. And just like Doug, another could-have-been Hall of Famer bites the dust. You hang up your skates and move on. You're toast.

This "toast" cycle for realtors is what truly breaks my heart and that is why I have made it my mission to help every new realtor on this planet, starting with you, make it to the big leagues. YOU are talented! You are unique! YOU are meant to do this! You DO have what it takes. If you are passionate about selling houses and you like houses, the rest is easy.

The Edge is your selling system. As you grow five, ten, fifteen years from now, you will develop your own style and flair, but for now, this is your system. You with me? Learn it. Use it. And make it your own.

Edge Rule: Learn it, use it, and make it your own.

Unlike hockey, this system is one you can learn easily and with very little money. Don't get me wrong, you will crash and burn, have some ups and downs, but it is a system you will use for life. With practice, practice, practice (Repetition! Repetition! Repetition!), you will soon be kicking some serious real estate ass all the way to the bank! The reason most agents *don't* make it is that they don't have a system that works for them. They don't learn to fish! **The Edge** is your system. And it's one that you will be designing – you will customize it. I will give you the Six Steps, but you will make them your own.

As you know by now, **The Edge** does not use any scripts. We don't use any hard closing techniques. Why? Because that is like putting a square peg into a round hole. That is old school training. Buyers and sellers are all on to that hard closing stuff and see it a mile away. If you look like a salesman, you are toast. Burnt toast! **The Edge** teaches you how to be yourself, by giving you full-on permission and encouraging you to be your unique authentic self on every occasion. Once you've homed in on who you are and what you like, then we get to developing relationships, not "selling" people. With **The Edge**, we don't try to "sell" anyone. You cannot "sell" anyone a house. They either like it or they don't. We do, however, learn how to develop relationships and that is what Step Two was all about.

Steps One and Two lay the foundation, Step Three is your magical filtering system to decipher who you will spend your time with professionally and who simply stays in the "friend zone." In real estate EVERYONE will want to talk to you about real estate and people may appear to be real buyers and sellers, but with Step Three of the **Edge** you will be able quickly to DIS-Qualify people that will waste your time. Steps Four, Five and Six are designed to make you better. It's that simple. I will say it again. Steps One and Two lay the foundation. Step Three is your filter system. Steps Four, Five and Six make you better.

These are Six Steps and Four Cornerstones that will change your life, your relationships, your bankbook, and beyond. And, guess what? Anyone with a car and a pulse can follow these Steps, develop their Cornerstones, and make a lot of money selling houses. How can I be so sure? Because I'm living proof. I wouldn't say I am more talented or any better than any realtor out there, nor do I have some kind of amazing abilities or magic secrets. I did have one thing, however: I learned the "system." I was one of the lucky ones who learned what really matters. I learned this thanks to years of huge mistakes plus crossing paths with the right people. It took me fifteen years and I am sharing it all with you in hopes that it saves you ten years of heartache. If you embrace this program, you will avoid the huge mistakes that new agents make and it will get you to where you want to go ten years faster than any other program out there today.

The Inner Game starts when we are small children and grows from there. It is how we think and how we process and it comes from our environments that we were in and around when we were young, as well as who and what surrounds us today, like family, friends, parents, and more. Due to a rough upbringing or perhaps a difficult relationship that you are currently stuck in, you may think that you are doomed or can never change, but I am here to tell you: you can and you will. As easily as you could change your hair color, you can change the way you think. And how you think and what you think about is what the Inner Game is all about.

The Inner Game is about learning how and what to focus on, taking full responsibility for everything in your life, and eventually letting go of any expectation, so that you can perform at the highest level. When you are detached from the outcome, you become unstoppable. The Four Cornerstones are like a lighthouse that keeps you heading in the right direction. The first three steps are designed to get you moving and get you into action. The last three steps hone your mental game help foster big thinking, healthy thinking, and completely eliminate any limiting beliefs you may have. (Or don't know you have.) Focus, Own It, and Have Fun are steps four, five, and six of **Selling on the Edge**. It took me twenty years to realize their importance, but looking back, I first learned them when I was sixteen years old. And I learned them all from my good friend and first best friend ever. Vinh. (Aka: The Vineman)

THE VINEMAN

My Dad had a thirst for self-help that was insatiable, and a passion for bettering himself and others that was contagious. My Dad was a seeker, so he would study coaches, take lessons, take sales classes, go see psychologists, read the Bible, study the Buddha, talk to priests, socialize with older people, younger people, whoever. My Dad knew he could learn from anyone and did not discriminate. When he needed help, he knew the power of asking others for it. He was an entrepreneur and businessman, so he wanted every edge he could get and he believed in always "learning and growing, growing and learning." He was and still is the most coachable person I have ever met. Even though our family was always very happy, he always wanted to make things better for us and for himself.

I remember being around ten years old and finding an old cassette tape that my Dad made with positive affirmations on it about financial independence, health, and joy. At eleven I remember seeing a copy of Earl Nightingale's motivational book, *The Strangest Secret*, and trying to read it. At twelve, when I was just starting to love tennis, my Dad gave me a tape on visualizing the perfect serve and perfect match. I would listen to it on his Sony Walkman and wonder what was wrong with my Dad, but then the next day I'd have the best game of my life and found myself beating all the kids on the block! "Wow," I thought, "does this stuff really work?" Nah.

You see, I was one stubborn kid. No matter what my Dad told me to do, I'd never listen – until much later in life. That didn't stop my Dad from being a great father, teacher, and mentor. I believe the challenge all parents have is the following: How do you get your kids to do what you want them to do without telling them what to do?

My Dad was brilliant at this. He figured out that his stubborn little son wouldn't listen to him, but would listen to others, especially if I thought they were better than me. You see, my Dad knew that besides being stubborn, I was also the most competitive kid on the planet and I loved to win. He used that desire of mine and slowly but surely taught me the power of being coachable.

So here I am about fourteen and I finally smoked my Dad on the tennis court for the first time. I ran home and told Mom, "I JUST WHOOPED DAD!" That made me the expert in my own eyes, and even though my Dad had taught me to play, I wouldn't listen to him anymore. Was I a little punk! The next day I went down to the tennis courts ready to take on all challengers. Some of the older boys were playing but no one wanted to play me as they all thought I was a pushover. They laughed at me as I practiced my serve in an adjacent court. Every time they'd laugh, I'd focus more and hit it harder, hoping they'd ask me to play. They never did.

I was just about to call it a day when something awesome happened. The girls' senior high school team had just finished practicing and one of the girls, Tammy Olson, happened to see me practicing my serve. She came by and asked if I was up for a game. Oh boy, was I ever! What a great opportunity. A chance to show everyone how good I was! I was gonna whoop Tammy Olson big time and the big boys next to us would see it all go down. This was to be my shining moment. I just beat my Dad and now I was going to beat Tammy Olson, girls varsity champ. Next stop – like Doug – I'd crush the big boys, then national tournaments, then the finals at Wimbledon where I would destroy Andre Agassi in straight sets to win it all. (Ah, we know how to dream as kids, don't we?)

Tammy proceeded to not only crush, but humiliate me. She outran, out-hustled, out-served me. Better shots, winner after winner after winner – I was done, destroyed, buried, it was a total massacre. I was laughed off the court. Not by Tammy. By the boys. Tammy was a class act. She played better and she was better. She thanked me for the match and encouraged me to keep playing. She was humble in her victory, something I would learn to admire and imitate later in life.

However, none of that mattered at the time. Although she was the better player and she deserved to win, I had bigger problems at that moment. In the eyes of the big boys watching, I had just lost. TO A GIRL! And let me tell you, at fourteen years of age that is very tough for a young man to deal with. I packed up my racquets, picked up my water jug, grabbed my towel and off I went down, head down, spirit crushed. It was a walk home I would never forget.

As I crawled up the driveway and into the house defeated, I tried to sneak by my family unnoticed. My parents could tell something was wrong. I was almost in tears. I told them what happened and they sat listening with compassion and understanding, as they always did in my darkest moments. Later that night when the wounds hurt less, my Dad said, "You know, maybe this was a good learning experience."

"Yeah, right, Dad!" was my thought, but then my Dad asked, "What did you learn from Tammy? Maybe you should ask her to play again. Ask her how she got so good." He went on, "Sometimes to win, you have to lose." I wanted to run away. My Dad was suggesting I ask her where she took lessons and asking me what did I learn from her? Was he nuts? I said, "No way, Dad. I don't ever want to see her again." I was a fourteen-year-old boy who just lost to a sixteen-year-old girl. Humiliated in front of the big boys, and Wimbledon was nowhere in sight. I was done! Quitting for good, this time. Adios. Toast. Maybe tennis was not for me. Band camp was looking pretty good right about now.

Somehow I managed not to quit, and a few weeks later my life would forever change. I was at the court practicing my serve, hitting balls against the wall, and sure enough there she was. Tammy Olson, not only one of the cutest girls I had ever seen, but one of the best tennis players I had ever played. Should I ask her out? Should I get my butt kicked again? There she was, serving like a goddess, ripping one-handed backhands with ease – and with the cutest brown eyes and hair I'd ever seen. Yep, I'm definitely going to avoid her, I thought. I can't go through that embarrassment again. So that was the plan: I would just hit the road, Jack. Then as I was walking off the court, trying not to look at her, my Dad's words of wisdom echoed in my head as they always do.

My Dad was right and I knew it. I could either humble myself and ask for help, or forever keep my head in the sand. I decided to take my parents' advice, swallow my pride and ask for some help. (Humility: Cornerstone IV.) None of the big boys were there that day, so I thought what do I have to lose? Nothing. No one will ever know, and worst case, maybe she'll ask me to the Sadie Hawkins dance. (The one where the girl asks the guy.) I was a dreamer.

So I sucked it up and walked toward her. My heart was pounding like the tennis balls I had just been smashing into the wall, but this was it. I knew it was something I had to do. Pride was not going to make me a better player or get me a date for the Sadie Hawkins dance.

I walked up to Tammy and figured I'd just open my mouth and be myself. What else could I do? I said hello and told her she played a great game the other day and I learned a lot from her. She thanked me and even blushed a little. "Oh wow," I thought. I thought I'd be the one blushing. I asked Tammy about her game and how she got so good. She told me she practiced a lot and was also in a special group coaching class called STP, at another park. She said the next session was starting soon and told me how to sign up. After some teenage chitchat and no invite to the Sadie Hawkins dance, I was still feeling good. I didn't have a date but I had a new friend and she was a lot cuter than Doug, and for whatever reason, I felt great.

I ran home and told my parents, "I have to join STP!" I didn't know what it was, but I knew that if Tammy was in it, I had to be in it too. Did I have a crush on her or did I want to be better at tennis? Who knows? Who cares? God moves in mysterious ways. Either way, this stubborn kid was becoming coachable. For the first time in my life, I asked someone for help and it felt good. It felt great. It was so cool because asking for help did two things. First off, I could tell Tammy was flattered that I complimented her on her great game, and secondly, she was pleased that I asked for her advice. This learning stuff had its points. "Maybe Dad was on to something," I thought.

My parents commended my humility and courage in asking Tammy about her game. They were happy that I had learned the lesson of paying respect to others when you lose, and even happier that I had the nerve to ask for her help and advice. All these life lessons from one simple tennis game! Heavy-duty principles like Courage, Humility, and Respect were in the picture. Concepts I didn't really understand at age fourteen, or their importance and relevance in life. However, I sensed that I had great people in my life teaching me things for a reason. (Reasons I would understand twenty-five-plus years later when I realized my destiny was to help realtors.) My parents may not have known the hockey system, but it was dawning on me that they knew something else even better: a life system. They were just using tennis to help me get the message and learn what they always hoped I would learn, the Inner Game. The mental game. The other stuff is easy. Master of the Inner Game was the difference-maker and game changer. And with Tammy Olson on my mind, everything was changing! My life was getting interesting, that was for sure. It was about to get even more interesting.

Life is an inside job. Inside the mind and inside the heart.

THE VINEMAN

My parents went on to put me in STP where I got to play with better kids, get better coaching – and, my favorite moment, I met my friend, Vinh. Aka: the *Vineman*. If I was Andre Agassi, Vinh was Michael Chang. That was my joke because he was Asian. Vinh and I dreamed big dreams of going pro together. Dreams of being the number one doubles team in the world. Dreams of winning Wimbledon. None of that ever happened, but it didn't matter because Vinh became my best friend on and off the court.

Vinh was ten times better than me at tennis, so every time we played, he would crush me. He didn't mind, he played with me anyway. He would spend hours upon hours teaching me the game. Always putting my game before his. He taught me how to move better, serve better, volley better, constantly feeding me balls to improve my groundstrokes, mainly my disastrous backhand. My backhand was soooooo bad it was embarrassing. If you are right-handed, have you ever tried throwing a ball with your left hand? That is how bad my backhand was in tennis. It was the worst part of my game. It was so bad that I used to try to run around the court and hit a forehand. That meant I got to be very fast, because by running around and hitting a forehand I learned to run faster and faster. Vinh recognized this. He said, "If you want to get good, you have to get a backhand." He said, "I'm going to teach you how to hit the best backhand anyone has ever seen." In tennis you need to have the basics down, and hitting a backhand is one of those basics. I said, "Good luck with that, Vinh," pretending it was no big deal, but deep down I knew he was right.

Our families didn't have enough money to rent ball machines, but to Vinh, it didn't matter. He was a natural-born teacher at age fifteen or so, so money or no money, he always found a way, no matter what. (Another characteristic of a winner that I would later recognize as an extremely important key mindset: never making excuses or letting other people make them.)

Vinh would feed me ball after ball until the sun went down and even beyond. In the dark it didn't matter. We didn't need light or no stinkin' ball machine. Vinh would somehow pack 32 balls into his pockets and keep them coming. He would push me from one side of the court to the other, stretching me farther and farther, speeding up his feeds and running me until I could run no more. I would complain how bad the balls were and Vinh would say, "If you can hit these rocks, you can hit anything." He never let me make excuses or be negative. Along with a better physical game, I came to see that Vinh also had a better mental game. An edge. An *inner* game.

Vinh's game inside and out was infinitely better than mine, yet he was always happy to play a game or set with me whenever I wanted. He was always coaching me along the way, though he'd whoop my butt every time. I'd get frustrated and Vinh just laughed, saying, "Someday, Mark. Someday." I could see that while I enjoyed winning, Vinh enjoyed teaching – even though at this point, he was doing both.

Like all great coaches and teachers, Vinh enjoyed watching me grow and get better. He genuinely did. I didn't really understand at the time how someone at age fifteen could be so patient and enjoy being a teacher. He had a gift. He loved sharing it. At 15 he was way ahead of his time. He made me faster and smarter – and, yep, ultimately helped me develop, you guessed it, one of THE BEST backhands he or anyone in STP had ever seen. I became known as the kid with the lethal backhand. Vinh taught me this not by showing me one or two things that magically changed everything. He told me what I needed to do consistently, every day, to get better. What I needed to do was to practice hitting backhands over and over. He gave me some basic pointers like how to move my feet and how to hold my racquet, but beyond that he told me I needed to FOCUS on one main thing, and that was hitting more backhands rather than running around and using my forehand.

I was focusing on winning and Vinh said, "Forget about winning! Today you are going to hit 500 backhands!" He fed me backhand after backhand, and each day and week it got better and better. My game changed. I was getting better – a lot better. Vinh had a gift. Like Doug with his raw talent on the ice as a skater, Vinh, at 15, was already a natural-born coach.

We became inseparable in high school. We would play at night, in the morning, Epic 5 set wars we called them: in the hot, in the cold, indoors, outdoors, wherever we could sneak onto a court. One winter we even tried playing in the snow by shoveling out some of the courts. We were nuts, but having the time of our lives. And I was coming to understand what true friendship was and what it meant to really give.

In high school we continued to practice hard, but could never make the varsity team. Senior year was approaching and this would be our last chance. Our high school class had some of the best tennis players in the country. With a class of over 800 students and only ten boys allowed on the team, our final shot to make the team was once again slim.

Vinh and I had tried out sophomore year and didn't make it. We'd tried out junior year and didn't make the team. So now "Coach Vinh" decided to step it up to a new level. Vinh said, "If we're going to make it our last year, we need to learn from the best." We needed to spend all summer playing better players, college players, whoever players, as long as they were better than us. We had to play whoever was bigger, stronger, faster. Bottom line, we hit a wall and Vinh knew his coaching would only take us so far. Vinh DID know what we didn't know. He knew we didn't have the skills to make the team and unless we went out there and found them, we were going to fail yet a third time and graduate from high school without having made the varsity tennis team.

FORGET ABOUT WINNING!

Vinh decided that we had to do something drastic. He entered us in a very high-level tournament for a local sporting-goods chain. He fibbed about our ages and skill level, but we were in the tournament. I said, "What are you, nuts? We're going to get slaughtered!" Vinh's response: "So what?"

"We need to forget about winning and let's worry about what we need to DO to get better. And what we need to DO is play better players to get better, or we are not making the varsity team!"

-Vinh Tran

Vinh knew our level as compared to others better than I did, and he was doing a hard-core reality check. He said "we" didn't have the skills at this point to make the team. I knew he had the skills, but he was being nice about it in saying "we." The fact was, "I" didn't have the skills. Vinh was a great wingman. We were in it together. I honestly think my making the team was more important to him than making it himself. Either way, he had incredible talents that I wouldn't fully comprehend until later in life. Meanwhile, it was time for our first adult tournament as minors.

We proceeded to get destroyed in that tournament, and I was ready to call it quits. Not Vinh. Vinh had a plan. I was just along for the ride. He said, "Even though we lost, we won." Sounding like Yoda, he had a point. Getting slaughtered by the better players helped us see our weaknesses. Vinh saw the holes in our games, and, like all great teachers and coaches, Vinh knew exactly what we had to DO next. Get more help! Vinh convinced our parents – mine and his – that they had to help us get to a well-known summer tennis camp a few hours outside the Minneapolis area, that summer, before senior year. It was called Tennis and Life Camp (TLC). How appropriate. Well, this TLC was no cheap deal. We needed to come up with almost $400 and our parents weren't exactly thrilled as they had kids to feed, mortgages and all the rest of our bills to pay.

That didn't stop Coach Vinh. "We will find a way. We might have to make some sacrifices, but we will find a way." Was he kidding me? This kid was 17! Where was this magic coming from? Yet I knew he was right. Vinh never made excuses, and never let me make excuses. He wanted the best for us and I can hear him asking me, "What can we do to make this happen?" Vinh's "no excuses" policy was something I would never forget and it would become a keeper for me as Step Five: Own It in The **Edge**.

I had been going to music lessons all my life and loved playing drums, but it was time to make some sacrifices. We had to focus on playing more tennis and what we could DO to get better. Camp would make us better. Camp: in. Band and drum lessons: out. I had been in Marching Band the previous two years, but I told my parents that tennis was more important to me and drumming was over. I would even sell my drumset to help pay for the camp. Giving up music lessons, selling my drumset, doing a part-time job at Dairy Queen with Vinh, together with some help from our parents, we both managed to raise the money and get enrolled at TLC Tennis Camp.

We came home from camp and fall tryouts were here before we knew it. I was scared. Vinh always knew the right thing to say. "We did everything we could, now let's just go out there and have fun!" And fun we had. The rest . . . is history! Vinh and I both made the team our senior year, and we lettered in tennis. Unbelievable. Even our friends couldn't believe we finally made it. I don't think even our parents could believe it. The irony was that we had to play against each other in the final team tryouts to see who played first seed and who played second seed. For the first time ever, I beat Vinh. I thought I won Wimbledon! I would never forget it. I'm not sure whether he was happier or I was happier. The student had beaten the master. It didn't matter to either of us because we had both made the team. Vinh had taken a poor-to-average player with mediocre skills and made him great. That player was me. Vinh had the selflessness to share his skills over the years to help me grow and become better. Vinh had The **Edge**.

There is no doubt in my mind that, without Vinh, I would NEVER have made that varsity team my senior year in high school. Vinh knew the steps we had to take to get us to where we wanted to go.

Focusing on what we needed to DO, never making excuses, and having fun were the three things that got us there. Little did I know it at the time, but these three key concepts, twenty-five years later, would become the basis of Steps Four, Five and Six of the **Selling on the Edge** program. **Step 4: Focus. Step 5: Own It. Step 6: Have Fun.** Also known as: *The Inner Game.*

To this day I will never forget my friend Vinh for his kindness in teaching me the game of tennis, his willingness to put my game ahead of his game, and his generosity in teaching me for no other reason than to see me grow and get better. And this biggest lesson of all from Vinh: If you really want something, you have to be willing to make sacrifices. He changed my life on and off the tennis court. Without Vinh, my first real coach and best friend, I can honestly say I would not be doing what I do today. Vinh had The **Edge** and will always have The **Edge**. His *state-of-mind* to believe, focus, own it, and have fun, changed my life and I am now passing these principles on to you as you begin your career selling houses. Thanks, Vineman.

THE EDGE IS A STATE OF MIND

Let's rewind. If I don't learn about courage from Doug, I don't stand fearless in front of the bigger boys on the tennis courts. I then don't lose to Tammy Olson of the girls' team that fateful day, humiliated on the tennis courts at age fourteen. Then my parents don't encourage me to humble myself and ask Tammy for her help and learn from my losses. I never hear about STP from Tammy. I don't meet Vinh, a new best friend who is a natural-born coach and teacher, I never elevate my game to a whole new level, I never make the varsity tennis team, develop relationships and learn the core values and life lessons over those five years that change my life and destiny. It all started with a shift in my state of mind. A change on that cold day on the ice when Doug inspired me to change my mindset from "We can't" to "We can."

I share these stories because all these people had The **Edge** long before I ever did. Thanks to Doug, Tammy, and Vinh, I learned it and now I am passing it on to you. The **Edge** is a state of mind that says you *can*. You *can* be coachable, you *can* be humble, you *can* ask for help, and you *can* be fearless like Doug. You *can* do it. You *can* make millions selling houses and sell tons of houses this year. Why not you? **Selling on the Edge** is understanding that you *can* win. It is also understanding that sometimes you will lose today in order to win tomorrow. The **Edge** can be whatever you want it to be, but for now the **Edge** can be your selling program, your coach, your roadmap to selling houses. Yes, it is flagged as a real estate selling program, but if you take a closer look, you could probably make an argument that it is a ten-step personal growth program. (Don't tell anyone, wink wink ☺.) If you use this program, live with the Four Cornerstones in your life, and work the Steps, I guarantee it will not only boost your bankbook, it will change your life, your relationships, and your future . . . IF you use it.

Edge Rule: Use it or lose it.

After years of crashing and burning and almost not making it as a real estate agent, then weathering some of the toughest markets in real estate, I finally had some huge revelations that would change my future. Bottom line: I was beat-up but still standing. I was winning. All my challenging experiences were helping me formulate the **Edge**. I knew I had something I needed to share with other agents. You now hold that system in the palms of your hands.

I wanted to come up with a system that helped people. My only requirement was that it must be simple. Like Vinh's fundamentals that he taught me on the tennis court, the **Edge** is six key fundamentals that you must make part of yourself if you want to make the varsity team of the residential real estate world. You've learned the first three. Be Yourself. Get Out There. DIS-Qualify. You are now about to learn the final three steps, inspired by Vinh and all the many great mentors, coaches, friends and family members I have been blessed to have in my life.

You are blessed with your own unique gifts and talents that you may not even know yet. The Main Mission from day one is to always bring out the YOU in you. I know you have dazzling abilities and incredible skills and limitless potential beyond what most people ever imagine. I want to bring out that part of you! I want to see you shine in your own inimitable way. There is absolutely no one like you on this planet, and that, my friends, is – and will be – your **Edge** as you start your new career selling houses.

I love real estate agents. I am one, through and through. I have been blessed with some good fortune and now it's time to give back. I have a passion for helping agents, I love working with agents to make them better, happier, healthier, wealthier. Just like Vinh had a passion for helping me on the tennis court, I have that same passion for helping you learn about selling houses. Toward the end of senior year in high school, I finally grasped that getting the right guidance from the right coaches has the power to change your life. I was no longer the stubborn kid I had been. Like my Dad, I came to believe in always being coachable, learning, listening to others, and asking for help. Even more importantly, I was getting the bigger picture. Maybe it was time for me to worry a little less about *winning* and focus more on *helping*. Vinh's words stayed with me as I headed off to college . . .

"Forget about winning and let's focus on what we need to do to get better."
-Vinh Tran, aka The Vineman

CHAPTER 18

STEP 4: FOCUS

"This is your time. Now go out there and take it!"

-Herb Brooks (1937-2003)

Head Coach, 1980 US Men's Gold Medal Winning Olympic Hockey Team

Step 4 Main Mission: **Avoid Weapons of Mass Distraction (WMDs)**
So You Can Consistently Do What You Must Do.

Step 4 Main Moves: **Find Trauma Victims**
Build a Success Triangle

Herb Brooks told his team and the US Olympic Coaching selection panel, eight months before the 1980 Olympics began, that no one had ever beaten the Soviets, as the Russians were then known, because no team had ever done the hard work necessary to beat the Soviets. He said no team had ever trained hard enough and got to the physical level necessary to outlast the Soviets in the final stretch. He said no team, group, or player was ever willing to do what it took to beat them.

Instead of putting together a team of individual superstars, Coach Brooks said he was going to put together a group of individuals who were *willing* to do whatever it took to get in the physical shape they needed to be in to win. To do that would take *focus* like never before. Herb Brooks's team did not focus on the Gold. His team focused on what they needed to *do*. (Go rent the movie, *Miracle*, with Kurt Russell starring as Herb Brooks, and see how the story ends.) Without giving it away – they beat the Soviets, won the Gold, and it became the greatest upset ever in all of sports. It was coined the Miracle on Ice.

"Do you believe in miracles? . . . YES!!"

-Al Michaels, legendary sportscaster

Herb Brooks passed away in a fluke car accident in 2003. It shocked the entire world and especially all the people of his hometown in Minnesota. Herb's legacy lives on to inspire not only hockey players, student athletes, students of all kinds, adults in all walks of life, business leaders, coaches, teachers, and, yes, now even real estate agents, and specifically, me. Herb Brooks is someone I never met, but always wanted to. He was gone before I was able to meet him. Life said his time was done and that was that. Everyone always asks me why I am holding a hockey stick above my head in that main photo on the old cover or often keep one in my office. The answer is that it's a tribute to Coach Herb Brooks and all the lives he changed by being himself and never veering off the path of what he felt was right. Here's to you, Mr. Brooks. Thank you for the lessons you have taught me and countless others. #gogophers

We don't know how much time we have on this earth. We really don't. We like to think we will live to 100 or 80 or even 65, but the truth is that we just don't know when Universe could decide our time is up. Although most of us will never have an Olympic Gold medal moment, it doesn't matter. YOU are just as important to this world as anyone else is – and you could be gone tomorrow, so I have news for you, my friend: this really *is* your time. I got news for y'all. Life is not a dress rehearsal. This is it. This is your time. Right here. Right now. No matter where you are in life, or where you think you are, this is it. It's game on today. Herb Brooks died a legend as his team beat the Soviets in the *Miracle on Ice*. Your miracle starts now. It starts with the power focus.

This IS your time, so why not figure out what it is you really want and go for it! If you can first decide exactly what you WANT, you can then put your entire focus on what you must DO to get it. Most new agents don't know what they want. They think it is the money, but it's not about the money. What would you really do if you had more money? Write three things down now. Just knowing what you want does you no good, do you agree? You have to do something to get what you want. The key word in that sentence is DO. *Knowing what you want and then focusing on exactly what you need to do is the magic formula.*

Know your want. Focus on the do. Focus on what you must do and you will get more of what you want. FACT: If you constantly focus on all the negative in your life and what is wrong with it, then guess what? You will get even more of that negativity. The Main Mission in Step Four is to avoid distractions so that you do what you need to do. Distractions like negative thoughts about people, places or ideas can drag you down if you focus on them. Train your mind to focus on the good and you will get more of the good!

Edge Rule: What you focus on expands.

How do we get better at focusing on what we must do in order to get the good stuff in life and train our minds to avoid the zillions of distractions we all face every day? Answer: Repetition! Repetition! Repetition! Focus is like a muscle. The more you exercise it, put it to work, and are aware of it, the stronger the muscle will get. Again, many new agents think focus is about spending time focusing on what you WANT. "I want a big car, a diamond ring, a million dollars." Focusing on what you want is only half the battle. You will learn here that the primary point of Step Four, FOCUS, is to focus on your behavior. Focus on what you need to DO.

*Focus is more important than goals. I see people confuse goals and focus all the time. Goals are good, goals are what you want, but **focus** is what you need to do to attain those goals. Focus must be on consistently doing the necessary behaviors that will get you what you want (goals) and where you want to go. Successful people focus on what they need to consistently and specifically DO to get the prize; they don't focus on the prize itself. So yes, focus is more important than goals.*

Michael Phelps is a great example of this. If you see him in any interview, he never discusses his gold medals, he discusses his training regimen, his nutrition, his coaches and drills and what he is going to DO to get those medals. Michael Phelps knows EXACTLY what he must DO to get where he wants to go. His "do" is something like this: 10,000 meters per day of free-style swimming, 500 meters of sprinting, 5000 calories of healthy nutrition, 60 minutes of meditation and visualization, weight training 5 days per week, 9 hours of sleep every night, and on and on and on. He knows his "DO." Do you know your "do"? You will.

Edge Rule: Focus on the "do," not the "want."

WEAPONS OF MASS DIS*TRACTION*

Along with knowing you "DO," you are going to learn how to protect yourself from distractions. Weapons of Mass Distraction I call them. (WMDs for short.) These weapons of mass distraction can be so debilitating that they can wipe out your entire career and you won't even know what happened. You will be quitting the business without understanding why. The reason: WMDs. They come in all shapes and sizes and they kill careers. Get this through your head now. WMDs can be disguised, cunning, and powerful.

They can drag you down and pull you away from your important daily behavior and you won't even realize it. Many new agents have the best intentions, but because of surrounding environments that distract them, they can never successfully do what is necessary to make it. By building a proper FOCUS muscle, you will have the ability to protect yourself from WMDs and continue doing what you need to DO to get whatever it is you want. You will learn to recognize WMDs from a mile away, and this awareness is half the battle.

For me, WMDs have come from all over the map. I was the type of person who initially had zero focus skills – mainly because no one ever taught me anything about focus. They always used to accuse me of having A.D.D. or people told me I couldn't concentrate. I used to tell people:

"I am so sick of everybody always accusing me of having A.D.D. – oh look, a kitty . . ."

I used to joke about it, but in fact I didn't know or understand focus and its importance. I used to say, "Maybe I do have A.D.D. or maybe I actually don't and the truth is that you are just boring." That never went over well. I didn't care, I was young and I never believed I had A.D.D., I was just so thrilled with life and happy and always excited to see and hear new things. Life is precious and I'm lucky because I have always been able to be happy and enjoy it even in the darker times. However, like everyone, I had many things that were my WMDs. For me it was certain people that pulled my focus. Going out to bars was always a distraction, parties on the weekend, even little things like video games, my bed always distracted me, new movies that were being released, the computer, my phone, someone else's problems, breaking news stories, the list was endless. Basically, anything I could come with as an excuse to NOT work, I would allow to distract me. I had no defense against WMDs and they are everywhere when you are a self-employed real estate agent. Was it A.D.D., or was it simply that no one ever taught or trained me on the power of Focus?

Although I learned eventually that focus was something one could learn, early on I was as helpless as you will be if you don't regularly build your focus muscle. WMDs come in zillions of forms and everyone will have to identify their own, but some well-known WMDs come in the form of things you may think are important like emails, paperwork, Facebook, tweeting, busy work, eating, drinking, smoking, talking, shopping, and on and on and on . . . who knows, whatever they are I call them all "weapons of MASS distraction." Part One of learning about focus is mastering the art of avoiding WMDs at all costs.

WEAPONS OF MASS DISTRACTION (WMDs): Anything that pulls you and your focus away from what you need to DO.

In real estate, my friend, you don't have a boss, you don't have a time card, and it is up to you if you are going to even get up that day. If you don't learn about focus and how lethal WMDs can be – how to spend your time and what to spend it on – you will be gone within twelve months and I will have failed you.

Focus was for me the toughest thing to master, but once I did, it was immensely fulfilling because I learned to turn it on and off like a light switch. If you can master this step, everything else will fall into place. This is one of the toughest steps to teach, to master, and to put into practice. Why? Because in society today there are so many WMDs. A WMD could be another opportunity, some new idea, a place to travel, things to see, a girl you just met, a boy you think is cute, an ad online, your cell phone, your computer, your email, certain friends or neighbors, the mailman, work, co-workers, television, movie theaters, newspapers . . . they are endless. Only you know what your weakness is and what is holding you back. Your number one Main Move is identifying these distractions so you can avoid them. Anything that pulls you away from doing what you should be doing is a WMD. Even your feelings can be WMDs. For example, let's pretend you are feeling depressed one day. Who cares? Go out there and say hello to some new people and you will forget about your feelings. Have you ever felt like dog meat one morning and then for whatever reason you decided to go to the gym, and ended up walking out of that workout feeling like a million? You changed your feelings by Doing something. What you *do* will change the way you *feel* every time.

Edge Rule: How you feel doesn't matter. It's what you *do* that matters.

Feelings can be the subtlest of all WMDs, so don't let them wipe you out. You will discover your WMDs the more you get to know yourself, but now you're aware of them and how WMDs will destroy your business. It's critically important to know yours and avoid them. I hope I have made my point. OK, you are now probably asking, "What is it that I must DO, exactly, in order to crush it selling houses?" Answer: Spend eighty to ninety percent of your time finding trauma victims.

FIND TRAUMA VICTIMS

I asked my five-year-old niece what focus meant and she said, "It's shutting the door and doing whatever." Is that amazing or what? The key part there is "shutting the door." I love that. It says it all. When Kobe Bryant was on the court, he had the ability to magically shut the door on everything around him so that he could focus on the task at hand, which was to score the next bucket. For you to score in real estate, you have to know where to spend your time, who to spend it with, and HOW to spend it. If you don't, weeks and months can go by doing "busy work," or "miscellaneous crap" that has nothing to do with making money. Don't beat yourself up. You are now your own boss and you are going to learn how to handle these things. If you find yourself being consumed by a WMD, that's OK. Just get out of there: "shut the door" like my niece says. Don't be upset, just congratulate yourself that you are becoming more aware of your WMDs and are now very dialed-in to what has been holding you back. Know that you are on your way to big success and making more money because you are now tuned in to what can drag you down.

To make money in real estate, you have to spend 80% of your time DOING Steps One, Two, and Three. Spending time knowing thyself so you can be yourself, attending your passion arenas, getting out there, and running **Sales Triage™**. What you will be left with is real buyers and sellers. Your job as a realtor is not to sell houses, it is to get very good at finding and identifying real buyers and sellers. Aka: Finding trauma victims. Your "DO" is to consistently spend your time doing whatever will lead you to more trauma victims. Got it? That is it. If you only take one thing from this book, it is this. Spend eighty percent of your time looking for trauma victims and you will be a real estate rock star.

Once you find trauma victims, let me tell you, my friends, they close themselves. How? They want your help! They call you back, they show up to appointments when you schedule them, they write offers for very close to asking or even at asking price; when they see a house that is right for them, they pull the trigger. If they are sellers, real sellers will price their homes at fair market value or lower, they will listen to you when you tell them not to be there during showings, they will reduce the list price of their house if it is not selling. Real buyers and sellers do what you tell them to do and they appreciate your service. Real buyers and sellers don't try to haggle about your commission. They don't try to take advantage of your service, they don't act like drama queens, they will be extremely grateful for your help. Your mission as a realtor is not to sell houses; that's the end prize. Your Main Move and daily behavior in Step Four is to Find Trauma Victims. Everything else is secondary.

Edge Rule: Spend 80% of your time finding Trauma Victims.

THE 80/10/10 FOCUS RULE

What is the 80/10/10 focus rule that you must master? It means that you must spend 80 percent of your time *doing* things that make you money. Ten percent on your own personal health and well-being. The remaining ten percent can be on whatever nonsense you want. As we just learned, finding real clients and selling them is what makes you money. Writing offers for 90 percent or more of asking price is also something that leads you to more money. Spending time developing relationships is something that will lead you to money. Any activity in Steps One, Two, and Three will eventually lead you to money. So if you are feeling frustrated, as yourself: how are you spending most of your time?

What about people that you think are viable clients but who are really WMDs? It can happen. Certain clients can actually become WMDs. It is your job to figure out who needs your help versus who is a waste of time. **Sales Triage™** and DIS-Qualifying will help with this. These steps are all intertwined, but in the end I will direct you back to Step One if you have questions. Questions like, "Does my gut tell me I should be working with this particular client, or not?" Or, "Do I like this person?" Or "Do they fit the criteria of a client I want to work with?"

I will always send you back to Step One, which is BE YOURSELF. Then I will ask you what you like and what don't you like? If your answer is that you don't like some particular client for whatever reason, then why are you still working with them? There is no realtor commandment that says you have to work with everyone who wants your help. Doctors and lawyers turn down potential clients all the time. If you feel someone is going to drive you nuts and affect your quality of work with other great clients you do enjoy working with, then by all means cut this whackjob loose! That is an example of avoiding whackjobs of mass distraction.

The whackjobs I didn't like working with included anyone who asked me to "Find me a deal." This was a major red flag for me and I would run from these lowballer-time-waster-WMD types faster than you could say Billy Bullsh*tter. My personality did not go well with these types of people. I have never been a haggler, never been interested in salespeople's reducing their commissions, and I never ask. I am not a coupon collector and I don't ask people to give me deals – so I don't work for people like that either. Once I got well into my career and learned the hard way, I realized I must DIS-Qualify these people instantly. I learned how to avoid them. Learning how to focus was the key. How did they pull me away from making money? Simple. I would spend all this time finding them a deal and then when I found it for them, it was never good enough. Can you think of someone in your life where no matter what you do, it is never good enough? These types of relationships are no good. DQ them!

Finally I figured out a great way to get rid of these bottom feeders. Anytime anyone approached me with a request to find a "deal," I said, "My fees are triple and I require a $10,000 advance." (That was some line I heard an attorney say in a movie, but it worked!) My confidence went up, my time freed up, and DIS-Qualifying these people quickly helped me to keep my focus on the most important thing: finding clients I liked working with, focusing on who I wanted to work with, where exactly I wanted to specialize as my area, and what kind of houses I wanted to sell. I was forming my ideal lists and didn't even realize it.

YOUR THREE "IDEAL" LISTS
1. Ideal client.
2. Ideal area.
3. Ideal house.

If you could sell any type of client, work in any area, and sell any price range or style house, what would all of these things look like. You have to see it before you will ever sell it. You have to know what you like, then make your three lists, and you, my friend, are now specialized! It's that easy. Your ideal client list is the most important, but then it's important that you figure out your ideal area list and your ideal house list. Let's talk about each.

FOCUS is what I want you to be constantly aware of, but all the steps are so intertwined that you will see how one can affect the other. Step One is to be yourself, so you have to know what you like; and, specifically, what your idea client looks like – or even better, what they DON'T look like. Make sense? Make your ideal client list now. Write down five things that your ideal client would have, look like, and/or act like. This will help you spot the ones you want to work with and avoid people that you don't care to work with. Traditional training will teach you to go after everyone, throw out a catch-all net, and believe anyone is a potential client. This is simply not true. The sooner you learn this, the faster you will make money. You need to specialize. When you're new, you specialize in whatever area, neighborhood, client type, or type of homes you like. Doctors specialize. Lawyers specialize. And **Edge**-trained real estate agents specialize!

A good place to start is with your ideal client list. Make your ideal client list now and pin it to your wall! If someone doesn't meet your criteria, then don't work with them. It's that simple. It's up to you. Got it? This is *your* system! Easy-peazy hug-and-squeeze me!

IDEAL CLIENT LIST: (Write 5 characteristics you would love all your clients to have.)

1._____

2._____

3._____

4._____

5._____

Would you date someone who didn't meet your criteria? Would you date someone you couldn't stand? Would you date someone who was verbally abusive toward you? Would you marry someone who didn't seem committed to you? No, you wouldn't. But, guess what? I see new real estate agents tolerate similar behaviors and worse. It's unfortunate, but I see agents put up with the most inappropriate things from potential clients and they justify it with, "Oh well, I am new, and I don't have anyone else I'm working with right now." You've heard how this story ends. A corner suite at the Death Valley Inn. You have to be willing to pass on these *less than ideal clients* in your first year. They will suck you dry and take you out. Focus on finding the winners, working with the winners, knowing inside and out what your dream client would look like, and then focus on attracting more of them. What you focus on expands. If you think big and think of amazing, kind, appreciative, loyal, financially ready, honest, committed clients, then that is what you will get.

"If you think you can or you can't, you are right."
-Henry Ford

You are just as entitled to work with the easy, kind, appreciative, loyal, big, dream, ideal clients as the next guy, so if you think you can – or think you cannot – you are right! So choose CAN! Make an ideal client list and hold the line. They will come. Knowing what they look like is a great start. Spend 80% of your time going after these people and developing relationships with them and I promise you, the prizes and medals and money will come.

Once you have your *ideal client list*, then make your *ideal area list*. Meaning what kind of neighborhood would you love to work in? Where is your dream area where you would love to sell homes? Make that area one of your passion arenas!

Lastly, you will build your *ideal house list*. Meaning what kind of houses would you love to sell? Price range? Style?

Now you have three specific criteria and specialization lists. Ideal Client. Ideal Area. Ideal House. You now know your specialties. Do you see the power of that? You just became an expert with certain clients, an area, and a type of house. I now anoint you Super Specialist of your ideal lists. Most agents spend five years before they ever start to specialize or even know what they prefer. By making your own ideal lists right now, as opposed to listening to someone else on what to do, you add the passion factor in there. If you are passionate about something, people will recognize that and you will start attracting the exact type of clients that you describe on your list, as well as attracting opportunities in your ideal neighborhood: your chosen area. If you are working with people you love, in an area you love, and selling houses that you love, you cannot lose. Spend 80% of your time focusing on your three ideal lists. Clients.

Area. Houses. You will crush it! Why? Because you now know your passion in this industry and no one can beat you at your passion. People will be drawn to you because you will know what your specialty is and clients will see that you are clear on what you do and who you are. Most agents are unsure of who they are, who they help, where they sell and what they sell. Your being clear will help you land more clients because real clients will see that you are focused and know what you want. Real clients want a leader. Do you like working with people who are unsure of what they do and where they are going OR are you attracted to people that are focused, have a good sense of self, and know what they want? Of course we are all drawn to the latter. So are people buying and selling houses.

Get your lists written down in blood. This will help you spot these clients and opportunities when you get there. How could you ever find a tiger if you didn't know what one looked like? Knowing what you are looking for is vital to success.

Edge Rule: Know your ideal customer.

I see new realtors get started and they spend their first year on things that are not vital to survival. They spend normal business hours and every waking moment trying to understand every single line of the contract before they ever even talk to a buyer or seller. Just go find ten buyers to write offers and you will learn the contract in thirty minutes. Call me, I will do it for you. Name, Price, Close Date.

Could the contract be a WMD? Absolutely! Could sales training? ABSOLUTELY!! Overdoing it on any one thing could be a hidden form of procrastination or even a WMD. If you spend all of your time learning scripts or mastering fancy sales techniques or all day every day in sales courses, you are in big trouble. Step Two is what? GET OUT THERE! Go out there and fail. That is a good use of time. So many people ask me about WMDs and what are the worst ones. Only you know what is preventing you from doing what you need to do, but in my opinion, the two worst weapons of mass distraction for new realtors today are smart phones and social media! These things can ruin you and too much time with emails, FB and fiddling on your cell or the Internet will end your career. Yes, you will be toast, gone, buried, and out of this business in twelve months or less; I guarantee it, unless you can learn to avoid these huge WMDs. Anything that pulls you away from Steps One, Two, and Three is a deadly weapon of mass distraction –

and WMDs are designed to do one thing: kill your business. Social media, cell phones, the Internet, email, and websites are some of the deadliest disguised WMDs ever created.

However, don't be confused about what I'm saying here. I am not saying that websites, FM, Twitter, social media and the Internet are not amazing, revolutionary, helpful tools. But in your first year or two, you have to learn and get really good at the fundamentals first. The rest of the hoopla can come later. If you focus on all that too early on, it will affect your long-term ability to sell houses, because you will not have the fundamentals. I never had a FB account when I was selling houses, although Facebook was available for a good chunk of my fifteen years in the business. I never even had a website when I was selling houses EVER! I used to brag about how I didn't need a website to sell someone's house or get a lead – because I didn't. Experience and great coaching along the way taught me how to catch fish. They taught me the fundamentals, and that was all I ever needed. I never needed FB, Twitter, websites, techy lead-generating Internet tools, drip campaigns, magnet mailers, or recipe cards with market updates on them, and neither do you. Not yet, anyway. If you want that later, fine, but in Year One, Two and three, they are all WMDs. Master the fundamentals first, then we can worry about your fancy-schmancy website.

FUNDAMENTALS FIRST:
Being Yourself
Getting Out There
DQ/Gut-Check/**Sales Triage™**
Focus
Owning It
Having Fun

That's it. That's your focus. Steps One, Two, and Three are your action steps, the Outer Game. Steps Four, Five, and Six are your mindset and mental steps, the Inner Game. Eighty percent of your time should be spent on the Outer Game. Master that and you will be winning gold medals in real estate. This is your time. Most realtors will not do what they need to do in order to get what they want. Will you? Are you coachable enough to follow these suggestions? I believe you are. That's why you are still here.

Congratulations, you are doing great and it's about to get even better. You are now very close . . . to the **Edge**!

FOR ANYONE WHO IS STILL STUDYING FOR THE STATE TEST

My good friend Patrick has been studying for his license for almost two years now. He came to me and asked for my advice on passing the state test and any insight I might have that would help him get this done. The advice I gave him was simply to sign up for a test date; fail it, and then sign up for another test date. Forget about what is on the exam or if you pass the first time or not. It's a hoop that they want you to jump through before they give you your license. Just go take it. Fail it and sign up for another test as soon as possible. Eventually you will pass it. Most new people spend months and months trying to master the material and put off ever taking the test. Or they try to analyze all the material and understand every single example and definition. I have news for you. *Nothing* on that test will ever apply in the real world of selling houses. The test is a screener to weed out people. And maybe they will weed you out if you don't hurry up and set a test date.

ANALYSIS PARALYSIS

Many people, like my friend Patrick, are suffering from what I call analysis paralysis. Almost five years now have passed where he could have earned hundreds of thousands of dollars selling houses if he had taken the test in his first six months, but he wants to ace the test. Acing the test will not make you any money. This I promise you. Checking email will not make you any money. Talking to other realtors about how good or bad the market is will not make you any money. Getting out there and finding buyers or sellers in your passion arenas and selling them houses will make you money. You cannot start doing any of that until you pass the test. Analysis Paralysis can be a WMD if you let it. It can cripple the most talented new realtors. It is natural to want to know everything you can, but you must be careful when studying anything, even this program, that you don't over-analyze and over-think it, or you may become a training junkie. (note: Version 2 edit…in 2023 Patrick finally got his license! Nice work kid!)

Selling on the Edge has a ton of material and I want to share it with you to help you save ten years of heartache, make more money selling houses, have a little fun and hopefully change your life for the better. However, there are certain personality types that will want to use "studying" and "getting prepared" and "learning the material" as an excuse NOT to Get Out There. Many new realtors use "learning" as an excuse to never talk to people. They are waiting for everything to be perfect or "right" or whatever excuse they use. You may not even realize this, but if you look at other realtors, you will see them everywhere. Ones that seem to know everything about everything, but the reality is that they never leave the nest. I call them professional training junkies. They attend every single class or seminar possible and that's great – but they never spend any time in Steps One, Two, and Three. These people suffer from a severe case of analysis paralysis. A simpler way to understand it is they are spending all their time "getting ready to get ready" and they never get to the "do." They never take action. And Action pays the bills, my friends. So be careful not to fall into this trap yourself. If you do, then make the adjustment, get your ass out there and get your fail on! You were born ready.

ONE FINAL WARNING TO THOSE WHO WORK AT AN OFFICE

Discussing office drama will not make you any money. Arguing with the office manager about the copy machine will not make you any money. Yet new agents become obsessed with office politics and company parties and even award ceremonies. All these things I just mentioned are examples of weapons of mass distraction and you have to check your focus daily to make sure you are not getting sucked into this nonsense.

Your first year, you will be susceptible to all the office chitter-chatter. Remember, you don't have to be friends with everyone in the office. You are here to make a living. If you want more friends, find them in your passion arenas, not at the office. The office can be the most deadly and deceptive WMD, so heed this final warning about WMDs. If you doubt me, ask any realtor how much money they ever made sitting in the office. Eighty percent of your time where? The Outer Game. Out on the field! Get Out There!

Now what about the other twenty percent? Great question, ten percent of your time should be spent on improving you. Visualizing success, meditating, mentally and physically getting stronger. Things like going to the gym or yoga or whatever stimulates your mind, body, and spirit! Elite athletes spend at least ten percent of their training time on visualizing what they want and meditating on the WIN. This helps them focus on what they want, and when it's game time, they have already been there 1000 times and their body knows what to do. In their mind and subconscious, they've already won.

In real estate you can get caught up in working 24/7 and you will burn out quickly, so allow ten percent of your time for your well-being and doing things that will improve you. One of the top agents I worked with would not leave his house in the morning until he had meditated on the perfect day. He would spend thirty minutes before walking out the door, no matter what. He knew that if he didn't do this, he would immediately get caught up with weapons of mass distraction.

Here is a simple way to remember the 80/10/10 Rule:

80% on your DO and what makes you money.
10% on YOU and your well-being.
10% on all the other bullsh*t.

Regarding that remaining bullsh*t ten percent of your time, OK, fine, check those emails, rock and roll on Facebook, check your Match.com account, Google your brains out if you must, do the paperwork, whatever the "other sh*t" is, you have ten percent of your time to blow on this stuff. You want to chitchat with the new hottie at the office, fine, but make sure you have spent ninety percent of your day on what matters. Got it? I'd call it the 90/10 Rule, but I think we all need some time for goofing off and having a little fun throughout the day, so by all means, do! The 80/10/10 Focus Rule: Learn it, live it, love it. It's the real deal. And soon you will be too if you learn to master your time by using the 80/10/10 Rule.

If you are committing to real estate full-time, then you may be working 5 days a week from 9-6 p.m. From 9:00 a.m. to 6:00 p.m. I am saying 80% of your time should be spent doing things that will make you money. To be sure you are doing this, ask yourself the following question: "Is what I am doing right now going to dramatically change the quality of my life and massively increase my bank account in the near future?" If the answer is "no," then you are not doing what you must be doing. Focus on the DO! Here is a cheat sheet in case you forget:

80/10/10 FOCUS RULE

80% - Steps One, Two, and Three

10% - Steps Four, Five, Six

10% - BS, paperwork, social media

THE TERMINATOR FOR REAL ESTATE AGENTS

I had a very successful year selling houses in 2011 and to prove than even I can be an idiot, I decided I should invest in the stock market and try to make even more money. Oh dear, hello Mr. Greed and Captain Ego, how are you today? Little did I know, even the stock market could and would become a major WMD.

"I'll be back."

-The Terminator

It was early 2012 and I had lunch every week with a friend who supposedly was killing it in the stock market. He suggested I invest the money I made the previous year in the market. Me, being completely OUT of focus, agreed with him. I figured, how hard could it be? I would day-trade in the early morning and sell houses as usual from 9:00 to 6:00. Before I knew what was happening, the stock market became a Weapon of Mass Distraction and I didn't even see it. I put money into a brokerage account, got up at 4:30 a.m. to obsess over stocks, read books and articles, check the market every twenty minutes: was it up, was it down, should I buy, should I sell? It was like I was on crack, I had no clue what I was doing so of course I lost money hand over fist, but that didn't stop me. Dumping more and more money into the account, I thought any minute now I'd get it right.

The whole time, I was completely disregarding all my real estate work. Even my intention to work in real estate from 9:00 to 6:00 went out the window. Not only was I consumed by a WMD and totally out of focus, I was out of control.

What happened exactly? I stopped going to all my passion arenas, I was too tired to talk to clients, I was upset if I lost money, and my attitude of gratitude disappeared. I didn't care. All I cared about was my brokerage portfolio. Apart from the money that I had in the account, the opportunity cost was adding up. I woke up one day to realize I had not sold a house in four months. Didn't matter. I was going to master this stock market stuff. I was *magna cum laude* in college. I weathered the toughest real estate market. I crushed it the year before. Somehow I started thinking that because I was good at one thing, I was now good at everything. Not so much.

I wasn't out of control, my ego was. My focus was gonzo.

I had lost sight of the Four Cornerstones: Gratitude, Service, Humility and Forgiveness. I was heading toward Death Valley. Then, by the Grace of God, it hit me! I needed to do a reality check and start taking responsibility. I took a serious look in the mirror and asked myself, "What in God's name am I doing investing in the stock market?! I know NOTHING about the stock market!" I was completely derailed and blind-sided, and this weapon of mass distraction was about to destroy my business and me. The next day I sold everything at huge losses and I didn't care. I knew what I had to do and everything was to go. I closed the account and I was done.

It was brutal to dump all those stocks and lose all that money. Many people said just hang onto it and wait for it to rebound, but you see, I knew that was not me. It was pulling my focus and I had to get out. Because of this **Selling on the Edge** system and Step Four (Focus), I was able to get out of the stock market and back on track.

You may not have the stock market; you may have other WMDs in your life. I don't know what they will be, but be aware because they are out there. I cannot stress enough that WEAPONS OF MASS DISTRACTION are the number one career killers among realtors. They are out there and will never stop coming at you. Weapons of Mass Distraction are the Terminator for real estate careers. They will hunt you down, never stop coming at you, and get you when you least expect it. Developing your focus muscles, understanding the 80/10/10 Rule, and making a success triangle are your tools to stay on the high road – OR – if that is too difficult, you can simply remember what my six-year-old niece says and just . . . "shut the door!" Whatever you do, beware of *The Terminator*, which is code for any and all Weapons of Mass Distraction. He'll be back.

Important Warning About WMDs: *As you are now aware, some people have to actually be reminded to stop spending so much time studying and training because they become what I call "training junkies." They spend all their time learning and forget about the Outer Game and Getting Out There and executing and selling houses. They hide behind classes, and books, and more and more learning and, believe it or not, even training can become a WMD. WMDs are the Terminator for real estate agents. They never stop coming, they never quit, and they come disguised in many different forms. WMDs are cunning, baffling, and powerful. They will get you if you are not focused. It's your job to make sure you are aware of anything that is, or potentially could be, a WMD. Then you make sure you terminate the Terminator before it's too late.*

Edge Rule: Avoid WMDs.

ARE YOUR GOALS REALLY *YOUR* GOALS?

Or are they someone else's? It's a fair question. A lot of people spend their whole lives living someone else's dreams. I have seen hundreds of people trying to please someone else and achieve a goal that someone else wanted for them. For example, there is the young girl who goes to medical school only because her parents and grandparents were all doctors and they insist she must be one as well. However, the reality was her dream was to be a dog walker and painter. Then there is the boy who spent fifteen years working at his father's company because his mother felt that was best for him. She laid the guilt trip on him, his whole life, that he must help his father. The reality here was this young man's passion was teaching kids and he always wanted to teach grade school, but never did because he was too worried about pleasing his parents. How about the woman whose husband pressured her into being a stay-at-home mom and housewife for twenty years and the reality was that this woman always wanted to start a fashion company but never had the courage to go against her husband's wishes? She ended up waiting thirty years to finally do what she always wanted to do. For most of us, by the time we realize our goals are not our own, it can be too late.

Why do we live other people's dreams and strive for goals that were never ever our own in the first place? Answer: We don't have the courage to say NO. The inability to say no to others, combined with social pressure, family pressure, and society's expectations has put many dreams on permanent hold. Limiting ourselves to others' expectations is a speed rail to Miseryville, population: one. Doing this over and over and never living your own life the way you want to live it eventually wears you down and before you know it, you don't even remember who you really are. Now you're lost along the way, going through the motions and wondering, "What ever happened to those goals and passions I had when I was a kid?" **The Edge** is about you! This is your time and it's time to start living YOUR dream and setting YOUR goals that you want for yourself. In Step Four we are going to figure out goals. Your goals. Goals that the real you has always wanted.

SUCCESS TRIANGLE

Most selling systems and self-improvement programs ask you to immediately state your goals and dreams and everything you want in life as the very first step. In case you haven't noticed, *we* have never even mentioned goals yet. Why not? Because if you are new and you still haven't mastered Steps One, Two, and Three, you might not even know what it is you truly want. Mastery of these first three Steps means you know who you are, through and through, and are living that way. You know your passions inside and out and you're involved in those arenas. And you have learned how to say NO and how to Dis-Qualify people, places, and things that are not healthy for your well-being and future success. Simple, right? OK, even if you are still working on those steps, take some comfort in knowing the only step you really have to master in this program is Step One. Until you do that, we're not going to worry about goals, because you might not know who you even are at this point, let alone what you want. Here is my question for you. Are your goals and dreams really yours? Or are they someone else's?

Edge Rule: Master Step One and you will always get it done.

Step One: we teach you how to bring out the real you. Once people do that, they realize that what they truly want is very different from what they "thought" they wanted. When I first got into real estate, I wanted a 500SL Mercedes, I wanted a million dollars in the bank, I wanted to own a penthouse suit on the Wilshire corridor . . . and then I realized that I only wanted those things because that's what everyone else wanted. I was caught up in the hype of my perception and image of success and I never really knew what I wanted. After some time, I realized that spending time with my family in Minnesota was the most important thing to me. Seeing my friends on a regular basis was a goal. Spending time fishing for bass was my dream vacation and driving a fully paid-for Jetta was a perfectly satisfying goal for me.

I have intentionally not brought up goals until this point because when you are getting started, I don't want you to get caught up in what you want, just yet. The number one reason realtors fail in their first year is that they focus too much on themselves and not what their DO should be. Once you can confidently tell me you are being yourself, through and through, and have really mastered Steps One, Two, and Three, then OK, we can talk goals. Because then I will believe they are your goals, not someone else's.

First and foremost, the new realtor must focus on simply "doing" and mastering Steps One, Two, and Three. Being yourself is very difficult for some people. For years you may have been living your life in somewhat of a disguise. I am giving you the green light to absolutely let loose in Step One and come out of your shell. You get to be you again. I need you to be you. This is the key that surprisingly will ATTRACT people and customers into your life. It's the nucleus to this system. Being yourself and doing your own thing will launch everything else, but it's going to take some practice, especially if you have been bottled up for the last few years.

Getting out there and attending passion arenas each week can also be scary. Telling someone they do not qualify as a client will be VERY difficult for most agents. However, these are the things that will make you money and get you earning money out of the gates. I want you to start EARNING while you LEARN. If you start out with goals, you will never get on the bike and try to ride it. For now, just get on the bike! If you are dead set on having some goals from day one, then set goals to master Steps One, Two, and Three. Set what I call "behavior" or action goals. Take action your first year. As you begin to figure out who you really are along the way and you start bringing out the real you in you, then it's goal time. For then and only then will these goals truly be yours. You will have a confidence and a calm about who you are, you will be in sync with life, and THEN we can set some goals.

You will know you are doing Step One correctly when people start asking you what's your secret, or when you find yourself *attracting* others into your life. Everyone is drawn to someone who is totally comfortable in their own skin and not afraid to be themselves. You will know you are doing Step Two correctly when you are comfortable using the "best friend" exercise on *everyone* and people start telling you that you are a great listener. You will know you are getting good at Dis-Qualifying people when you are *not afraid to ask difficult questions or turn down some business.* And you will have mastered Step Three when you are *listening to your gut and using* **Sales Triage™** *on everyone who passes the gut check! Are you paying attention to your gut these days? Or are you ignoring it?*

Do these things sound familiar? They should, because this is what you want to focus on for eighty percent of your time. Focus and goals (DOs vs. WANTs) can easily be confused by most people. If you focus on your goals, you will most likely never get your goals. You have to focus on what you must DO to get those goals and then get good at DOING whatever that is. By now, if you're not clear on what are the most important things to spend your time on as a new real estate agent, then I suck at writing and just call me.

Yes, I believe writing down goals is paramount to success, but truly knowing who you are must come first, or the goals you write down may not truly be your own.

So what about this success triangle? What is that all about? It's very simple. For those of you who have been dying to write your goals down, now is your time! Draw a triangle in the space below or on a separate sheet of paper. At the top point, write the word PERSON. At the lower left point, write PLACE. At the lower right point, write THING.

PERSON

$$$

PLACE   THING

In the middle of the triangle, put a number – how much you want to make over the next twelve months -- with a dollar sign in front of it. You have to put $200,000 or more. I don't care what you put, but it MUST be $200,000 or more. Why at least $200,000? If you recall, my guarantee was that you would make at least one hundred thousand in the next twelve months with this selling program or you can send the book, the CDs or the DVDs back (within twelve months of purchase with your receipt) and I will refund your entire investment. So . . . by putting at least $200,000, then if, for some reason, you only get this half right, you will still have a hundred thousand! ☺ Got it? Nice job! Think big, my friend! THINK BIG!

OK, so what is your number? Got one? Good, write that sucker in the middle of your success triangle in big bold ink! Now, above the top point of the triangle – PERSON – I want you to write the name of a **person** you want to have in your life, or the name of a person you want to spend more time with, or the name of someone you want to help in any way, or you want them to get better in any way or just have a better life. For me, I was single when I came up with this and I put, "A beautiful loving **girlfriend**." That was a person I wanted in my life. You can put anyone. Ask me at the seminar how mine turned out. ☺

For PLACE, I want you to write a place you want to go over the next year and spend more time or see for the first time. Not necessarily a vacation spot, but pick a place you really want to see and where you want to spend time, about which you feel that if you did this, your life would change dramatically for the better. And don't say Vegas! ☺ This one should be easy: Hawaii, Italy, the Moon, or even your home town where you grew up. Some of the agents I have worked with even put a particular lake or countryside. It doesn't have to be Rio. Keep it simple. Mine was **Grand Canyon**. I have never been. If my success triangle works, then by the end of the year I will have seen it. Make sure you are putting a person, place and thing that you truly want. Not what I want, or what your spouse wants, or what your parents' goals are or even what some guy writing some six-step selling program tells you to write. You have to ask yourself what it is *you* truly want. This is *your* success triangle.

You now should have a dollar amount in the middle, a person you want to attract into your life on top and a place you want to visit over the next twelve months at the lower left point of the triangle. Lastly, we have our "**thing**." Your "thing" could be anything material that you want. Here is your one chance at a material item, so indulge! A car, a house, a cabin, a new 50-inch plasma TV, a new whatever, I don't know, only you do, so put what you want. For myself, I have put "a cabin on Cross Lake, Minnesota." I love that lake and have spent many summers fishing there, so over the next twelve months, my goal is to own a cabin there. I can't wait to hear what you put.

OK, you're almost done . . . underneath the triangle, write the date of exactly one year from today! And sign it! This is more important than anything else in your Success Triangle. Signing and dating. So get your signature and date on there! It's worthless unless you sign and date it! After all, this is real estate. (Everything has to be in writing!) Take your Success Triangle and put a copy of it in each of three places. Place one in your wallet, one on your wall in your office/work area, and one on your bathroom mirror, then let your subconscious get to work. You now have four goals that you can rattle off in 15 seconds, boom, if anyone ever asks you. Ninety-nine percent of the world cannot do that. You now know your goals and they are in writing. Pat yourself on the back. I'm serious. Great job. This whole process should not take you more than five or ten minutes. Keep it simple. The Success Triangle is an effective way to achieve goal-setting and it is all you need for your first year or two.

Are you with me? Can you handle that? When I first got started, the company I was with, held a two-day seminar on goal-setting. I showed up at 8:30 a.m. on a Saturday and spent the next two days sitting with other realtors discussing goals, dreams, how many homes we were going to sell, how many signs we would make, where our bus benches were going to be strategically placed. We then wrote over twenty pages in our journals, made vision boards, sang kumbaya, blah, blah, blah. By Sunday night I was so exhausted and brain-stuffed with things in my head that I couldn't go to work for three days. By the following week, I forgot everything I did, was overwhelmed and confused, and couldn't state one goal I had ever written down, nor did I care. This kind of goal-setting not only became a WMD, but it was burning me out by spending so much time on it. Don't make this huge mistake. Get your person, place, thing and money goals down, and that's it. Having a few clear, concise goals as opposed to three hundred things in a forty-page journal will help you focus. With goal-setting, less is more. Olympians understand this perfectly. Whenever I get overwhelmed, I study Olympic athletes, their mindsets and their daily behaviors. I have realized that they have it easy when it comes to goal-setting because there is only one goal: The Gold Medal.

Edge Rule: Keep It Simple.

Step Four is all about keeping your focus and understanding how you spend your time. It is worthy of its own step because it is vital to becoming a great realtor. All the skills you have learned up to now will help you focus. For example, learning how to say NO and Dis-Qualifying certain prospects will help you focus because you will now be able to say NO to certain social events that might otherwise drag you away from your 80 percent.

IF EVERYONE ELSE IS DOING IT, STOP DOING IT

At one point in my life, I loved to drink and go to bars. I had heard it was a great way to network with other agents and that to sell a lot, you had to go out and socialize all the time. I would eventually learn that this was anything but true. I realized this was not helping my business at all. Going to the bar, talking about the other agents, gossiping about the manager, who was sleeping with who, drinking to oblivion, then more gossip and ultimately nothing was ever accomplished but a giant hangover. I finally realized it was a giant weapon of mass distraction. So then when other agents pressured me to go throw a few back at happy hour, I started saying NO. I would go to the gym instead, or attend a passion arena. This ability to say NO helped me focus and my focus muscles were getting stronger. My determination to go my own way began paying dividends. As I got really good at focusing and avoiding WMDs, my business skyrocketed. No more wasting time at bars, no more hangovers, and laser focus was my new mission.

Focus was my most difficult step to master. I was an ADD trainwreck when I first got started. I was a people pleaser and believed you have to work 24/7 and go to network events, and dinners, and office meetings, and happy hours . . . and after two years I was burned out and had not sold one house. I was not DO-ing anything that would make me money. I was doing what everyone else was doing. Not good. I was doing what I thought realtors were *supposed* to do. I was certainly not doing what I wanted to do. I wasn't being myself by doing the dinners and happy hours. I never liked any of that stuff, but someone taught me that if I was going to make it, I would have to wine and dine. They would say things like, "It's the only way," or, "You have to schmooze people to make it," or my favorite, "Everybody's doing it." (It was like peer pressure back in junior high.) I was no better than the girl who went to medical school against her own will, or the young man who worked for his father although he never wanted to. I certainly was not being me. Here I was, years into the business and I was still the square peg trying to jam myself into the round hole.

After a long stretch of zero results and many, many failures, it hit me what my new plan would be. It became my mantra moving forward as I started getting great results. My confidence surged and I knew I was on to something. My new mantra was this:

If everyone else is doing it, I will stop doing it immediately!

This new belief gave me an edge. It helped me focus. It allowed me to feel good about being myself. Most of all, it made me stand out. I wasn't standing out because I was a rebel, I stood out because I was being me.

One of my interests and passions was the higher-end market. I knew people who were selling fifty homes per year, but for me, that sounded like a lot of work. I decided that I would go for the big fish. As I expected, everyone told me that I had no business selling the bigger homes and that I certainly would not be able to do that driving what I drove (VW) and dressing how I dressed (t-shirt). But my mantra of doing the opposite of what everyone else was doing bubbled in my soul. The more people told me I couldn't do it, the more I knew I could. They told me I had to have grown up in Beverly Hills to have the right kind of connections. They said, "The high-end market is for elite, experienced agents." I said, "That is nonsense," and went on my way. I knew I just had to meet some people that were capable of buying that kind of real estate and I could do it. And so can you!

Edge Rule: If everyone else is doing it, stop doing it.

I started going to places where I thought these high-end buyers and sellers would be. I took a part-time job as a caddy at Bel Air Country Club. I went to lunch once a week at the Beverly Hills Hotel (I ordered a Coke and a small salad; I couldn't afford much else.) For me, this seemed like a better idea than going to a 7:30 a.m. network meeting with other realtors or a happy hour mixer with mortgage lenders that were trying to schmooze me. And I was right! Caddying at Bel Air Country Club, I met some amazing people and developed relationships with them. It was a nice way to forget about real estate. The BH Hotel was exciting and I never knew who I'd meet there or see. I knew it was more productive than some after-hours mixer with other agents who simply wanted to complain about how bad their commissions splits were or how their office printer was never working. I was becoming a familiar face at certain hotel lounges and got on good terms with concierges who were happy to keep their ears open for anyone discussing real estate. I just kept showing up. Week after week. Little did I know that I was prospecting without even trying and passion arenas were forming. I was authentically developing relationships. I would rarely even tell people I was a realtor until I had crossed paths with them a few times. I'd just say I was taking a break in style. I would order a Diet Coke because I certainly couldn't afford anything else. But they had nice air conditioning and I felt like a high roller. It was fun. I didn't have any magic networking technique or golden introduction or fancy way to talk to anyone. I did one thing every week and that was to show up. I kept showing up week after week. Sometimes twice a week. That was all I had to do. Good things started happening.

"Ninety percent of success is just showing up."
-Woody Allen

I had just had enough with traditional networking venues and I was now going to do things my way. I was officially going to follow my gut from here on out, and, more importantly, use focus to avoid weapons of mass distraction. (1) Go with my gut. (2) Do the opposite of the pack.

This behavior would eventually prove to be a one-two knockout punch, skyrocketing my real estate success to a whole new level. I want to sell high-end homes. So I hung around places where people who could afford high-end homes hung out. Before I knew it, I was selling high-end homes. I know what you are thinking: "But that sounds so simple." It was. Keep it simple.

If I thought something was a waste of time, I said, "No." I went and did what I wanted and was passionate about. I had fun like you will if you attend passion arenas that you choose. I followed my heart, not someone else's orders or the herd mentality. This is a great lesson that I want you to take with you and embrace, your first year and beyond. The lesson is that just because everyone else is doing it, that doesn't mean it's going to work for you – or that it even works. Social parties and agent events can drain you dry, so pick and choose carefully where and how you spend your time, my friends. Next time someone insists you attend some networking mixer or agent expo and you are not feeling it, rock a "Dean Malevich" and say no!

CHAPTER 19

THE THREE PERSONALITY PITFALLS

When new realtors have some success or are putting deals into escrow, a whole new emotion can change who they are. Money starts coming in and you're going to feel on top of the world. But beware. Proceed with caution, as even success can pull focus and be a WMD. My good friend Thanos has his Ph.D. and is a well-known teacher now in Italy. He gave me some words of advice that sum up my point nicely here:

"Success, the Mother of all ruin."

-Thanos Pappadimitriou

Success can lead to ego, and ego can wipe out your career quicker than anything. People sometimes achieve a little success and then quickly dismiss the hard-work ethic and excellent customer service that got them there. Ego takes over, and they stop doing what they did in the first place to earn that success. Thus the downfall, for some, can follow right after success. This often involves three very distinct personality pitfalls that will kill your deals, your character, your reputation, and even your finances if you don't watch out for them. Keeping the Four Cornerstones as your foundation will help you avoid most of these pitfalls by easily spotting them. Don't fall into these traps!

The Three Personality Pitfalls:

1. The Baby Sitter
2. The Control Freak
3. The Big Spender

Focus in real estate is about spending 80 percent of your time doing what makes you money, and you are now very aware of WMDs (Weapons of Mass Distraction). So what happens when you get a deal under contract and you have to spend time making sure the deal closes? This is where new realtors typically fall off the track and all hell breaks loose. New agents put a deal in escrow and they are very close to selling a house so they STOP doing everything they did prior to this to get the deal. They stop prospecting, they stop building relationships, they stop doing everything except babysitting this one deal. What is even worse is they stop getting out there and attending their passion arenas (Step Two). There's danger ahead when this happens. Threat level red! You are on a fast track to Death Valley. Why? Because if you stop developing relationships and spend all your time handling this "one" client, your well will soon run dry. You've not only taken your foot off the gas, you have pulled over to the side of the road, abandoned the car, and started walking through the desert in the wrong direction without a compass, map, or water. #notgood. Guess where you are bee-lining toward? You guessed it, amigo! Valle de la Muerte.

If you go back and read the Main Mission of the Focus Step, the key word most people miss is "consistently." You never stop attending your passion arenas, developing relationships and finding new trauma victims, no matter what! Not even to handle an escrow. Not even if your ass falls off. Got it? I've seen it happen with extremely experienced agents as well. Once they get multiple deals going, all of a sudden they become big shots, rock stars, and they put everything else on hold while they micromanage their deals, run the escrow department, get short with their clients, and yell at other agents. They are out of control and it is usually because they have been caught in one of the three pitfalls. You will see many personality pitfalls as realtors make sales, but these are the big three. Let's break each one down so you can spot them when you start doing them. Because I promise you, you will – but knowing them and knowing what to look for will keep you light years ahead of the pack and help you avoid the pitfalls. The Babysitter pitfall is by far the most common trap that new agents fall into when they start doing deals.

THE BABYSITTER

Let's talk about the first character, The BABYSITTER. New agents typically get a deal going and then spend all their time holding the client's hand: hours on the phone with this one buyer as they are freaking out. The agent feels obligated to "be there" for every emotional up and down that comes with buying a home. Buyers, thinking you are their therapist, ask you to come over at 9:30 p.m. because they are scared about this big step. You go over there and drink coffee with the buyer until 1:00 a.m. Then the next morning the same buyer calls, asking if you can be at the inspection; and they want you to show their relatives the house too. You are basically holding the hand of the client and babysitting every single step of the deal. You are now either so busy babysitting that you're too exhausted to do anything else, or you are neglecting your passions arenas and your "80 percent," as you feel you cannot do another thing until this deal closes. You must watch every single step and babysit the client to make sure it does close. This "making sure" and micromanaging will kill your future business. It pulls focus from your 80 percent. Don't let it.

Here is what new agents don't understand. Once you get it into escrow, it is either going to close or it is not. If you found a great house, they made the offer, you are in escrow and their loan is on the way, then your job is over. You have done your job. Now get back out there and put another one in escrow before this one closes. Your job is to SAVE TRAUMA VICTIMS. If you are stuck babysitting one, you are not being the person the universe wanted you to be. You are excellent at what you do. So help a lot of people. That is your job. Buyers and sellers will try to get you to babysit – and the more you give, the more they will expect. You have to draw the line. You want their respect; you don't need to be liked. Just like doctors: you don't see a doctor helping only one patient a month. They work with many patients. That is your goal. (Remember: Act and think as if you were a doctor.)

Many new agents and, yes, even experienced agents will do only one deal at a time because they think they have to babysit each deal. The reason they do this is that it is natural to babysit during your first few years. New agents have what I call severe "buyer empathy" that makes them feel they must be there for clients 24/7. Buyers and sellers perpetuate this myth because so many realtors DO this kind of thing. It's your job to draw the line when buyers and sellers ask you to do things that are not your duties. Say no. This does two things for you. First, it commands their respect. Second, it makes you look different. New potential buyers and sellers don't necessarily test you consciously to see if you are strong, but they will do it in one form or another, so be ready. In a transaction like this, people want to know the agent they work with is strong and confident. If you come across as weak – even though you may not be – you will not get their business. Think about it. Think about the last person you worked with professionally. Lawyer, doctor, nurse, teacher, anyone. Were they confident? Did they jump at your every request?

Clients will ask you to pick up kids, come to dinner, lend them money, drive them to the airport, do their laundry, fix their roof, and walk their dog. And you, being new, will be tempted to say yes, as most agents think it will lead to business. But I am here to tell you it will not. Know your part. Your job is to what? Save them! By either finding them a home or selling their current home. Your job is not to babysit. Babysitting one deal at a time will ruin you.

You have lots of potential and, trust me, you can easily have ten deals going at once. You have to trust that the other people in the game will get their parts done. The escrow company, the lender, and the inspector all are getting paid to now take over and do their part. Let them. You are not an inspector, an attorney, an accountant or a banker, so once you have done your part, which is to either find your buyer a great home and negotiate a great deal, or find your seller a real buyer and put it in escrow; then you are done. You will still review the inspection and check in with the client to make sure everything is going well, but not 24/7. What would a doctor do? Remember the PRE-OP and POST-OP steps in **Sales Triage™**? These two steps are all about managing expectations. Post-Op is the step you take the minute a house goes into escrow so that your clients are clear you will not be babysitting them during the whole escrow period.

(For those of you who are extremely new, "escrow" is a period where the house has been put under contract, but not officially sold. It is roughly a thirty-day period where the new buyer has time to inspect the house and the seller has time to move out and let the new buyer know any problems – disclosures – with the house. After this time period has passed, the lender sends over the money to the escrow company, the title company changes the title to the new buyer's name and gives the money to the seller, and then it's closed.)

An escrow company is kind of like a referee. They hold the deposit and make sure that both sides abide by the rules of the contract until it closes. Just like in sports, real estate has a referee, and it is the escrow person. (Unless you are working on the East Coast; then you guys just use attorneys to play ref.) My point is that you have done your part and now others are involved, so have faith in them and let them do their part. To return to the doctor metaphor, think of it like this: you had appendicitis and the surgeon just finished taking out your appendix. When you wake up in your hospital room, you won't find the doctor standing by to feed you soup. Though he or she may come by and check on you after the surgery, someone else will bring your food or help you go to the bathroom. In real estate, if you act like the doctor, your clients will understand what your role is. Doctors are great at delegating and letting others handle their parts.

Some doctors can also develop a god-complex, and this can be trouble. We have a similar character in real estate, the egomaniac also known as . . .

THE CONTROL FREAK

I am sure you know people like this. The control freak is super-dominant and has to have everything their way. Ever heard the phrase, "my way or the highway"? Yeah, we're talking about that guy – the one who has to get everyone to do things his way. When you are new, you will get emotionally involved in your first few deals, but I am here to teach you to keep your cool. Do you know what unflappable means? This is how you want to be during an escrow. Here is another example: everyone knows Tom Brady is one cool cat who knows his role. His greatest strength is that he respects all the members of his team and he lets them do their parts. He knows his part is to play quarterback. And, yes, as a realtor you are essentially the quarterback. Once Tom Brady has passed the ball, he doesn't tell the receiver how to catch it. He doesn't tell the blockers how to block. Similarly, in real estate it is a team and you will learn to work with escrow companies and lenders that you like and trust and you have to let them play their parts.

New agents have a tendency to hold the reins too tightly and that's the first symptom that you are becoming the next Control Freak. If you find this happening, loosen up. Remind yourself of the Four Cornerstones, especially Humility and Gratitude, and this will keep you grounded. Shift your focus back to your DO and trust in others' abilities. My experience has been that the elite of the elite agents are typically the most humble, grateful, and most willing to let others do their parts. The egomaniacs come and go.

BE NICE

The real estate community is very, very small. The best agents know it takes a team effort to close every deal. And the best agents know that the agent on the other side of the deal has to be their biggest ally if they are going to close the deal smoothly and successfully. I have worked with all types of agents and I am never more thrilled than when it is with someone I know is a team player. I want to point out to you, the newbie, something they do not teach in traditional real estate training. When it comes to putting together a deal, the "other agent" needs to become your best friend. I am referring to the agent representing the buyer if you are representing the seller, and vice versa. This agent on the other end needs to become your ultimate ally. It is NOT "you vs. them" as most agents tend to think it is. It can't be they lose, you win. That doesn't work. It also can't be your client wins, their client loses. That's trouble too. You will never make deals happen that way. **Your goal should be win/win/win**. When you are putting together any and all deals, your goal should be three objectives. 1. Your client wins. 2. Their client wins. 3. Both agents win. It is a team effort and if you can master the art of working with other agents to close a deal, you will close more deals and close them much more easily.

Traditional training does not even address the importance of having good relationships with other agents. I attended every training possible and not once did someone cover the need for working and communicating with, and always respecting, your peers. I am here to tell you that WIN/WIN/WIN is key. How do you achieve this? With communication and humility.

Edge Rule: Think triple win.

Communication is crucial. Talk to them, don't live and breathe via emails and texting. People misinterpret texts and emails; then, next thing you know, they have a grudge for no reason except that they misunderstood you. Pick up the phone, introduce yourself and be real. Meet them for coffee or lunch.

Humility is helpful. If you are dealing with egomaniacs, I don't care, humble yourself and stick your hand out. Ego is no match for humility, your authenticity will be contagious, and you will get more done as they start to see you as an ally. Most agents will never grasp this concept of win/win/win in their entire careers and neither will your clients. It is your job to make sure it happens. You're not involved in a litigation or a case in a trial court. It is not a football game where there will be a winner and a loser.

In residential real estate, everyone must feel they have won in some way or another or the transaction typically will never close. The buyer must win, the seller must win, and, yes, even the agents must win. When there is win/win/win happening, you can put that sale on the board, it's going to close.

Don't fall into the trap in real estate where you think the other agents are your competition. There are plenty of houses to sell and plenty of trauma victims for everyone to work with. If some other agent closes a big deal, celebrate their victory and pay your respects. That abundance mentality will help you breed more success as well. See other agents as your allies and your peers, unless of course they give you reason not to.

Many realtors have told me they have even used the "best friend exercise" to talk to agents. Sometimes when you are new, you're going to encounter some hugely famous and big-time agents that can be intimidating, and you may be awestruck when you cross paths with them. But I encourage you to talk to them just as you would with your best friend, and be yourself. Treat them with respect, as you would want to be treated. Before you know it, you will have yourself an ally in the industry. This ally may become your business partner one day, or even your wingman. Believe me, you will be seeing the same agents over and over, so you want to start building healthy relationships with them. One day you are going to need them to help you out, and vice versa. If you were an asshole or treated them disrespectfully when they were a lowly assistant, they will remember. So, in a nutshell: Be nice. It's a small, small world . . . after all!

Edge Rule: Be Nice. (Even when you are having a bad day.)

THE BIG SPENDER

The last personality pitfall to avoid is my favorite because this was ME all the way! The Big Spender! The Big Spender is an agent who closes a deal, goes out and blows his entire check, and comes back three weeks later and starts over. Yes, I confess, that was me. I would close a deal, get a check for $15,000 and I was off to the races! I would go gamble in Vegas, ski in Vancouver, or party in NYC and piss away 80% of the money and come back three weeks later saying, "Oh boy, I have to get another deal now." Only to come home realizing I have neglected all my prospecting duties, have developed zero new relationships and haven't attended a passion arena in over a month. Not Good.

This was the equivalent of Kobe Bryant scoring twenty-seven points in the first quarter, and then in the middle of the game while the clock was still running, he would just leave the game. Imagine that! Kobe rocks out 27 points in the first quarter and now it's the start of the second quarter and he is not there! The fans are freaking out, his teammates are confused, and Phil Jackson is scrambling for answers. The assistant coach runs out and says Kobe just tweeted the following message: "Hey y'all, I had a great first quarter so I have to run now, I'm going to zip over to Ruth's Chris for a steak, then to Armani and buy a suit, then I'm off to visit Italy with some friends and I'll be back sometime next month for our road game against The Heat . . . or not. Have a great second half, but I have to go celebrate my record first quarter. Peace, out – Kobe." (Since original print, we lost the great Kobe Bryant but kept this as tribute.)

    OK, it sounds ludicrous when we put it that way, but that is what the Big Spender does. They close a deal, get a check and then check out of the game for two, three, or even four weeks or longer. I'd have a banner quarter where I sold three or four houses and made more money than I ever dreamed of in that short amount of time, so my nature was to stop playing. This is something that not only I did, but I see it all the time among other agents as well. I realized I was going from deal to deal doing this, never getting any momentum going and not only letting down my clients, but I was letting down myself. Why did I feel the need to check out after every deal? Well, mainly because I was exhausted. Besides being a big spender, I had moments where I struggled with all the pitfalls. I'd babysit, micromanage, suffer from CEO syndrome and even have days where, I admit it and I am sorry, I was an asshole. I did, however, recognize that these behaviors were not appropriate or conducive to making it in the real estate world so I corrected myself and used Humility, Service, Gratitude and Forgiveness (the Four Cornerstones) to get me on the high road and keep me there.

    You will have these moments too, and that is why I am sharing them with you. We are all human and that is why we can sometimes get off-track. It's important to recognize it when you find yourself teetering on the edge of one of the pitfalls. My biggest pitfall was being the big spender. I knew this was not a healthy way to make a consistent living, so it was time to put a stop to it. It wasn't until I got sick and tired of always back-pedaling and playing catch-up that I really decided to look at my behavior and take full responsibility for everything in my life. I realized the problem was <u>me</u>. In real estate we don't have bosses, managers that watch our every move, employers keeping us accountable, punch cards, time clocks, bankers' hours, or sick pay. You may hang your license at a brokerage, but agents are essentially self-employed and that means you have to be self-managed. Yes, you will have a manager, but the reality is that they will be there for you if you choose to take advantage of their help. You are the one who is running the show now. And running a good show starts with taking a look in the mirror. It is important, as it is in all good businesses, to take inventory – only, as a real estate agent, you are going to take inventory . . . on *yourself*. I started doing a personal inventory on myself every Sunday night and I would ask myself, "How can I get better?" This reality check, as I call it, helped me avoid the pitfalls and got me improving on all levels. These pitfalls can wipe you out if you are not careful. They can pull focus from your moneymaking eighty percent, so be on high alert.

After closing a deal, your confidence will be at its highest, so instead of leaving town for a big-spending break and killing all that momentum, keep doing what you are doing. There is no better time to attend a passion arena or to make another sale than right after you've made a sale. Why? Because you are on fire. You're in the zone. The confidence is rolling. Instead of being a Big Spender, pay your taxes immediately and get back to Steps One, Two, and Three, ASAP!

Let me repeat: pay your taxes at once. You are now a business owner and I have news for you, if you are a new realtor, you will come up with every excuse in the book NOT to pay your taxes as the commission checks come in. You will rationalize a way to keep the whole paycheck for now and worry about the taxes on April 15th. You will spend that money and when tax time rolls around you will be jammed! Jammed big time. Trust me, pay your taxes immediately. For those who may not be grasping this bold command, let me explain. When you close your first sale, you will be paid a lot of money and zero taxes will be taken out because you are an independent contractor for your broker. Unlike normal jobs, your broker will not deduct one penny for taxes. It is your responsibility to pay your own state and federal taxes. So pay them ASAP. You don't want to learn the hard way.

Edge Rule: When you close a deal, pay all your taxes immediately, no exceptions.

They do not teach this in real estate school and I have seen more realtors get upside down after their first year or two because they make a sale, get a check for ten grand and figure, "Well, since I am new, I will just keep the tax portion of this commission to invest in my business. Then, on the next sale, I will use that entire commission to pay the tax on both deals." And blah blah blah and ten other silly excuses. Then . . . disaster strikes. They get their next sale and they forget how they spent three grand on a credit card over the holidays, so they decide not to pay any taxes out of their second deal either. T-R-O-U-B-L-E. "But I have another deal in the pipeline" may be your excuse. New agents kid themselves by saying, "I'll just close another deal and that entire check, every single penny of it, will pay for all my past-due taxes and I'll be set." That sounds all fun and dandy, but before you can say "Uncle Sam," that deal goes south and the market is now dead. Crickets out there.

And guess what day it is? Yep, April 15th, and not a client in sight. It's April 15th, only to find you now owe over eighteen thousand in taxes and your bank account is at zero. Taxes have now become a WMD as you need to pay them and the pressure wears on you. I have rarely seen realtors recover when they get upside down in taxes. The pressure pulls focus and it's hard to be yourself and get out there and work when you now have a giant debt on your shoulders. Realtors in this position get desperate. They start selling hard, they start looking for the quick fix, the fast money. They are unable to develop genuine relationships; they try to push people into buying a home they don't really like and this is how bad reputations begin. It isn't long before realtors like this are out of the business. Such agents, who had so much talent, end up going back to their old jobs to make money and try to pay their taxes. Another "could have been hall-of- famer" bites the dust. Out of the industry. Gone. Done. Not because they weren't good enough, but because no one ever taught them the importance of paying their taxes without delay.

Edge Rule: When you close a deal, pay all your taxes immediately, no exceptions.

(That Rule is worth repeating.)

TAKE FIVE

Before we move to Step Five, let's take five. I want you to close your eyes and think about everything we just talked about here. Take five minutes to focus on what you will consistently do every day. You're going to meditate each morning for the next thirty days with your Success Triangle in front of you. Focus is like a muscle. Focusing on what you are going to do every day is like exercising a muscle. Consistently doing what you need to do every day is like making a muscle stronger.

Focus on what you must do consistently each day to lead you to your goals. Focus on the DO. This muscle will strengthen, your ability to focus will get better, and your ability to identify and avoid WMDs will get sharper. Your **Edge** will sharpen. Your ability to say NO will strengthen. You will build momentum because you are growing and you will feel it. Others will see it in your confidence and appearance. I promise you, the more you practice these tools and techniques, the better you will get at being focused and staying focused.

I was taught you either have the ability to focus or you don't. I was taught that focus is a talent, not a skill. I was taught wrong. It is actually neither. It is something that you can either choose to learn or not choose to learn. Like playing the piano, focus can be learned, taught and mastered by anyone! Even people with ADD. Like anything worthwhile, it takes practice, so don't beat yourself up if you get off-track or a WMD wipes you out for a few days. It will happen even to the best of us. For now, just be aware of what derails you easily and pulls you off the tracks. It will be different for everyone.

The great news for you is that you are now extremely aware of the importance of Focus. It's not always easy out there, and there can be a lot of rocks along the way. If you ever get out of focus and need to recalibrate and re-focus, I encourage you to simply take five. Take a break. Go to the library. Go to a church. Sit in quiet. Let your soul catch back up to your body. We can fly so fast in real estate sometimes that we even leave ourselves behind. I encourage you to really enjoy studying focus and have fun with it. This step changed my life when I learned I could learn it. When I realized it wasn't some magic gene that people either had or didn't have, I began practicing and I got better at it. Focus is where you find the answers to come of your toughest problems and it starts by quieting your mind. You know your favorite peaceful place: a lake, a cabin, or even a local library. Use these places, recalibrate, get re-aligned, get *in* focus so that you *can* focus and your dreams will start materializing in ways you never imagined. Never underestimate the power of focus. I promise you, nothing can change your life faster than mastery of this step. Nothing.

Nothing can change your life faster than focus, but nothing can ruin your life faster than being around the wrong people. We are all susceptible to our surroundings, so unless you are Superman, who you surround yourself with is vital to success. In Step Five we are going to build your dream team. It's time to take a good look at the roster and see who makes the team and who gets cut. Ever tried out for something and gotten cut? It's not pleasant, but sometimes it's for the best. Sometimes it's a wake-up call.

Chapter 20

THE BLAPPA BLAPPA BLAPPA INCIDENT

Throughout college I fell in love with devouring self-help books, spiritual books, and sales books. My Dad would read them, then send them to me. I've read and been inspired by all the greats, like Tony Robbins, Thomas Merton, Andrew Carnegie, Earl Nightingale, Eckhart Tolle, Brian Tracy, Napoleon Hill, Sandler, the *Men Are From Mars, Women Are From Venus* guy (John Gray, Ph.D.), T. Harv Eker, the *Chicken Soup for the Soul* franchise, the *Seven Habits of Highly Effective People* guy (Stephen Covey), the *Seven Spiritual Laws of Success* guy (Deepak Chopra, MD) – I loved it all; it was endless. I studied all that good stuff, then got into Jesus, Jews, Catholics, Gandhi, Martin Luther King, Jr., Dr. Seuss (Theodor Seuss Geisel), athletes, professional sports coaches, relationship books, sports medicine, and more. You name it, whatever it was in the field of self-help, I was learning it and I was passionate about it. I soaked up all this because I enjoyed it. It was helping me get better grades, so I kept reading and reading. At one point I was convinced that I was going to be an accountant and that reading this material would help me get a job. Fate had different plans for this kid.

Although during high school my grades suffered, in college I was flying high, whizzing along with all As and Bs. I had a part-time job at the information booth, which happened to be next to the Dean's office. He helped me get that job so he could keep an eye on me and make sure I wasn't shooting off any more fireworks in the dorms or getting kicked out of school again. Students would come to the info booth for directions or what not and I'd end up helping them with homework or teaching them something from Stephen Covey or whatever the book of the week was. It was comical. They'd ask me where the bathroom was and I would tell them about Tony Robbins's latest book or give them my quote of the day (usually made up by me). The Dean noticed that I had a knack for helping others, so he suggested I become a tutor. That was funny to me cuz I NEVER saw myself as a tutor. Tennis player, waiter, accountant, rock star maybe, but never a tutor.

However, mentors and other good friends, a lot of times, see things in us that we don't see in ourselves. (You are going to learn how to identify a mentor in your life and how to find one in Step Five.) I became a study skills tutor, since I was fortunate enough to ace all my classes without too much struggle. The Dean said to me, "You have a gift, you need to share it." Off I went, a few hours each Monday and Thursday, working at the Reading and Study Skills Center. I used to laugh, because I barely got into college and now I was teaching others how to study and learn. Dean Malevich was right. He said, "You have a gift, you should share it." It felt good to give back. I thought of Vinh.

In college I enjoyed studying the teachers almost more than the subjects themselves. I would say, "This teacher is good, that one is bad," and I began really paying attention to what the difference was between great teachers and mediocre ones. Was their advice good? Was it bad? Or were they just there to get a paycheck? Did the students learn? Did they connect? Like the Dean, did they see things in us that we students didn't see? Was the lesson real-world street-smart or was it bookworm-smart? The latter bored me, so I vowed to teach practical stuff at the study skills center. People would come in for help in history or English and I would teach them about time management, being pro-active, or something else I learned from one of my Dad's tapes. I had people lining up and I wasn't even teaching the subject; I didn't care, I didn't know anything about half the subjects – but I knew how to get As and it started with good time management.

It started with students' knowing their DO. (Sound familiar?) I didn't know anything about most subjects, but I knew a system to get As and Bs and students kept coming back. Not bragging, but I felt good about making a difference in others' lives and it was helping me pay my tuition.

A.D.D. MOMENT – STOP!!!

You need a break. Put the bookmark in and take a breather. Why? It's movie time. OK, stop reading this book right now, put it down for today and let this soak in. Rent *Coach Carter* tonight and come back tomorrow. You'll understand after you watch the movie. Seriously, go see it. And in case you forgot the other movie recommendations that I've been mentioning because they can inspire you and really complement everything we're learning in this program, here they are again:

ROCKY I, II, and *III* (Nothing touches these three.)

TOP GUN (Vintage Tom Cruise.)

GLENGARRY GLEN ROSS (Greatest real estate movie ever.)

COACH CARTER (Samuel L. Jackson in the title role.)

MIRACLE (U.S. gold medal-winning men's ice hockey team, 1980 Winter Olympics. Kurt Russell as Head Coach Herb Brooks.)

Amazing movies, right? Now for your break, see *Coach Carter*. This guy has **The Edge**. If you want to learn the meaning of coachable and focus, I highly recommend you see this movie tonight. It will teach you focus. You will also enjoy the other ones and they will help your real estate career. *Rocky* will teach you to be yourself. *Top Gun* will teach you to get out there! *Glengarry* will teach you to DIS-Qualify, and *Miracle* will teach you to own it and have fun!

. . . OK, welcome back, hope you took a break. Anyway, where were we? Oh yes, college, and the power of good teachers and coaches. I was also learning that you had to seek out the right coaches, because not everyone had your best interests at heart. That was just how life was, and I was learning some lessons like that the hard way. I had met some awesome people in my first year in college and was cruising along nicely when I decided to really screw things up my second year . . . and join a fraternity. Bad move, McLovin (*Superbad*)!

I don't know why I did it. I was never the fraternity type. I was more of a band-dork/bowling team type of guy who was shooting for Spanish Club officer and was happy about that. I simply got sucked into my first WMD. I heard about the parties and saw the girls and thought, "Oooooh, fraternities!" – maybe that was where all the cool people hung, and who doesn't have insecurities and a desire to be cool when they're nineteen?

My college was a Division Three college, private, and Catholic. We were like a Notre Dame wannabe, only a lot smaller, and fraternities were actually not even allowed. But there were a few private ones. Sure enough, I was approached by some slick upper-classmen who told me that Blappa Blappa Blappa (I'll call it that to protect the innocent) was having interviews (their version of Rush Week). I was young, away from home, and as smart as I was in class, I was the biggest idiot when it came to life. Let me remind you about my being kicked out of the dorms my third week in college. This next milestone would prove far worse. I was longing to "belong," as all teenagers and young college kids do at some point. I didn't feel like I fit in too well, got cut from the tennis team, and was feeling pretty vulnerable. Maybe a fraternity would be worth checking out. I was looking for some group-type things to get involved with. When I was ultimately asked to pledge in what was supposedly a business fraternity, I figured that this might be the ticket! It would look good on my résumé. I could be a part of a group and, long-term, it might really help me in my career, since it was allegedly a professional business fraternity.

I would soon find out that Blappa Blappa Blappa had less than zero to do with business and was nothing more than a cover and excuse for a bunch of kids to get together to drink and party. That is what we did. All. The. Time. I literally almost died at one of the pledge parties from drinking more than was humanly possible. Somehow I didn't, and the next morning when I woke up – half-naked in a ravine outside someone's cabin in northern Minnesota – I was informed that I had officially made it in! What was I even *in*? I now had the privilege of drinking with people I never really said two words to, sober? We were drunk three days a week and it was supposedly cool. I was hanging around older guys who drank heavily, made us do stupid stuff, hazed us, and as sophomores, we were supposed to be like, "This is so cool, I'm so honored to be here." Well, it was bad news. My grades went down, my original great friends disappeared, and I didn't understand why. I was now running with a bad crowd. Very bad. I was in big trouble and didn't even see it. Then came the Pete and Janice moment. A moment that would forever change my live.

PISTOL AND JANICE

In college I never made the tennis team. I was up against a crop of athletes from all over the country, and although Vinh got me to the varsity team in high school, Vinh was now off to Boston and I was on my own. I tried out my second year in college and didn't make the team, mainly because I didn't train. I was drunk half the time, hanging out at the Blappa Blappa Blappa house, resting on my laurels and thinking I would somehow luckily make the team. Just as there is no luck in real estate sales, there is definitely no luck in tennis. You either work hard, have a system, and make the team – or the sale – or you end up out on the tiles. That's what happened to me when I was the last person to get cut from the team. The silver lining in getting cut was in a friend I met along the way.

Edge Rule: It's not about the final destination. It's about those we meet along the way.

During tennis tryouts I met someone who would become a longtime friend, whose name was Pete. "Pistol," we called him. "Pistol" Pete was a freshman and boy, could he hit the ball. I saw greatness and knew he would make the team easily. I befriended Pete, as I knew he was salt of the earth the day I met him. (Gutcheck.) We would practice and laugh together, and since Pete was in his first few weeks of college, I knew he didn't have a lot of friends. Pete was cool, down-to-earth, but the thing with Pete was, he was a young-looking little nerdy freshman. Just like I was when I started college, so I could relate to Pete quite a bit. We also had a mutual spark and love of tennis and we would practice and practice and practice and Pete gave me hope again.

Anyway, Pete's freshman nerdiness was a recipe for someone who was going to get picked on a lot. I thought this high school nonsense had ended, but soon realized that there would always be mean people out there, even in college. I could relate to Pete's problems because I was pretty short in high school as well. I was even a nerdy band dork as well. I never ran with the popular kids. It just wasn't my scene. But my parents had taught me to be kind to everyone, and Pete and I became instant friends. He would come to the dorm to watch my TV and I'd let him hang out. He felt cool and it felt nice to look out for someone. I'd been a freshman too and I remembered how awkward it was. Although Pistol got picked on, I always had his back. No matter what.

I never made the tennis team, but Pete did, and in some roundabout way I felt like I had passed on what Vinh had shared with me. I don't know if I made Pete's outer game of tennis any better, but I'd like to think I helped his inner game by befriending him, being there for him in his first year, and helping him feel included during an awkward transition from high school to college. I know that this gave him confidence and sometimes a little extra confidence is all it takes. Pete went on to become a great college tennis player. Vinh helped me. I helped Pete. Although I didn't make the team, I got to see the joy in helping others.

Shortly thereafter, I had this great idea that Pete should join my fraternity. I would then have someone I was really good friends with in the fraternity, and not just bogus-drinking-pretentious-frat buddies I had nothing in common with except booze. (In hindsight, I should have left the fraternity, but I was too young to know I was running with a bad crowd.) I suggested Pete try to get in, which started by coming to the pledge meeting where the fraternity members on the board would decide, along with a vote of the whole fraternity as to who gets to pledge and who doesn't. Looking back, it was like some insane reality show. A brutal entry process to what? The right to drink and ruin your grades and hang around with pompous assholes? Yippee! I was nineteen and didn't have a clue what was going on. I didn't know what I didn't know and thought this was life in college, so I stayed in the fraternity. It was fine because I figured I would get Pete in with no problem and all would be well.

Then came Pete's interview. You had to be "referred" to pledge and I spoke up for Pete, stating that he was my new good friend and I wanted him in. He came in and sat down in the center chair in front of a large group of strangers. After grilling him with dumb, condescending questions for about twenty minutes, the three board leaders asked Pete to leave the room. The board then all looked at me and said, "Are you nuts, Williams? We don't think he's Blappa Blappa Blappa material." I remember saying, "What does that even mean? 'Material'?" They were not going to let Pete in? This was B.S.!

The whole fraternity would eventually vote on who got to pledge and who didn't. Because everyone just did what the board kind of inferred they should do, out of thirty-six people in the room, the only ones who voted for Pete were two: me, obviously, and then this one girl whom I barely knew. Yes, a girl. Oh, did I mention it was a co-ed fraternity? Bizarre, I know, but it was. We were not allowed to have fraternities on our campus, so people did crazy stuff to start clubs and cliques and Blappa Blappa Blappa had some girls in it. (Probably the one redeeming thing about it.)

Thirty-four to two? WTF?! Are you kidding me? Pete was denied? How could this group that I thought were my friends not accept my good friend, Pete? What did they mean, they were not going to let Pete in? They let everyone in. It wasn't even a real fraternity. I was furious. Yet, because I was young, I wasn't too clear on what really just happened. I walked out of there knowing two things: one was that this fraternity and thirty-four of the thirty-six people in it were bullshit; and the other was that whoever that girl was who also voted for Pete, I was in love with! I fell flat-out upside-down crazy in love with her the second she stuck her hand up and voted for Pete. It blew me away that she, besides me, was the only one in the room who had the courage to vote for my friend Pete. She put her hand straight up. I could not believe my eyes. It was the two of us with our hands straight up and Pete had himself another vote! Everyone else stared at her like she was from Mars. Not me! I was floored. Janice wasn't afraid to stand up for the underdog. I would never forget how good it felt knowing someone had your back, and how important having someone else have your back was.

I walked out of the meeting to tell Pete he was not allowed to pledge and we were both kind of in shock. We sat on the bench outside the room in the quiet empty hall with our heads hung low in disbelief as to what just happened . . . until it hit me! If they rejected Pete, then they rejected me. I was all about loyalty, so I had to get out of that fraternity. Real friends came first. I knew that Pete and I were the true winners in that situation. Thus the good news was: I got my wake-up call. Nobody messes with my friends or family. Pete and Janice helped me see the light. Light bulbs went off everywhere. I was running with a bad crowd. Blappa Blappa Blappa was a social environment that was killing my grades, killing my real friendships, and in hindsight, it was probably the reason I didn't make the tennis team. I was out. Thank God. Years later, when I read about how this group was disbanded at our college, it came as no surprise.

The biggest lesson I learned from these experiences was to pay attention to who I was hanging out with. I don't blame Blappa Blappa Blappa for anything; I was the one who made the decision to join. It was nobody's fault but mine (a famous Led Zeppelin song, by the way). I took full responsibility for my actions. I was grateful because I met Pete and Janice: two great friends who would change my life.

"If you are not present during my struggle, don't expect to be present during my success."

-Wil Smith

Before long, my old friends were back in my life and I was back on track. Loyalty and defending others was something I would make part of my core values and character from then on. Sometimes when you are in a tough situation, you don't always know it – so how do you check yourself and find out? You have to have a support group. Do you? You will in Step Five. We are going to find your "Dream Team"! Blappa Blappa Blappa taught me that not everyone in this world is going to have your best interests at heart. And if that is the case, what are you doing in relationships with the ones who don't? Be it a work relationship, personal relationship, or any type of relationship. Bad news people are bad news people.

Check yourself before you wreck yourself.

You have to do an inventory and reality check on yourself before you wreck yourself. If your friends are bad news or your significant other is bad news, it's time to take a serious look at the situation and honestly answer the question: Why are you with these people or this person? Reality checks and Dream Teams are two concepts you are going to learn about in Step Five. If you are going to make it big in real estate, you have to surround yourself with excellent people that have your back and lift you up, inspire you, make you better, and vice versa. As you embark on your new career, it's crucial that you constantly assess your relationships. It's important to find out: are you in healthy ones or are you being dragged down? Are your friends really friends or are they just exciting, perhaps appearing to be something they really are not; possibly influencing you negatively?

RULE OF FIVE FRIENDS

I want you to take the income levels of the five people you hang around with the most. Take everyone's income and then average that number. My guess is that your income is that number or very close to it. That is called the Rule of Five Friends. I am not saying you should choose friends based on their income; I just want you to be aware of how susceptible we are to our surroundings. Success has zero to do with income – you could substitute the word "income" with dreams, happiness, drama, health, or values – what I want you to do is to be aware of your surroundings, including the people around you. Take the fix people you hang around with the most and ask yourself, are they genuinely happy? Joyful? Doing what they love to do? Are they friends who are lifting you up in life, or are they Negative Nellies? Drama queens? Dragging you down, draining your energy every time you hang out? The Rule of Five Friends: Learn it. It is the first step of your reality check. You can do a reality check on any area of your life. You can stop whatever you are doing now, look in the mirror, and ask yourself: "Are my surroundings healthy?" Where do you work? Where do you live? Are you happy? Is there something you need to change or someone you need to stop seeing because it's just not healthy? Only you can answer these questions. They will be different for each of us. For me, the Pete incident helped me realize the importance of my surroundings. From that moment on, I would always take responsibility for my choices, my surroundings; and, in fact, for everything in my life. That was the new plan. It was time to own it!

CHAPTER 21

STEP 5: OWN IT

"Your excuses are your own, pal."

-Richard Roma, *Glengarry Glen Ross*,

- written by David Mamet

Step 5 Main Mission: **Take Full Responsibility for Everything in Your Life.**

Step 5 Main Moves: **Reality Check**

Build Your Dream Team

If you are not where you want to be in life, my question is, why not? What do you think is holding you back? How do I ask you this next question without upsetting you? My question is: Is it you? Is it *you* that is holding you back? Or is it your excuses? You can have excuses or you can have results. You cannot have both.

Step Five, Own It, will help you figure out and continuously assess what might be holding you back or where you can make adjustments to recalibrate. It's time to take a long hard look in the mirror so that we can see our excuses and get rid of them for good. It is very hard for most people to take full responsibility for exactly where they are in their life. Michael Jackson knew what he was talking about when he said:

"I'm starting with the man in the mirror. I'm asking him to change his ways."

-Performed by Michael Jackson (1958-2009)

(Written by Siedah Garrett, Glen Ballard)

It is easy to blame others, blame the market, blame the economy, blame an old boss, a father, mother, sister, brother, uncle, ex, in-law, kids, neighbor, dog, weather, and on and on and on! Blaming others is the easy way out. It takes all the responsibility off of you for your current situation. Owning it means accepting full responsibility for exactly where you are in life at this very moment. *Full* responsibility. I know. It's brutal. Who wants to take full responsibility, especially if your life is a disaster right now? The only way to change it is to know that changing it starts with you. There is no other way out. The formula is simple. To change it, you need to own it!

Edge Rule: To change it, own it.

As a new realtor, you are now on your own as the CEO of YOU, INC., and, guess what, it's all on you now! Step 5 is all about taking everything that comes in and out of your life and being fully responsible for it. The good, the bad, and the ugly. Your relationships suck? Guess what? It's your fault. I know this may sound harsh, but in order to change anything in your life, the first step is to take ownership. This is *owning* it. It is taking full responsibility for not only the good in your life, but the not-so-good, as well.

Victory has many parents, but failure is an orphan.

The line above has been written or spoken in this or similar forms over the centuries by, among others, John F. Kennedy. It's true because nobody likes to take responsibility for anything that is bad. Especially failure. "It's not my fault, he did it." "They totally screwed me out of that deal." "Boy oh boy, did I get ripped off." I can think of hundreds of excuses; so can you. When I wanted to make excuses to my friend Vinh about not having enough money to go to tennis camp, his response was: "Option One: don't go, and you will never make the team." (Yikes, reality check!) Option Two: figure out a way. Sell your drumset, get a job, make some sacrifices, but if you really want to make the team, then nothing can be an excuse. Nothing." (Own it.)

Edge Rule: Nothing can be an excuse. Nothing.

That means from this point on: No more excuses. None. Zero. Nope, not even that. Or that. Especially not that. No more blaming your sales managers. No more blaming the other agent for blowing up the deal. No more blaming the economy for not bringing you buyers or sellers. Play the victim and I promise you, it's dinner at the Death Valley Café by the end of the year for you and your pity party table for one. OR, the other alternative, take complete responsibility for EVERYTHING in your life and the sky's the limit! Owning it means the full realization that, "If it is meant to be, it is up to me!" Owning it empowers you; it gives you the power to change. Empowerment eliminates fear and gives you confidence to take charge. Once you BELIEVE, you'll be unstoppable.

OWNING IT GIVES YOU THE POWER TO CHANGE

Owning it empowers you. Empowerment casts out fear, which gives you confidence to change. Change leads to belief. Once you believe, it's game over.

It's game over because no one can stop you at that point. Once you believe you can, you will. The hardest part is changing one's limiting belief from "I can't" to "I can." I understand, though, that you may be in a difficult situation. The good news is that you are going to learn how to deal with difficult situations. First let me clarify that if terrible things have happened to you, I am not asking you to admit that it is all your fault or even partially your fault. That is not what owning it is. Owning is doing your best to make the best of what you have. Bad things happen to good people and it is tragic. Owning it is about what we do when adversity comes our way. It will come. It will come in many different forms. The question is, when it comes, what are you going to do about it? What can you do about it today to change where you will be tomorrow. The Four Cornerstones will really come into play here, especially Humility and Forgiveness. Have you ever tried to forgive someone who wronged you or your family? It's not easy. Humility helps you to forgive these people. If you cannot forgive, it's very difficult to move on, as the resentments can eat you alive. Forgiveness heals the one doing the forgiving. It can be more beneficial to the one who can step up and forgive than the one being forgiven. This is heavy-duty stuff, I agree, but you can see that it lets bygones be bygones so that we can make a fresh start.

TO TURN IT AROUND, LISTEN TO YOUR HEART

I found myself struggling in 2009 when the market was at a very, very, ugly, low point that wiped out hundreds of thousands of agents. Sure, I was blaming the market, other agents, friends, L.A., you name it. I had fallen into the trap of blaming others and playing the victim. I was even thinking of moving out of the city of Los Angeles to another state because I wasn't doing well. I wanted so much to blame it on where I lived and that I didn't fit in and that if I only moved to a different area, like Minnesota, or Colorado, maybe things would pick up. So that is exactly what I decided to do! After all, it was California's fault that I was failing, not mine. I had been rocking and rolling in real estate the previous years and although I didn't realize it, my glory days were about to end. About to? They did end. I was broke, homeless, and so embarrassed that I was going to run away from L.A. and my career, and go home to Minnesota with my tail between my legs.

I didn't want to admit that the problem was me. So . . . in denial, I started packing my things and was dead set on moving back to Minnesota. I had family there, I knew more people, and I figured life would be easier there. Anything would be easier than trying to sell houses in Los Angeles. I'd had my run in L.A. and it was over. Screw this town! I blamed my demise on "L.A. people," "the economy," "flakey West Coast buyers and sellers" . . . My attitude was negative, I was extremely bitter, resentful, and angry but I knew it wasn't my fault. I never had a chance out here. This business is cutthroat, and there is no way a small town punk like me would ever have a chance. That is what I kept telling myself. I remember pausing for a moment before I took off and thinking, "Wow, have I become the bitter, negative, resentful Angeleno that everyone used to talk about?" I had become the person I vowed never to become. My heart knew better and it ached. At a deep, deep level it hurt, but my ego had taken over and made me blind, no longer running the ship. I was disregarding my heart and my gut. "Screw 'em all!" was my motto. "I'm outta here!"

My solution? Run away. I loaded up my car and the next day I drove all the way to Palm Desert, California. Stopped to see my friend Bill one night so I could tell one more person how much I hated L.A. and that I'd be better off moving back to Minnesota. The next morning I hit the highway flying and drove for nine hours straight. I hated L.A. It turned on me and that wasn't fair. It was Obama's fault. "Poor me," I thought. I was loving this pity party, though. I was really, really liking it. Blaming everyone else made me feel good and my ego feel even better. It was so easy playing the victim. I kept justifying it and saying to myself that none of it was my fault. That was an easy out. This was fun and I was feeling good . . . for a while. Blaming something and someone else helped me believe that running away was the right solution.

But my heart didn't buy it for one second and I could feel it. At some level I felt like I had broken my own heart by leaving California. Ego quickly shunned that thought and kept me driving.

As I was driving, I looked at the mountains, reliving how much I enjoyed California, the friends, my life, my success in real estate; even the rough days and how I had learned in those dark moments. It made me a bit sad. As much as I wanted to get to Minnesota, I never ever told anyone in my family I was coming back because I didn't want to concern them or get their hopes up before I actually arrived there. As much as I missed my family and Minnesota, something happened to me as I was driving through Colorado. I had the pain inside of what it feels like to give up. To quit. And quitting was completely against my nature. I knew deep down that my life was not a disaster because of where I lived or who was President and what industry I worked in or because of "L.A. people." I knew I was blaming others and remorse was sinking in. Never before in my life had I ever played the victim. Never. I was on the verge of tears as I felt like a failure at that moment. My heart beat as if it were speaking to me, and as I came up over a ridge, I came upon the most amazing snow-capped massive Rocky Mountain view you could ever imagine. I could feel my heart pounding, telling me something. Slamming on the brakes, I pulled over to the side. I had a good cry and sat there on the side of the road sobbing like a child and wondering where it all went wrong.

My heart finally settled down and after some time I looked outside again to see the beautiful snow-peaked mountains everywhere, a lonely highway in front of me and behind me, and not another car in sight. I got out and looked up, looked around, took a few deep breaths, looked straight up into the sky and remember just saying the words, "Thank you." It was the first time I had said thank you in months. I don't know how the words even came out of my mouth. I said it again and again and finally bowed my head to the humbling Rocky Mountains, closed my eyes – and felt serenity for the first time in years.

Then . . . KABLAM!! Like a bolt of lightning, something shot through me like a laser beam and I knew right then that I had to turn around. Running away was not the answer and I knew it that instant. Changing cities would not change my life. God had big plans for me and it was that moment of clarity, that exact moment of Gratitude that helped me finally see the light! I was flying! Super-powers were back! I jumped in my SUV, kicked Ego's ass out the door, left that little pissant on the side of the road, spun out as I ripped the U-turn of my life and started my ass BACK to California! My heart had turned me around.

I loved L.A. and belonged there. I had a mission and a purpose and it was becoming clear to me. I just needed to slow down and do some deep introspection and find out why, when, and how the wheels came off the bus. My situation got bad for one reason:

Me.

I was not being the best I could be, and I knew deep down that if I took full responsibility for my situation, I could change it. Step Five was born.

REALITY CHECK

The first part of Step Five is to do what I call a *reality check*. This means literally looking in the mirror and asking yourself, "What is my part in this situation and what must I do now to change it?" That is what I did. I got back to L.A. and really looked at my life, my surroundings, and how I had derailed my business, my life, and my dreams.

I wanted so badly to blame the economy, the big city, the people; but the truth was that there were tons of realtors making a killing. Realtors always came and went like a revolving door, in with good markets and out with the bad. I saw this as an opportunity to help. I knew I was not your ordinary realtor and my "come to Jesus" moment in Colorado told me to MAN UP! It was time to start being of service, start helping other realtors, starting getting back to what really mattered. Service! (The Four Cornerstones). I asked myself, "What do I need to change about me? What can I learn from the past year? What do I need to do to start selling again?"

Doing this reality check accomplished two things. One was that it humbled me very quickly. It made me see my faults, my flaws, where I needed help. Admitting you are at fault takes courage as well as humility. I will tell you right now, it is impossible to do a reality check unless you are humble and coachable. It's not possible to admit you are wrong or at fault unless you can humble yourself and admit that YOU are the problem. I realized I had many problems, but at the end of the day the reality was that I was the problem.

Edge Rule: If you don't know what the problem is, look in the mirror.

As I looked in the mirror and got out some paper and started writing, I'd ask a question, then write down an answer. Feverishly I wrote about how I lost certain deals, how certain clients didn't use me, how I ended up blowing all my money and finding myself at less than zero. Then I asked myself the million-dollar question. What could I do to make things better? I didn't know. I couldn't think of one thing. It was like I forgot everything. I was housesitting for my friend Sara and her husband, who were out of town, because I had no place to stay and no money for a new apartment. Crushed and utterly defeated, I curled up in a ball on a bathroom floor, wondering what I could possibly do to get out of this mess. Finally after the tears subsided and I was coming out of my near-catatonic state, I sat up and leaned my head against the wall. As I slightly bumped the wall, I jarred a picture frame loose that was directly above my head and it fell to the floor. Luckily it didn't break so I picked it up to place it back on the wall. As I stood there with it in my hands, I looked down to read the words that would change my life. I had seen them before, we all have; but this time they sank in with a new impact.

God, grant me the serenity to accept the things I cannot change, the courage to change the things I can, and the wisdom to know the difference.

I read it again. And then it hit me! *The courage to change the things I can.* That was it! What was the only thing that I had control to change? Myself. In my heart and soul I felt my troubles were over and my prayers were miraculously answered. The keys to the kingdom were all right there in that prayer in the picture frame! It made perfect sense. The only way out of this hole was that I had to change myself. Nothing else. If it was meant to be, it was up to me. I put myself in this predicament and I was going to get myself out.

What was I doing to sink my own ship? For starters, my health was deteriorating because I was neglecting my body, mind, and spirit. I was drinking a ton, I wasn't developing myself and I had let it all go. I looked back on 2008 and 2009 and realized my drinking had got out of control and I didn't even see it. Second, I wasn't attending any passion arena-type events. I was on autopilot, hoping for referrals and/or a miracle sale. In real estate there are no miracles. You either consistently get out there, consistently attend your passion arenas, and consistently develop new relationships, OR, in a few months or at most, a few years, you will consistently be broke. I promise you, your well will dry up. Your pipeline will be completely empty. And that, my friends, is a nightmare you don't want to live if you are a real estate agent.

But that is exactly what happened to me. Third, I realized I was taking clients for granted, assuming they would use me. I wasn't nurturing or developing any relationships. Personal or professional. (Shocker: I was single.) I was becoming selfish; getting cocky and defiant. Could it be that I was that "entitled L.A.-asshole-realtor-guy" that my friends warned me not to become?

As bad as I felt things were, a ray of warm light and a feeling of confidence was slowly washing over my mind and body like nothing I had ever felt. The more I unloaded my issues, the better I felt. For the first time in my life I saw the power of taking full responsibility for EVERYTHING in my life. Just getting all these things down on paper gave me a sense of relief. I felt like Popeye eating spinach; the more things I took responsibility for and wrote down, the better I felt. The awareness and bringing these problems to a head was healthy. So what could I change? It was all right there in the prayer on Sara's bathroom wall. I would later find out that this prayer is famously known as the Serenity Prayer. It was time to use courage to change the only thing I had control over. Myself.

Boozing and partying hard was a problem and I knew it. The next morning I walked into my first AA meeting, admitted I was an alcoholic, and asked for help. That was humbling. I wouldn't "get" AA for quite some time, but that's OK because eventually it "got" me, and I have not drunk since. Also, I faced the fact that I was being extremely unprofessional and rude with clients, so I got busy calling them one at a time to apologize. I had forgotten how to be myself and develop relationships. Many of the Cornerstones had completely crumbled. I called my old sales coach and asked for help. I told him I felt rusty and scare and could really use a hand. I called old friends, apologizing for losing touch and asking them about their lives by way of reconnecting. I even called my parents, told them I was struggling, and let them know I was sorry for being so distant. I was building new bridges to old clients, friends, and family, and it was well received. The reality check and the humility to reach out to others and apologize, ask for help, and start fresh appeared to have stopped the damage. I was becoming me again. I had got lost along the way, but the Four Cornerstones were bringing me back. Gratitude, Service, Humility, and Forgiveness. The four musketeers had returned to save me and reset my mind, body, and spirit. Thank God.

STEPS FOR A REALITY CHECK

1. Look in mirror.
2. Ask yourself two questions: What must you change? What is holding you back?
3. Be brutally honest with your answers.
4. Write those answers down.
5. Go ask someone or something for help with these issues.

The last one was the toughest for me. I used to think asking for help was a sign of weakness; saying you're sorry was a sign of insecurity, and admitting it's my fault was something I should never do. I now see it as a sign of strength. The key to a great reality check is the brutal honesty. You must be ruthlessly honest with yourself. Got it? Remember our old hangout called Denial Isle? This is the time to be unsparingly honest with yourself.

The more honest you are with yourself, the faster you can get to work doing something about your issues. The more reality checks you do, the more you will write down. The more you write down, the better you will become.

Lastly, asking someone for help is how we remain humble and learn about accountability. Asking others for help and sharing your shortcomings will make you accountable, since sharing with others does that organically. The winning process gets under way with the relief of admitting you can't do it alone and need some help. Ever heard the phrase, "Admitting you *have* a problem is the first step toward *solving* the problem"? Admitting it to yourself in your basement while eating pizza watching CSI reruns at three in the morning doesn't count. You have to tell someone else!

You may be saying, "I don't know who to ask," or "There is no one I would want to share my weaknesses with." That is not unusual. We are going to help you build a support group. A dream team. It's important to have a support group, someone to share your stories with, someone who has your back, and someone who holds you accountable. You may already have some great people in your life, or maybe not. Either way, we are going to build this dream team next – but one final warning first.

A WARNING TO THE NEWLY LICENSED AGENT

For as long as you are in real estate, you will see agents blaming the market, their office, where they live, that they never get to be on "floortime" at the right time, how someone else is always getting the "good leads," that they never get a high enough split, the corporate office fee is outrageous, the realtor across the room is annoying, the realtor across the street is annoying, the DRE is driving them crazy, the MLS is not helpful, and on and on and on, blah blah poor me . . . STOP!

I am here to tell you that you are not going to be that person, ever. How do I know? Because you are learning how to sell on the **Edge**. You now have a system and mindset called *owning it* that allows you to rise above and beyond that negativity and victim mentality. My warning is to be extremely cautious whom you hang out with in and around your office during your first year. Most new agents will want to use the excuse that they are not supposed to do well because they are new. Most will want to socialize all day long. Did you know other agents can be WMDs? Most of the people you meet will be gone in less than twelve months, so it's critical you monitor your surroundings. I wish it were not true but it is. I'm hoping my training will change that; but, until then, remind yourself of The Rule of Five Friends and how it applies here. Don't feel the need to get to know every single agent in your office in your first year. Your mission in your first year is to focus and master Steps One, Two, and Three – not to be *Buddy Buddy Who's Your Buddy* with everyone in the office. That guy never sells a thing.

Remember why you are getting into this business. New agents have a tendency to spend a lot of time schmoozing with all the other agents in the office and spending time worrying about who in the office likes them and who doesn't. With **The Edge**, in your first year, focus on Steps One, Two, and Three: Your 80 percent! Keep your head down, listen as much as you can, and march to the beat of your own drum. Then, get your ass OUT of that office and fine Trauma Victims!

The part that breaks my heart and that I am trying to change is that ninety percent of realtors will play the victim. Why? It's easier. It means you now don't have to do anything; that's why people like playing the victim. If someone feels there is nothing they can do about a bad situation, they can sit at home and be miserable. There is a point, however, where you can choose to own it and head toward **The Edge**.

Remember the Teddy Roosevelt quote? The man in the arena? If not, go back and reread it. It is the quote at the beginning of STEP TWO – GET OUT THERE. If you don't take responsibility, you will never have the courage to get in the ring. Or, in my case, back in the ring. I had let things get really bad in 2009 and part of me even had this great plan to move and start in a new career. Something completely different, because that way, no one would know it was my fault. I could sneak out of real estate, forget about my terrible year, and lie to people, telling them, "I'm going to do something new. Real estate is not something I ever really liked anyway." It was ludicrous. I loved real estate, but now I was going to quit and move to a different state, all to avoid letting anyone know I was failing and in trouble. It happens to the best of us, my friends. But the true champions admit they were at fault, ask for help, and get back on their feet and back in the ring. That's the direction I took.

Among the *Rocky* movies, *Rocky III* is one of my favorites. Rocky Balboa gets beat so bad, he says he is done and will never fight again. Adrienne knows he doesn't really mean that. She knows it's just an excuse, but she wants to know the real reason so she pushes him into a corner and forces him to do a reality check. "What is the real reason you're quitting?" You have never quit anything in your life! Tell me, Rocky! Why?" It's at that moment when Rocky screams out . . .

"Because I'm scared! OK? For the first time in my life, I'm scared!"
-Rocky Balboa, *Rocky III*

You will get scared some days, but admitting it is OK. Admitting you are scared, vulnerable, and sometimes don't know it all, only means you're human. The more honest, open, and vulnerable you are, the more clients will relate to you, because they will feel your integrity and honesty. This honesty will build trust and attract customers to you, as opposed to your always having to chase them. You are getting to a new level when you can do this sincerely. It is rare when someone can admit they are scared or ask for help, but opening yourself up like this is exactly what **The Edge** is all about. Be yourself. Be human. Clients will appreciate your humility all day long over the "super-closer slick salesman" who has all the answers. It worked out pretty well for Rocky. It will for you too.

REALITY CHECK SUMMARY

1. Look directly in the mirror. (Do this once a week.)
2. Ask yourself the following: What must change? What is holding me back?
3. Be brutally honest with your answers.
4. Wrote down your answers.
5. Ask for help.

In addition to the two main questions, you can add your own. For example: What can I do to be a better person/agent/parent/son? What current behavior in my life should I change right now because it is holding me back? What adjustments can I make today to work on these issues? If I could do one thing this week that would make a tremendous different in another person's life, what would that be?

You got into this business to work on your own, have more freedom and make more money. You will have all that if you take full responsibility for everything in your life: the good, the bad, and the ugly. If you forget, just remember the words of our friend Richard Roma, played by Al Pacino in the greatest real estate film of all time, *Glengarry Glen Ross*:

> *"Your excuses are your own, pal."*
> -Richard Roma, *Glengarry Glen Ross*

I keep this line on the wall in my office to remind me never to play the victim role. Do whatever it takes to remind yourself that excuses are deadly, because they prevent necessary change. This is where having a good wingman, best friend, or spouse who can call you out comes in handy. For now, you have to first learn how to be accountable to yourself. Most training programs will teach you to have accountability partners, and this is a good thing. I know agents that have thirty-two accountability partners for this, that, and the other thing, but none of it will make a difference unless you first take responsibility for your own actions. It starts with you. It starts with you taking responsibility for everything in your life. Making this decision will change your life.

Edge Rule: Your excuses are your own.

Someone who is crystal clear on this concept is Tom Brady, six-time Super Bowl Champion. (New edition of this book, he may be more by now! #GOAT) I love watching Tom Brady in an interview, especially after he loses, because he always owns it. When he loses, if you notice, he will say that his team played well and *he* made the mistakes. When they win, he credits his team and *never* talks about himself. It is an amazing thing to watch and learn from. Win: he credits team and others. Loss: he takes complete responsibility. Look around you in life and take notice of who plays the victim vs. who really owns it. The first step to mastering these 6 Steps of **The Edge** is to be aware of these concepts. You may take some time to *get* this program, but don't worry, the more you work at it, you'll find good things happening and I promise, eventually . . . it will get you. Don't worry, you won't be alone. You will have the help of your *Dream Team*.

CHAPTER 22

BUILD YOUR DREAM TEAM

Unlike Tom Brady and other professional athletes, you may not have a coach, a nutritionist, a trainer or an accountability partner keeping an eye on your so he can tell you what adjustments to make. Most pro athletes, like Tiger Woods, have a whole slew of people on their team. These people comprise their support groups that the athletes work with to get better and better because champions know that they cannot succeed alone. So how do we do it in early on in real estate? Maybe you don't have the money for a fancy real estate coach, or you may be single and don't have a spouse for moral support, or you are on your own and don't know many people. What can you do to build support for yourself?

You'll build your *Dream Team*. A dream team is your support group. It is your core group of three to five people who will love you, support you, be there for you, hold you up, lift you up, carry you at times, help you get better and maybe even safe your life. I have found that if you have three key people in your life, it is impossible to fail. DREAM TEAM = WINGMAN+BESTY+HERO

Real estate can be a long, lonely road. Most people think you will have tons of friends and confidantes because, after all, doesn't everybody love real estate agents? No. They don't. The truth is that it can be a long, lonely road, especially when you are new. I love what I do and there is no better feeling than helping someone buy or sell a house, but when the transaction is over, I have often felt like a cowboy that rides off at the end of those westerns. Everyone is happy, the buyer got their house, the seller has moved on, and once again, the cowboy-hero/agent has saved the day and rides off into the sunset. My good friend, Barry, who is one of the top agents in the Los Angeles/San Fernando Valley area often shared the same feelings. He has more clients and more deals than anyone I have ever known and he had this to say about his support group outside of work.

> *"I'm very selective about who I spend my off-time with. It's good to develop relationships and spend time with potential future clients, but too much and you'll burn out. It's just as important to forget about real estate for a while and spend time with your friends and family. They keep me grounded, keep me sane."*
>
> -Barry Dantagnan
>
> (Top 1% of all Coldwell Banker Agents, USA)

Tom Brady has a team. Kobe Bryant had his teammates and coaches. Even corporate salespeople have co-workers and managers on the sales team. Who do you have in real estate when you first get started? Just you. If you don't get some kind of support team on and off the court, or if you try to figure out this business all on your own with no support group at all, you will soon be gonzo. Time to build your Dream Team! Your goals will be:

1. To find a life mentor NOT in the business (HERO).
2. To identify or find your best friend NOT in the business (BESTY).
3. To find your wingman, like a best friend who IS in the business (WINGMAN).

For the ladies out there, you can call this last one your wingwoman if you want! For now, I will use "wingman" for both. These three key people will genuinely support your new endeavor and dreams and cheer you on, no matter what. They will stay loyal and true to you forever – and they will take some time to identify. The question now is, how do you find the right people? You have to know what to look for, and a key ingredient for anyone on your Dream Team is that they want NOTHING from you except to see you be happy. They will also make you feel safe, sane, smart, sexy, and successful! They will always have your back. Making sense?

Dream Team Member Requirements: **They want nothing from you.**
They have your back, no matter what.

Look around in your life for these people. Perhaps you already have someone like a hero, a besty, or a wingman already. The key is that you will now consciously build a support team. You may already have some of these people in your life or you may not. Either way, it's OK. It's time to begin building and searching for your Dream Team members. This group will play an invaluable role in your long-term success.

The Hero is a mentor, but not a mentor in your career; a mentor in life. Note the difference. A hero is usually well over sixty years of age (think lots of gray hair) and is someone you admire deeply. Grandparents make amazing heroes. The hero has had tons of experience in life; the rest doesn't matter. This person usually has nothing to do with real estate. Your hero is not some top agent you aspire to be like or someone in the field that is coaching you or helping you with work. I use the word "hero" because these types of people are the real heroes of the world today. They will make time for you just because. They will listen to your situation at any time and they have lived long enough on this planet and been through enough tough times in their own life so that they can advise you accordingly.

This person could come in many different forms. Yes, it could be your grandparent. It could also be a teacher or college professor from your past, possibly a neighbor woman who lives on your block and is now the "little old lady" you help with her groceries. Dean Malevich was the first hero of mine when I was in college (although I didn't realize it at the time).

Two very important distinctions of the hero are, first: they do NOT work in the real estate industry, nor have they ever; and, second, they are not one of your parents. The reason for these distinctions is that it's important to get a different perspective from those in the industry or someone in your immediate family. The hero is not to be confused with a mentor in your career. The hero is your *life* mentor, not a business mentor. You can usually spot them by their patience, tolerance, humility, kindliness, love, and unconditional support. I realize this sounds a lot like great parents; you're correct about that. For many of us, if we are lucky enough, our parents are our heroes, mine included. However, for your Dream Team, you need an additional hero for that different perspective. It's essential to get a different twist sometimes, and maybe you can be more open and frank with this other person. Make sense? #goodjob. When you need some wisdom and profoundly thoughtful advice, your hero will provide this every time. A hero will never tell you what you want to hear. They will tell you what you need to hear, and you can learn more in five seconds than you did in five years.

My Uncle Wilfred (one of my many heroes) was in his final days at the hospital. The family members were all sitting around his bed. It turned out that I was the only one of the younger generation in the room who was not married. My older cousins were giving me grief and poking fun and one of them said in front of us all, "So Mark, when *are* you going to get married?" Everyone laughed and I responded with, "When I find the right person, I guess." At that moment, Uncle Wil slowly raised himself a little. Everyone stopped talking, as he hadn't really been moving or saying much up until that point. He leaned toward me, looked me in the eye and said:

"Mark . . . it's not about 'finding' the right person. It's about 'becoming' the right person."

-Fr. Wilfred Illies (1923-2003)

My Uncle, Hero to me and many others.

The Besty is simply your best friend. Do you have a best friend? Maybe not. Not everyone does. It's OK. However, you are going to start looking for one. The Besty is crucial for when you just want to forget about real estate and go have fun or let loose if you're hanging on too tightly. Besties allow us to be ourselves and will always keep us in check. I love my best friends because they keep me grounded and down to earth. They also remind me to stay true to myself when I drift off the path. "Besty" = best friend.

The Wingman is your partner in real estate victory! Your Goose if you are Maverick. Your Butch Cassidy if you are the Sundance Kid. Your Jerry Rice if you are Joe Montana. Your Jimmy if you are Robert (for you Led Zeppelin fans). This person is DEFINITELY someone in the real estate world. Definitely a real estate agent. The Wingman does not necessarily have to work at your same office or company, but you two are inseparable in the work world. For me, it was my friend Joe Convery. I met Joe during my first week in real estate. He had already been in the business for almost five years when we met, and later on our careers would cross paths and he became, still is, and will always be my Wingman.

So this is a brief picture of each, but let's talk about why you need to start with these three as your dream team, and how to find them. In the beginning, you may not have any of these people in your life; however, don't beat yourself up. It's OK. You may not even have been aware of the power of a good mentor or hero, or understood why you needed a wingman, but most people understand a "Besty," so let's start with that as we explain each team member in more detail.

THE BESTY

The Besty reminds us that just being ourselves is more than OK and always enough.

If you recall, the very first step in **Selling on the Edge** is to be yourself. As you begin this business, the money, the new freedom, the entrepreneurial world can change you, sometimes in good ways; sometimes not so good. Having a best friend that you can stay in touch with and see on a regular basis will help keep the real authentic you intact. The Besty usually has absolutely nothing to do with real estate. Just be careful if *all* your best friends are people who are in the real estate business. That can make it hard to get away sometimes when you need a break. It can make recharging difficult. There will be days when you want nothing to do with real estate and those are the days when you can just go kick it with your BESTY! If your besty is also a real estate agent, it could be hard to forget about the business for a while. So I recommend finding someone outside of the real estate industry for this vital Dream Team position.

When I first got started selling houses, I didn't have a Besty in L.A. yet. I had a lot in Minnesota, so when I wanted to take a breather and get away from real estate for a while, I would fly back to Minnesota to see my best friend, Hawk, whom I met in college. Hawk was my besty and he had a way of keeping things in perspective. We could go two months or two years without seeing each other, and within seconds of getting in touch it would be like we never skipped a beat (a true sign of a besty).

Another true sign of all of these people on your Dream Team is that they don't want anything from you except for you to succeed and be genuinely happy. The common thread of everyone on your Dream Team will be unconditional love and support. The best part about having a best friend is that you can just be you. You don't have to play any role or act any certain way, because you can always be yourself around your Besty. This kind of quality time is essential for remaining authentic. Being yourself is at the core of this program and your Besty always keeps you true to yourself. Spending time with your best friend keeps you grounded because they help you remember who you really are and that you are perfectly acceptable exactly the way we are.

As you grow in real estate and gain some success, it might be possible to forget who you are and lose your original authenticity and sense of self. That spark, that edge, that uniqueness that makes you different is one of the most important keys to this system. Maintaining that unique spark that only you have is your secret weapon. It will be tempting to go in directions the real you doesn't want to go, just because everyone seems to be doing it. Remain true to who you are deep down and hang on to that unique dimension. Your Besty will help ensure that this happens – as well as keeping you in check and reminding you where you came from. Most importantly, their unconditional love of you, exactly as you are, ensures that you always keep being that same person. **The Besty reminds us that just being ourselves is more than OK and always enough.**

THE WINGMAN

When sh@#*t would hit the fan in life and in real estate, and I hit some rough patches, my best friend (Besty) was there, no matter what. Sometimes, however, Hawk couldn't help me with a real estate problem. So what was I to do then? Traditional real estate says go talk to the manager, or someone in your office or another agent. But this is easier said than done. What if you don't like the manager? What if the other agents in the office are threatened by you and don't want to help? (This is often the case with new licensees.) I am not saying that this will be true for you. People are very helpful for the most part, but this is about finding someone that you know, beyond a shadow of a doubt, has your back all the time. How about a loyal ally in the field that you know has no ulterior motive (like making money off you). How about someone who has nothing to lose by telling you the truth, because they are not making a penny off you?

Bottom line: most managers are making money off you. So, sorry, they cannot be your Wingman. Other agents in your office can be competing with you and may not tell you how it really is. I suggest finding a wingman at another company; or, if they are with your company that's OK, just make sure they are working out of a slightly different area or simply a different office within the same company. An ideal Wingman has the following characteristics:

WINGMAN CHARACTERISTICS

-Wingman must be a residential realtor.
-Wingman must be doing real estate full time.
-From the second you meet Wingman, you completely 100% trust them.
-This person will defend you to no end, cover your ass, have your back, and be there for you in life and especially in your real estate career, no matter what.
-Wingman cannot be your manager.
-Wingman cannot be someone in your immediate office.
-You can always count on Wingman.

This Dream Team member will take some time to find. When you do, you will know it and they will know it too. Do not rush this one. It will happen organically. Just as it did when you met your best friend. The only difference is that your wingman is a best friend who is also a residential real estate agent.

Remember meeting your best friend? Take a moment now to picture it. Go back to the very instant you met that person. Can you remember the time, the place, and the occasion? You probably clicked from the get-go. There was that magic spark and then later on that person surfaced in your life and you had yourself a BESTY! As you begin in real estate, the same thing will happen as you meet other realtors. You will simply know when you've found your wingman, as the relationship will develop naturally. Over time you will find someone you like talking about real estate with. You will like their perspective and they will like yours. A respect and admiration will develop and the two of you will have an uncanny, magical professional chemistry together. This magic will allow you to solve problems together that others may not. It will just flow. You will never find them draining to be around, and they will feel the same about you. Both of you will leave each other feeling energized and inspired after every time you hang out. Getting the idea of a Wingman yet?

Let me clarify one thing. This is not going to be someone you are partnering up with financially. A wingman is not someone you are going to list and sell every property with and share your commissions. Your wingman is a loyal ally and "best-friend-like" agent in the field, someone you keep an eye on in a good way, and vice versa. You have their back, they have yours. It's a relationship you will have forever if it is the right Wingman.

HOW I MET BIG COUNTRY

Your Wingman is probably the most pivotal and important member of your Dream Team -- vital to long-term success in real estate. Without one, you will not survive long. I was almost ready to give up when I met Joe "Big Country" Convery. I coined the name "Big Country" for him because he's six foot three, former MMA fighter and a guy you don't want to mess with, personally or professionally. Seemed like a good wingman to me! He felt like the older brother I never had. The moment I met him, I knew this was something different.

It was my first year in the business and I was seeing an open house forty miles from where I lived. I got stuck there, as I forgot my wallet and had only a few miles left in the tank. This other agent was walking out the door, quickly spotted the troubled look on my face, and asked, "Something wrong?" Before

I could even tell him the full embarrassing story, he was handing me a twenty and he zoomed off. I never even caught his name, but I remember thinking that he looked like some NBA star that ESPN was always referring to as "Big Country." Six months later I walked into a random open house and there he was. Spotted him instantly, couldn't mistake this guy. Huge smile, tons of energy, it was indeed Big Country! I told him I was the guy he lent twenty bucks to a few months back and asked if I could repay him or take him to lunch sometime. He opted for lunch and the rest was history.

He had a few years' jump on me in the business, and he worked at a completely different company. It just felt right. We started having lunch regularly. We cracked each other up. He really knew his stuff, and even though I was new, he liked my point of view as well. We had similar goals and dreams. We motivated each other to sell more, learn more, and be better agents. I trusted Joe with every fiber of my being. He would buy the sandwiches when I was broke and other times I would buy, it didn't matter. He was selfless, generous, and we wanted the best for each other. We both hated wasting time at office meetings, so we started our own at a local sandwich shop: just us. Office meeting of two. We would meet once a week and tell each other how our deals were going . . . or not going. It was like a sales class and therapy session all in one. All for free! It was good to have someone to talk out problems with and figure out solutions together. I felt it was the missing piece of the puzzle. I no longer felt like that solo cowboy. I remember thinking (like the pilots in *Top Gun*) I finally had a wingman.

Real estate can be very cutthroat. On days when you feel like it's you against the world, you need a wingman that you know is on your side. There will be some real life dogfights over your career and your wingman will be your one loyal ally in the field that you can always count on. Always. It will take time, but keep your head up and an eye out for this person. I promise you, they will surface over time, naturally, organically.

You will go through some deals which, through no fault of your own, will go haywire. Some deal gets cancelled and now a commission check for $15,000 that you were expecting just before the holiday is gone. Gone! You will want to quit and move to Mars. It can be painful. You will have some serious crash and burn moments and I am telling you that if you don't have a wingman to help you back on your feet, it can be hard to recover. You might not make it back. Real estate can be brutal, my friends. B-R-U-T-A-L.

It's not like the shows you see on TV. You will make mistakes, fall down, get yelled at, feel like quitting, lose out on a big listing – and your wingman is the one who will get you through. And if you hang on, I promise you, good things are coming your way.

"Never, never, never give up."
-Winston Churchill

Joe and I would go on to do some of the biggest deals of our careers together and it was all because of that fateful day I ran out of gas and met my wingman. Find a wingman . . . or you might not make it home . . . literally! ☺

Edge Rule: You never, ever leave your wingman.

THE HERO

Heroes remind us to be grateful for the one thing we can often lose appreciation for . . . Life.

I feel society today does not spend enough time with older people. Can you help me? People don't visit nursing homes much; they're scared to walk into hospitals and don't want to attend funerals. We gravitate toward youthful things, everyone is busy making a living, running and running and running, and most don't even know where they are running to. Over the next twelve months as you begin your new career, can you find time to go visit some elderly people? Wherever you choose to go; it's up to you. I know you are saying that this had nothing to do with selling houses, but I am telling you that it does. Because it has to do with you. It will make you better. It will give you an intangible edge that you cannot learn in the classroom, from a book, or even from me. The only way to find out what a Hero will do for you is to go and meet one. Can you commit to doing this just once per month in your first year, and then let me know how your experience was?

Most people do not like to face the aging and the dying. It can be uncomfortable, awkward; and, yes, sometimes even a little stinky. Well, I am asking you to step up and spend more time with older people, dying people. Take some time to go visit the sick or the elderly in assisted living centers. Get to know that old man or old lady in your building. Say hi, ask them to go to lunch, bring them flowers once a week or take them on a walk in the city. By doing these simple acts, you will learn innately what a hero is and what a hero can ultimately do for you. These people have paved the way for all of us. If you are lucky enough to find your hero (and you will), do everything you can to spend time with him or her. It will change your life.

A hero has a lot of wisdom because they have a lot of experience in one thing: Life. Your hero does not have to be someone who is in a nursing home or hospital, but they could be. The only rule about heroes is that, like all other members of the Dream Team, it's best if they are outside your immediate circle because it will expand your horizons; give you maybe a slightly different perspective. And maybe that will be just the difference you need in your life to change everything. This is the power heroes have. Like great parents, a hero will teach you things you never could have imagined, make you feel safe, secure; and leave you knowing that it will all work out. Your hero could be your grandmother, the dean of your college, your uncle or aunt that you love seeing but never spend enough time with. It could be someone you befriend at the hospital or in your neighborhood.

Heroes have already lived a long life and have done it all, so to speak. Things don't faze or frazzle them the way they might faze someone younger. Heroes offer wisdom, experience, and life knowledge that will help you in all areas of your life. They appreciate spending five minutes with you, and in return they will teach you things just by sitting with them and doing nothing. All you have to give them is your presence and you will walk away every time with a new appreciation of life. Spending time with your Hero is a magical moment between two people that you cannot find in the office, at work, or with friends. Your Hero will have a magical calm. It is called serenity. They won't *tell* you what you want to hear; they will *show* you what you need to see.

HEROES TEACH US WHAT REALLY MATTERS

My Grandmother Adeline was the first HERO that I can remember, although I didn't know it at the time. She was a strong, courageous, independent woman who raised two kids as a single mom. She raised my Dad to be an amazing father and I would get to see her every so often as grandkids do if they are lucky enough to know their grandparents.

I was a few years out of college and I didn't know what I wanted to do. I was having lemonade with my Grandma, who was not very well at the time. I told her I didn't know what to do with my life and asked for some advice, as she was quite the entrepreneur back in her day. She replied, "Do what you love, and love what you do." Then she stopped talking. That shot through my heart like a zinger. These HEROES have this magic ability to utter the most amazing one-liners that put it all in perspective. I said, "I think I love teaching but I am scared there is no money in it." She said, "Forget about money, Mark, you give it all away in the end anyway." Heroes do more for us than teach us about life. They help us understand compassion and patience, and this is essential to becoming a great real estate agent. Ultimately Heroes will help you keep your foundation solid. A solid foundation means your Four Cornerstones of Gratitude, Service, Humility, and Forgiveness are all intact.

*If your Besty keeps you accountable to Step One of **The Edge** (Being Yourself) and your Wingman keeps you accountable to Step Two of **The Edge** (Getting Out There), then the Hero will keep you accountable to the foundation of **The Edge** (The Four Cornerstones). In essence, the Dream Team is your accountability team that keeps you accountable naturally, organically, and unconsciously. The Besty keeps you true to yourself so you can continue to bring out the you in you. The Wingman makes sure you keep getting out there and doing what you need to do to sell more. Finally, the Hero puts life in perspective and brings you back to what matters most, like Gratitude, Service, Humility, and Forgiveness. The Dream Team helps us get back on track when we lose our way and takes us to new levels we never thought possible. The Dream Team is an automatic built-in accountability system. This is intense, so you might want to go back and reread this paragraph.*

For most new agents, it takes time to grasp the power of a great Dream Team, but just know that, without one, it is impossible to reach the highest level in business and in life. Besty+Wingman+Hero=Your Dream Team! Build one.

Edge Rule: No one succeeds alone.

If you get a chance, rent the movie *Scent of a Woman*, with Al Pacino; then pick up the book, *Tuesdays with Morrie*. Both stories will help you understand what a hero really looks like more than I could ever explain. They are similar stories in that both are about a young man who befriends a much older, dying man and the unique relationship that develops. Over time, you may have multiple Heroes, Besties and Wingmen, but the important thing is that you are becoming aware of who specifically is in your life and who you need in your life if you are going to make it big. If you have the right support team in place, life and work will be a lot more enjoyable and lucrative. If you have the right *Dream Team* in place, the possibilities are endless.

WHY WE CALL THEM "CRABBY"

What they don't teach you in real estate school (or in any school that I have ever been in, for that matter) is that who you hang around with the most can either make you or break you. I now see why my parents were so paranoid if my friends in high school drank, did drugs, or got into trouble. My parents always wanted to meet my friends before I spent too much time with them. They also wanted to meet the parents of my friends. At the time, it pissed me off, as it probably did all kids. However, now I am grateful that they watched over me like that. I came across some bad apples that I thought were fun and cool, but my parents pointed out that staying out late, drinking, smoking, and skipping classes did not make these kids cool. My parents knew that who I hung around with would affect me, and they wanted the best for me. Thanks, Mom and Dad. Nicely done.

As an adult, no one tells us who we can and cannot spend time with. Building a Dream Team will make sure you are surrounded by good people as you begin your new career. Don't take this step lightly. Take a moment now to take a close look at who you spend most of your time with. If you think you already have a great support group, that is great! However, now that you are running your own business, doing something exciting, and venturing off to do something with your life, it may rub some friends and even some family members the wrong way. (Believe it or not, sometimes even our closest friends, deep down, don't want us to grow or change as they fear they may be left behind.) You have to do a reality check on your relationships, just as you do one on yourself. You with me here? A reality check on yourself AND on your relationships. Are the people you are running with and hanging out with on a regular basis good for you? Do they really want the best for you? Be honest. You see, humans are funny creatures. People pretend they want the best for you, but do they really? I hope so and believe most do; but sometimes it doesn't work out that way.

Let me share a story about the seven crabs in the bucket. If you place seven crabs in a bucket, they will sit there for approximately two to three minutes to adjust to their new surroundings. Then, close to the three-minute mark, one crab will begin to climb up, attempting to get out of the bucket. However, just as the crab gets to the top, one of the other crabs will inevitably reach up with its own claws and pull the first crab back down to the bottom of the bucket. A few minutes will go by and a different crab will start to climb up the side of the bucket. Sure enough, another crab, or maybe a couple crabs now, will reach for that one and pull it down. This goes on for an extended period of time until eventually NONE of the crabs any longer even try to leave the bucket and they don't know why. I know why. They don't try anymore because they know they will just be pulled down. Ever heard someone say, "Why even try?" Now you know it's because they have been pulled down in life one too many times. Humans can be just like crabs. People can directly or indirectly pull you down and it's important that you be aware of this. Otherwise, you could unconsciously and unknowingly end up at the bottom of the bucket, with a bunch of crabs, afraid to even try. Make sense?

You have to build a Dream Team with people who want nothing but the best for you. No crabs allowed! A great Dream Team not only wants to help you OUT of the bucket; they want to see you discover new territories, reach higher ground, and achieve bigger successes than even they could have imagined for you. I am sorry to point this out, but some of your friends are not going to want you to succeed. They could be crabs. They are going to tell you that you are "making a mistake getting into real estate." They will even use humor to passive-aggressively pull you down, saying things like, "I thought people only got into real estate as a last resort." Or, "What do you possibly know about selling houses?" Or, "I am only saying this because I want the best for you, but don't you think you'd be better at something else?" They will tell you things like, "Maybe you should hang onto your old job, just in case things don't work out," or, "You aren't really serious about doing this house stuff, are you?" Or my favorite: "I love you, but don't you think it's time to get a real job?"

Edge Rule: Avoid the crabs.

Beware of the crabs trying to pull you down. A red flag for anyone who is trying to pull you down is anyone who makes you feel less than. Anyone who makes you doubt yourself. Anyone who says you are not good enough. Anyone who tries to keep you in the bucket. Be aware of this fact of human/crab nature and building your Dream Team will be that much easier. Remember the BLAPPA BLAPPA BLAPPA fraternity? That was one giant crab bucket that I was lucky to escape from. At the time I didn't realize it, but I had the Dean as my Hero, Pete as my Besty, and these people helped me see and do things that I couldn't see and do on my own.

I promise you, as you begin to change while you progress in this program, some of the people that you currently have relationships with will fade away. It's sad, but the reality is that as you change, not everyone else will want to adjust accordingly. You will undoubtedly part ways with some people in your life. Although it may be hard to let them go, there is no growth without change. This is natural and normal as you achieve success. Embrace it and know that it is a sign that you are on the right path.

The flip side to that coin is that although you will undoubtedly say goodbye to certain people, you will develop new relationships. Within twelve months, if you focus and own it (like Steps Four and Five teach you), you will find yourself surrounded by some amazing new people and doing things beyond your wildest dreams. When I started to do my thing and no longer care what others thought, I lost touch with some great people. It was unfortunate, but necessary in order for me to grow. While I love all the people I have met along the way, not everyone will be with you forever. Sometimes you have to let the crabs go or say goodbye to certain people who may not be healthy for you. If you want to change your life, you have to change it. Growing is never easy, that is for sure, but if nothing changes, then nothing changes.

Edge Rule: If nothing changes, nothing changes.

Agents come and go, deals come and go, clients come and go; and even certain friends will come and go. Your Dream Team will always be in your corner. No matter what. As you build your Dream Team, I have only one final piece of advice: choose wisely, my friends. CHOOSE WISELY. Be very careful whom you select as your Wingman, your Besty and your Hero. They must surface organically and you will know these people as time goes on. The important thing is to find and build this support group and stay in touch with them. Your Besty will keep you grounded and help you remain true to yourself. Your Wingman will help you soar to new heights in the real estate world. And lastly, your Hero will put it all in perspective and share with you from a fund of amazing stories and insights that will not only change the way you see the world and your situation in life, but how you see yourself. In the end, the Dream Team will help you bring out the real you in you! And that is what **The Edge** is all about: Being yourself, surrounding yourself with great people, and making a great living selling houses.

Caution, though: All work and no play makes Jack or Jill a dull real estate agent. So let's get to our last, but not least, very important Sixth Step. It's time to have some fun.

CHAPTER 23

STEP 6: HAVE FUN

"Be desireless."

- The Buddha

Main Mission: Detach from the Outcome.

Main Moves: Reward.

Recharge.

I sat in my apartment writing this chapter right after experiencing one of the biggest heartaches of my life. I had just been dumped. I met this girl at the airport over Thanksgiving and it seemed to be the match made in heaven. Both our flights were delayed, so we ended up talking all night as we waited for our flights home. I thought it was fate in the works for something bigger on my horizon. We stayed in touch and went on a date the next week when we got back. I could hardly speak when we saw each other for our first date and she seemed to feel the same. She was as stunning as ever, her eyes lit up the street as she walked out the door of her apartment. Her smell almost knocked me out; her scent was angelic. Her demeanor and presence sent an arrow through my heart just like at the airport that fateful day before Thanksgiving.

We saw each other almost every day until Christmas, getting to know each other. Everything was going wonderfully. We went to dinner during Christmas week to say goodbye, as we were both going home to see our families once again; mine in Minnesota, hers in Hawaii. We had a great night and I was going to drive her to the airport the next day, as she was leaving before me. Early in the morning I got a call from her. Her friend had the ride covered, as her friend was also going to Hawaii on the same flight, and I no longer needed to give her a ride. I instantly knew this was trouble. I was crushed. Buried. Game over.

I thought maybe there was a chance I'd see her when she got back. I never did. I never saw her again. You see, this amazing person did not want to move forward in the relationship. That is code for, "I got dumped." I can laugh about it now because it happens to all of us. If it has never happened to you, you are not human or you have never dated. For those of you who have experienced this kind of rejection, I feel your pain. There is no worse pain, my friends, than to be heartbroken. (Well, on second thought, falling out of escrow on a forty million dollar house one time was pretty bad, but heartbreak was up there in the top two for sure.) I was buried, but I knew I would recover. This girl and I were just not in the cards. I had to accept it. I was down, but not out.

Edge Rule: Disappointment does not equal disaster.

Having my heart crushed for the first time in a while reminded me that we have zero control over anyone or anything. All we can control is our own thoughts and actions. I took a risk, put myself out there, had a great six weeks with a new friend – but it didn't work out. I respected her decision, knew it was just not meant to be, and in the end I was OK with that. I thought about trying to push it, but I knew it was o er. Her actions told the story. Actions always tell the story. Although I was hurt and felt rejected, I accepted the situation for what it was and moved on.

In any relationship, you cannot force anything. With **The Edge** we don't "sell," "push," or "convince." That is old school antics. I have said over and over that you can't "sell" someone a house. They either want it or they don't. You may force one or two deals over the top or "convince" someone to buy, but if you push someone into something they deep down do not want, you will regret it. The client will also regret it and resent you for pushing them into something they did not want. The result is that you end up doing more harm than good by trying to force your way and the relationship will end. Not good.

THE ART OF ACCEPTANCE

When you are cultivating relationships out there, if someone just doesn't want to spend time with you, that is their choice and there is nothing you can do but accept their decision. Real estate is a lot like dating: not everyone is going to want to go out with you. Meaning, you are going to meet people who don't want to work with you. Not because you aren't professional enough or good enough or smart enough, but just because. The lesson here is to not let it stop you or make you pull focus or deter you from your goals.

In your first year, a lot of people are going to say no to you. This rejection can really take a personal toll on new agents personally. No one likes rejection, but I am here to tell you that it is the nature of the real estate beast. If you want to make it big in real estate, you have to be willing to get rejected, crash and burn, get your fail on, and understand it is by falling down that we learn. Remember the Main Mission in Step Two? Get your fail on! Embracing failure, combined with detaching from the outcome, will make you unstoppable in your new business and in life.

As painful as it was to be shot down by the girl from the airport, it reminded me that maybe I needed to start practicing the art of acceptance a little more in all areas of my life by *detaching from the outcome*. Clients may choose to work with you or not, just as you choose to work with some clients or not. Sometimes it works and sometimes it doesn't; that, my friends, is life in Real Estate City. No one bats a thousand, even Derek Jeter didn't, but if you keep getting out there and understand the important and value of "getting your fail on," I promise you that good things will happen. I don't like failing. I don't like being rejected. But I remind myself it's as important as winning, because adversity paves the way to our final destination. If everything were easy, great moments would not be so worthwhile. Working on your own, starting your own business, getting your real estate license and selling houses is not always an easy journey. But that is why your life will be so much more fulfilling when you do start kicking a$$. Embrace the adversity, the rejection, and the failures, and know inside that this is a necessary rite of passage for the great agent. This mindset will help rejection and adversity inspire instead of defeating you. The mindset that failure is your friend will change your life because it will allow you to do one thing that most agents are afraid to do. It will help you take more chances. Which is where I need you to be. If you can take chances every day, you will be rewarded. Take chances at your passion arenas, by sharing your ideas, or by telling a client how you really feel, even if you think it may upset them – or even by asking someone out on a date!

I will never forget when I did that with my friend from the airport that Thanksgiving weekend. I took a chance and it didn't work out. But I got something later. I got the inspiration to write this chapter, and for that I will be forever grateful. Yes, I'm single now, but I know someone is out there for me. I now know that God has other plans for me right now. He wants me to be focused on this book and this program, so that is how I'm looking at it. By detaching from the outcome, we learn that maybe something even better than we could have anticipated is going to happen. Can you think of a situation where this happened for you? I have learned to LOVE detaching from the outcome because I know that what's in store for me is better than I could have imagined. It is easy to forget this simple notion, and that is why it is a necessary step in this system. Each moment we have is a gift; expecting things to work out the way YOU want them to will sometimes get you in trouble. You will know you have mastered this Step when you can accept any situation and detach from the outcome, knowing God may have a better plan in store for you. I will take His plan over mine any day of the week and twice on Sundays!

TURN IT OVER

I want you to have a foundation (The Four Cornerstones). I want you to have a game plan (The Six Steps). I want you to have a specific selling system when you find potential clients (**Sales Triage™**). But then when you are out there working or meeting with clients, just throw it all away and be yourself. You can only do your part and the rest is in God's hands. So turn it over! Turn it over to the universe, to God, or to whatever higher power you want to turn it over to. "Turning it over" simply means you are letting go of the outcome. I have gone on hundreds of listing appointments expecting to get the listing, thinking I was going to "will" it my way – and my desire to control the outcome did one thing. It stopped me from focusing on the most important thing, which was not the outcome, but the person in front of me at that very moment. I would get buried time and time again, as all the traditional sales training I had taken told me to "GET IT SIGNED!" "Don't worry about anything else until you walk out with a contract!" "Always Be Closing!" It just wasn't working. Luckily, I learned to detach from the outcome before it was too late. Many who are new never learn.

What so many new agents do in the beginning is that they are so focused on what they are trying to achieve, or what they are going to say next, or where they are going to go next, or what the commission is, that they are completely absent mentally and before they know what hit them, the client is asking them to leave. That is why everyone in the industry jokes that all agents have A.D.D. The truth is, we don't. But if you are busy thinking of the outcome (the cash!) and not the present moment, you will look like you are not paying attention. Your client will sense this, and you are done. Letting go of the outcome will solve that problem by putting you in the moment and focusing your attention where it should be, on the person in front of you.

> *If you are thinking about winning the race while you are running it,*
> *you are not focused on what you should be focused on.*

As I write this, I have learned that relationships in real estate are very similar to those in your personal life. We have to surrender to the knowledge that we really can't control anything or anyone. People march to the beat of their own drums, and that will never change. When you are holding on too tightly and have too many expectations, it is a sign that you have lost sight of the Four Cornerstones. It has never failed me. Whenever things seem off or I find myself "expecting" outcomes, I now see it as a sign that I am off-balance. I know that kind of thinking will get me in trouble and I need to look at my foundation. The Four Cornerstones.

I was crushed that things didn't work out with the girl from the airport, but I was grateful for the chance of meeting her. Let's look back to the Four Cornerstones – Gratitude, Service, Humility, and Forgiveness – and see how they may have been off-center during that particular period. I can either be selfish, focusing only on what did NOT happen, or I can look at what DID happen and be grateful. With that frame of mind, everything changes. I can be grateful for how she made my time at the airport extremely pleasant. I can be grateful for how her smile made traveling during the holidays so much more tolerable. I can be grateful that we were able to have some time together before we moved on in our separate ways. I can thank God for apparently saving me time.

Who knows, but if this happens with clients, I want you to be AWARE of what is REALLY going on. Pay attention to their actions. Traditional training teaches you to chase, chase, chase clients and even be a pest. Not with **The Edge**. Be honest with yourself in the reality check and if certain clients are not going to happen, DIS-Qualify them. Or if you are feeling pressure or they are accusing you of being aggressive or pushy, ask yourself if your foundation is intact. Are your actions based on the Four Cornerstones? Or are you operating from another place? Like "commission breath" or WIIFM (What's In It For Me)? If things are not flowing, if you go back to the Four Cornerstones you will usually see why.

The Steps flow from one to the next, and you will get it more and more if you study them and incorporate them into your work and life. In order to have fun, you have to be able to laugh at yourself and at life. If you were playing some game, what would be the best way to guarantee you have fun no matter what? Answer: Don't care about the final score! In order to have fun, it's essential to detach from any outcome or expectation. I'm not saying don't have goals and don't build a Success Triangle and don't dream and don't love winning – but when you are actually in the game, in front of a client, in the middle of a listing appointment, or talking to the cute person in the mall, do the following: FORGET ABOUT THE OUTCOME! Let everything go, detach and turn it over to a higher power. Forget about what you *think* you should say, what you *planned* on saying, what you *hope* will happen and what you *want* to happen. Just be yourself and let 'er rip!

If you want to make God laugh, tell Her your plans.

Step Six is about more than just having fun, it is about detaching from the outcome and letting go. You must learn the latter to get the former. (Did I lose ya there?) *Detaching from the outcome is the key to more fun.* (Huge secret there so don't tell anyone.) You have done the work, you are in front of a buyer or seller, now just be yourself and have fun at that meeting. Enjoy opening the doors and let the universe handle the rest. When I would show property, I would simply open the door and let the customers look around. I made it a point never to talk about real estate when showing houses. I tried to make clients laugh, or I took that time as an opportunity to get to know them better. This threw people for a loop because they always expected the realtor to start "selling." I never did. (Remember, if other agents were doing it, I wasn't going to do it.) Clients appreciate that. Have fun! The client knows "this is the kitchen" and "this is a bathroom" without your telling them. Say what you feel, not what you think realtors are supposed to say. This will make it more fun for you and more fun for the customer.

Step Six is not just about having fun on vacation. It's important to make every day fun. Every day if you "love what you do and do what you love" (like Grandma Adeline taught us), you will soar to new heights. Most people work work work, focus focus focus, and are tense and stressed at work. Let it go. Do your best and forget the rest. The biggest take-away I can give you about this step is to make a conscious effort to have fun *on* the job! I'm not saying don't prepare and work hard, but once you are on the field, in the game, then let it all go.

Here are some ways to practice and help you detach from the outcome:

Daily: Meditate for five minutes on having *no expectations from others*.

Weekly: Journal once per week on the Cornerstone of Service and how you can do more things with *unconditional* love.

Monthly: At all your passion arenas, play a game where you try not to tell anyone you are even a real estate agent. Just get to know them for them. Forget about trying to sell anyone anything and instead, just really try to understand someone else's situation.

HOW DETACHING TURNS INTO WINNING:

If you watch professional sports, hindsight always shows us why a particular team ended up winning. It is usually because they were the team having the most fun. They were focused but they were also loose, enjoying the game, smiling. In 2012 when the L.A. Kings beat the New Jersey Devils to win the Stanley Cup finals, the Kings looked like a bunch of kids laughing and playing pickup in their backyards or on the frozen ponds in their hometowns. They wanted to win, but they were not attached to the outcome; they were attached to the moment. It was one game at a time. One shift at a time. They didn't concern themselves with the result. They just focused on playing their best each shift and enjoying the moment. And they ended up winning it all.

The Devils, on the other hand, were very tight, bunched up. They looked stressed on the bench and their game suffered. They were not in the moment. You could see it in their faces, their demeanors, and their play. They were scattered, out of control, had zero teamwork, and they lost big time. The Devils had incredible talent on that team, but come game time, they were wound up. They were holding on too tightly and it cost them.

Don't get me wrong, the Kings didn't slack off in practicing or training. They came ready and their goal was to win. But when the puck dropped, they forgot about the Cup and just played their game. Fast, fun, focused and furious – and they smoked the Devils in six games. Not to mention setting a record in their playoff run, losing the fewest games ever in a Stanley Cup playoff run. It was a run that had been unmatched in the NHL. When Captain Dustin Brown was interviewed after winning the first game of the final series, the reporter from ESPN asked him, "Dustin, how does it feel to be three wins away from the Stanley Cup Championship?" Dustin replied, "I don't know, I'm trying not to think about the Cup right now. It's just one game at a time right now. We want to stay loose, have fun, and get ready for Game Two."

"Stay loose. Have fun."

-Dustin Brown, Captain, Los Angeles Kings

(and oh yeah, TWO TIME Stanley Cup Champion)

I have been a competitive s.o.b. most of my life and it wasn't until recently that I really learned how to have fun. And by having more fun, I actually won more and so will you. Really having fun means enjoying every day, not just vacations or when things are good, but when you have not-so-good days as well. It all started with the mindset of detaching from the outcome, no matter what. Whatever the situation, whether it is a listing appointment, a date, a tennis match, a pickup hockey game, or just a trip to Target with my nieces, I was going to forget about how I would *expect* things to go and just have a great time. If you are not having any fun in life, then we have a major problem. It's important as you are launching your new career that you pay attention to your *Fun-Meter*. New agents can tend to overdo it during their first year and burn out. When things get stressful and worry and fear creep up, these could be signs that you are not having any fun. Cranking up the *Fun-Meter* means reminding yourself that sometimes we have to loosen up and not take things so seriously.

How you can practice this for the next few months is to make it a point to accept things exactly the way they are. When adversity and curve balls come your way, know that it's part of the journey and have a laugh. Appreciate whatever it is, how it is. This will free you up to be joyous in the moment. And Joy is what it is all about.

As I related earlier, my Grandma Adeline told me years ago to "do what you love and love what you do," and I always remembered that. The part I forgot, however, was something she threw in later in that same conversation. Let me explain. One day shortly after my graduation from college, I was telling her that I wanted to get into some sort of teaching for a living but was concerned about making money as a teacher. Her response was:

> *"Forget about the money, you give it all away in the end anyway."*
> -Adeline Williams, My Grandmother (R.I.P. Addy)

That was her way of telling me to detach from the outcome. If you are so focused on the money, I have news for you: you will have a hard time making any. You will continue to struggle until you shift your focus to doing what is best for the client. Do I want you to kick ass, have big goals, and make more money than you ever have in your life? YES! Did Dustin Brown want to win a Stanley Cup? Of course he did. Dreams and goals are important, but put them down in your Success Triangle and then get out there! Will you achieve your dreams and real estate goals? YES! If you keep this Step in your mind during your journey, you will indeed. If you cling to the thought of what the commission checks may be and what you are going to get from your customers, you will be headed down a dangerous road. *Commission-Breath Avenue* leads to nowhere.

This program has no scripts whatsoever because when you are comfortable being yourself, in an environment you love being in, and with someone you genuinely like being with, you don't need one! You will say the right thing. You will be honest. You will be blunt. You will be yourself. If you want a script, fine, use your own words. What YOU would ask people and how YOU would ask. It will make it authentic. People can tell when you are being genuine. People respond to genuine. This is the whole point and purpose of this program: to help you remain genuine. If you can do that, what you create and do will be amazing. People no longer want mumbo jumbo sales jargon. If your gut says, "Oh boy, this house is ugly and I don't like it," then SAY THAT! Don't pull out some script that teaches you how to overcome objections or how to make some fancy sales move to try to sell them. If you think it's ugly, tell them you think it's ugly! This system allows you to tell the truth to people and not care what they do or think because that is how you act when you are detached from any outcome. I promise you, in real estate THE TRUTH SHALL SET YOU FREE! And make you a ton of money in the process.

GINGER BREAD MAN

I had a client couple who were extremely high maintenance and I was at my wits' end. They were driving me nuts. She was driving her husband nuts. Nothing was good enough for them and one day I snapped. She was in a master bedroom and asked me if I could find a house with a Jacuzzi in the master bedroom closet. With a laugh, I looked at her and her husband and said:

> *"Maybe we can find that, sure. And maybe we can find a house with a goddam gingerbread man on top as well!"*

There was a giant pause and I thought I was in deep trouble. All of a sudden both of them burst out laughing. This client told me later that she appreciated my honesty and putting her in her place. She said it helped her realize finding something one hundred percent perfect would be impossible and my gingerbread man zinger made her see this. She ended up making some compromises and shortly thereafter they found a winner. To this day we all still laugh about the famous gingerbread man line that changed it all.

There is no script that teaches you that, but it's what I felt at the time so I said it. You have to be true to what you feel. It will only benefit you and the client. Telling the client how you really feel will lead them to trust you and know that you are their ally in this journey and not just a salesman trying to close a deal. You will become an ally, a partner, a trusted advisor and not merely your typical real estate agent. This is what you become to people if you detach from the outcome, be yourself; and, most importantly, speak the truth. Doing this will give you an extreme edge over your competition because you are now earning their trust and respect and this will help you win their business and loyalty.

Edge Rule: Earn their trust and you will earn their business.

I was showing someone a house two blocks from the highway and she said she was in love with the house. She was not from the area. She was not aware of the highway. I knew it was close to the highway and my heart said to tell her the truth and tell her my thoughts. (This is selling on **The Edge**, so I did exactly that.) I said, "I have to tell you I don't like this house for you and your family because I am concerned that it is too close to the highway. Don't you think maybe there is bad air and it doesn't seem safe for the kids? So we should cross it off the list, don't you think?" I was trying to Dis-Qualify the house for her, but at the same time I was being completely honest and saying what I felt was true. Her response was, "Actually, as strange as this sounds, my family loves the energy from the highway as we are all from New York and it reminds us of home. So no, the highway is not a problem."

Can you believe that? What do you think most agents would have done? Due to not having the right school district, they ended up not buying the house and three months went by in which I never heard from them. I figured it was over, but then came a phone call. *"Hi, Mark, sorry we disappeared. My husband and I were away on business but we found a house we want to see. We always remembered your honesty about the highway so we are calling to see if you can take us to look at this house this weekend."* Booyah! **The Edge!**

My honesty about the highway had earned their trust. Earn their trust and you will earn their business. Two weeks later we were in escrow for a house that was double the price of the one near the highway and it came out of left field. They had even found it *without* me! That is what can happen if you detach from the outcome, speak the truth, and keep the Four Cornerstones close to your heart. If you are the type of person that needs a script and you have to know what to say, then I will tell you this: You have one script to remember from this point on in your career. It's called THE TRUTH.

Edge Rule: Only one script for *The Edge* – The Truth.

Here is what you must take away from this that will change your life and your business: If you are talking to someone and while having a conversation you are thinking what to say next, how much the commission will be, or what this person can do for you, it will cost you. If you are focused on anything other than being in the moment and being of service (Cornerstone), you will say the wrong thing, you will come off as phony, and you will have a hard time developing relationships. Detach, listen, then speak the truth from your gut and heart and you will always come out on top.

I see realtors get so scattered because they meet someone who says they are looking for a million-dollar house then all of a sudden their demeanor changes because they are no longer present in the moment. They're thinking of the commission. Their body is there talking to the client, but their mind checked out and is counting the Benjamins. The client senses this shift in awareness and boom, they tell you "Thanks for your time, I will let you know." I WILL LET YOU KNOW means one thing. You are done. You just killed that deal. How? You lost their interest because clients can see when you get attached to anything other than what's best for them. If you get "commission breath," it's over.

If you think about it, most people do not want anything from their best friend. The "best friend exercise" is excellent if you're getting caught up in the money or feel the pressure to sell. Try speaking to the client as your best friend, be yourself, and stay focused on Dis-Qualifying them. This way you will do your job, which is to find out whether they are real or not, and it keeps you unattached and not emotionally involved.

Edge Rule: Whoever gets emotional first, goes home with product.

I try to remember this lesson when the heat is on. I remember losing my first big client because I hung on too tightly and got emotionally involved. My focus was not on the client. It was on payday! My brain was spinning out of control because the commission on this listing was going to be well over $100,000. I lost track of my purpose, which was to be of service and help someone out. They smelled my commission breath and I lost the listing. It can happen to the best of us and it could even happen to you, but if you keep the guiding principle in mind, you will hopefully avoid these tough moments. Come up with your own style to prevent this. My way is that whenever I am walking in to meet someone, I visualize my best friend and remind myself that I am here to serve. This lets me detach from any expectation and do one thing that I can do better than most: HAVE FUN!

So how can you one hundred percent ensure that you have fun? If you are grateful and you focus on the Four Cornerstones, you will be happy and stay in the moment. One sure-fire way not to do this and to get in a piss-poor mood is to look at other people's success and get into comparing. I live in L.A. and let me tell you, people drive nice cars, have big houses, beautiful spouses, kids, boats, and if I start comparing what I have to what they have, I will be depressed, paralyzed, and feeling worthless in a matter of minutes. But then I snap out of it and remind myself to DETACH FROM ALL OUTCOMES. Or, as the Buddha says, "Be desireless." This sums up your Main Mission in this Step. If you can get that down, the Main Moves will be a piece of cake. Reward yourself and recharge yourself.

REWARD

New agents can put a lot of pressure on themselves and forget to nurture themselves in their early years. It's human nature to be hard on ourselves, but I want you to do the best you can and reward yourself when you have a good week or good month. If you attend all your passion arenas for one month straight, buy yourself a nice dinner and celebrate the small victories. What you are doing is amazing and you need to reward yourself for it.

> *Don't wait to sell a huge house to reward yourself.*
> *Mini-rewards along the way are very important. They keep you happy.*
> *Happy keeps you fun. Fun keeps you loose, and staying loose means you will sell more because you are detached from the outcome.*

Each week I meet with Joe, my wingman, and we talk about what good things happened to us the previous week. We focus on what we did right and we focus on our mini-wins. I call it Focusing on the Ws! W stands for Wins. Focus on the Ws, my friend. It makes life so much more pleasant. It is human nature to let our thoughts fester on the bad things that happen. Joe had a week where he closed three deals in one week and he lost one. We were having our usual Jersey Mike's weekly sub sandwich and I could tell Joe was upset about something, so I asked what the problem was. He said, "I just lost a huge listing to another agent." I said, "Joe. Did you forget about the other three deals you just closed?" He said, "Yeah, but the one I lost still pisses me off." I asked him to tell me about the three that he closed and in no time his demeanor was back to his usual bright, positive, excited self. (The crabs were trying to pull him down.) If you will remember to focus on the Ws, you won't have time for the crabs or even notice them!

Edge Rule: Focus on the Ws.

Reward yourself as you go. Don't compare your business to anyone else's . . . ever! I promised you at the beginning that if you do the work, you stay focused, and detach from the outcome, your time will come. You will see others having tons of success and I encourage you to be happy for them and congratulate them. Reward others by congratulating them and know that in this business, those who have an abundance mentality are the ones who thrive. There is plenty of business for everyone, so the minute you fall into the trap of, "If another agent wins, I lose," you will be sliding down a slippery slope. You will be like those crabs in the bucket, only this time YOU are the one trying to pull someone else down. Your time will come. Reward yourself for what you did well this week. And even more important is to congratulate others when they succeed. This is something few realtors ever do. Make it a point to always extend sincere congratulations when others have a big sale or successful deal. This is not easy and it takes Humility to praise others. Your Cornerstone is Gratitude and that means when others succeed, you can do it too! Praise others and be inspired by others' success; don't be a crabby crab.

I suggest journaling each night before you go to bed, writing down what you did well that day. Your small victories will turn into big ones, and with an abundance mentality your success will snowball. What you focus on expands, so if you focus on your strengths, what you did well, and your successful moments – no matter how small – you will create more of those moments. This is Focusing on the Ws. Focusing on the wins.

How do you reward yourself? Simple. Stop and say "Good job" to yourself. Buy yourself a nice lunch. Give yourself permission to take a three-day weekend. It's up to you. But the point is to reward yourself as you go.

I used to reward myself with a large Mountain Dew from Taco Bell every time I had a listing presentation. I know it sounds silly, but I loved all that sugar and caffeine and it was a real treat for me to buy myself a large Mountain Dew as a reminder that I did good. This may sound simple and even childlike, but that is what rewarding yourself is all about. You have to have fun and nurture yourself in this business. At times you will feel like you just lost a kidney when a deal goes south, but I am here to tell you that if you are in the ring enough times you will eventually come out on top. I see so many new agents put unrealistic demands on themselves. A year goes by and they think nothing went well. This happens because they only focus on the bad days. Let those days go and focus on the W. Before you go to bed, give yourself five minutes to journal what you did well that day. After sixty days you will be amazed at all the great things you have done. The positive things are easy to overlook. One way to never forget them is to always focus on the W!

RECHARGE

Being new in real estate, you may find yourself working 24/7 and one day you wake up exhausted and burned out. You realize you haven't had a day off in nine months. This is not healthy, and we need you healthy and rested if you are going to succeed in this business. That's why Part Two of Step Six is to RECHARGE!

I don't mean take a two-week vacation each year. I mean each week, take some private time just for you. Shut your cell phone off and take a day off. If you don't, you will go insane. I promise you. This is one thing I wish I had done more of in my first few years. I never did. The training that I received had taught me to be available *all* the time for clients and I thought that meant leaving my phone on all day and night, responding immediately to emails; literally being ON CALL. Not good for the soul and, surprisingly, it is not good for business. Being Mr. Always Available Guy may seem cool, but it actually kills your credibility and lowers your clients' respect for you.

Edge Rule: It's not important if clients like you. It is important that they respect you.

Being available 24/7 is not something that commands respect. You are not 9-1-1. You are a real estate agent who plays an important role in helping people's lives. So many new agents try to get their clients to "like" them by doing whatever, whenever for them. That is not your job. This will fry you, not only physically, but mentally as well. My clients would call me day and night and even when I was on vacation. Finally, after a totally ruined family trip one year, I decided to man-up and take responsibility for this. I had to set boundaries. My new policy was to tell clients I was only available to talk on Tuesdays and Thursdays. The other days I was out working for them. In my Pre-Op Step, I told clients that I was not available on Sundays, when I would be resting and spending time with my family. As long as I managed their expectations (a useful function of Pre-Op), they were more than happy to comply. You see, I was formulating a selling system with all these new ideas and things started to soar. I made a commitment that each week I would take one personal day for me. I would shut my phone off, take a personal day, and stop being everybody's bitch. On my day off I would play hockey, go biking, call my friends, eat out, go see a movie. My rule was, I was not allowed to talk, think, or breathe anything real estate-related. I would even tell my clients that I was unreachable on this day, and the shocking part was that they loved it! They totally understood. In fact, their respect for me increased and they were impressed that I was not available 24/7. Does this make sense? I had to take time to recharge or I would be no good to anyone for anything.

"Be faithful to that which exists nowhere but in yourself – and thus make yourself indispensable."

-André Gide, Nobel Prize in Literature, 1947

Even today I can find myself burning the candle at both ends, and I have to remind myself that I need a break. That is what recharging is. For me, that means taking more trips to Minnesota to see my parents and sister and spending more time seeing my friends. Then I get to be me again and this has resulted in my being a better agent for my clients, better wingman, better teacher, and better person. Why? Because I am recharged! Reinvigorated, my enthusiasm back on high, the fire inside burning bright.

I was having a hard time finishing this book and I was sitting in a remote hotel room where I locked myself in for two weeks to help me finish. I was hitting a wall. I was tired, burned out. Although I knew I needed to stop what I was doing and recharge, I didn't want to. I was being stubborn. Sometimes we think that working harder is the answer, but if we overdo it, we may hurt ourselves, lose our passion and our zest. You end up getting sick, you can't work, and then you are no good to anyone. Luckily I realized this, so I put the writing aside and went to visit my Mom and Dad. After spending some great time with my parents, later that week I went on to finish the book. Looking back, I'm grateful that I not only recharged my batteries but got to spend quality time with my Mom and Dad, who might not be around someday. I made the right decision. You have to listen to your body and soul and when you need a break, take one – or pay the consequences. While you may think you will miss something while you're taking a breather, the reality is that you don't know how much you may gain. Always take time to recharge weekly; and, yes, even daily. Go take a nap, go to the gym, take a walk to break up your day

You see, realizing that *recharging is not optional* was part of formulating a selling system with all these new ideas -- and things started to soar. I was working FEWER hours and making MORE money. The more I recharged, the better I could be when it was game time. Being rested was only part of it. I got into the habit of watching what I ate and drank and noticing how my lifestyle was either keeping me charged or if certain behaviors were draining me.

Since I hated the late-night dinners with clients, I stopped doing them. Where in the real estate handbook did it say you HAD to go to dinner with clients? That was old-school training. My doctor didn't go to dinner with me after I had my annual physical; why did I need to go to dinner with clients? **Selling on the Edge** became a totally different way to work with clients. I was in control of my way of working. This new system was letting me do things the way I wanted to do them – and that is what I want you to do. I am not saying don't do dinners with clients. I am saying that if you don't like that kind of thing and it is not YOU, then DON'T DO IT!

Edge Rule: Recharging is not optional.

STAY COACHABLE FOREVER

Someone with average skills who gets on the right track and gets the right advice from the right coach, manager, or teacher will outperform someone with superlative skills who does not have access to the right track, the right guidance and the right coaches. The right track, the right guidance and the right help will lead you to the right opportunities. And even if you don't get ALL the right opportunities, your life will be a hell of a lot easier. You have to be willing to ask for help and directions, and that is the definition of being coachable. You have to be willing to humble yourself, realize that you may not have all the answers, and understand that to get better, you may have to ask for advice and help. (Just like I did with Tammy Olson, the girl who beat me in tennis.) It's important to keep an open mind forever and keep that desire to learn more. Stay thirsty, my friends.

Edge Rule: You can learn new things from anyone.

For real estate agents, the Six Steps of **Selling on the Edge** are what I have found to be the best advice and roadmap for success in selling houses. I am grateful you invested in **The Edge** and want to thank you for trusting me to help you. After fifteen years of selling houses, being around thousands of talented people in the real estate world, and learning from some of the best coaches, teachers, leaders, friends and family on the planet, I have given my all to delivering a program to you that I feel is the right guidance to put you on the right track, in the right environment, and among the right friends and support group, as you start your new journey selling houses. As you have seen in going through this book, **Selling on the Edge** calls on you to design your own program and your own way of doing things. That was my goal in developing this system. We are all different and you have to do what works for you. That is the key to mastering this system. Having fun is the sixth and final step.

HAVING FUN GETS YOU BACK TO STEP ONE

The most important thing about recharging is that it allows you to get back to being you. "It resets your soul," as Sandra Beck, **Edge** Graduate, puts it. When you are not thinking about real estate for that one day or one weekend and you are just being you, you will, without a doubt, have your biggest revelations. Your mind will rejuvenate and you will come up with new ideas that you never would have thought about if you'd been sitting in front of the computer or babysitting clients or frantically checking emails 24/7. That happened to me. Knowing I needed to get away and recharge, I booked a flight to Denver. I got a room up in the Rocky Mountains and decided I was going to take some time for Mark. Sleep in. See the mountains. Detach from selling and have fun doing nothing but enjoying nature. It was on that trip that I was able to completely detach from my real estate business and let my mind, body, and soul be free to recharge. Looking out on the beautiful snow-capped Rockies and hiking beautiful trails, it hit me that I needed to share my real estate ventures with others. I wanted to help new realtors and maybe even some experienced ones become better and happier in their businesses and their lives. This was it. I was going to write a book and lay out a system to help people who wanted to get into real estate. Thus **Selling on the Edge** was born!

In L.A. I was caught up in the hustle and bustle of everyday working life, and I knew God had wider plans for me. Just as He does for you. Spending that weekend alone in Colorado inspired me to write **Selling on the Edge**. Being of service was a value I cherished; it was time to give back. I had always been passionate about teaching, so I figured why not write a selling system based on my journey and see if I can help some people? You see how this shows that recharging doesn't just mean taking a day off; it means letting your mind be free so your unconscious can come up with stimulating ideas that will help bring out the you in you even more. You can unleash the you in you. As you go through the steps again, each time you will get better and better while you make this system your own. This process will bring you back to your core self and your core passions. Knowing thyself and "to thine own self" being true (Step One) is the most important part of making this system work. Being yourself. We are back to where it all began. Recharging naturally and organically takes you back to Step One and you know what to do from there. REPEAT!

Edge Rule: Reward, Recharge, Repeat.

ENCORE

Beyond the Edge

CHAPTER 24

EXECUTE

I have lived for a number of years now in the great state of California, in the city of Los Angeles -- home of Hollywood and some of the greatest writers, artists, moviemakers, creators and producers anywhere in the world. Driving to my office in L.A. one day in the heart of "The Industry," as they call it, I was not surprised to hear Steven Bochco, one of the most successful, influential people in TV history, interviewed on the radio. As the interviewer pointed out, Bochco was famous for shows that transformed TV storytelling. Shows like *Hill Street Blues*, *NYPD Blue*, and *L.A. Law*, as well as a long list of other hits in a career spanning decades. He was talking about the secret to his success. What he said transformed me. I have learned lessons from many different people in my life, none more life-changing than this one. Bochco said that in his opinion, success came down to one element: the ability to execute. He said that the only difference between him and a lot of other people who strove to be TV show creators, producers, writers, and more, but never seemed to make it, was one thing: "The ability to execute." I listened to what he said. Execute means "finish it." Don't just think about doing it. Do it.

Edge Rule: Execute

Finishing it means completing what you started. Completing what you started means doing what you said you were going to do. It's what Executing is! In Minnesota we are famous for the phrase, "Git 'er done!"

You got your real estate license, so now go sell houses. Your biggest roadblock as you get started will be your natural tendency to want to get everything perfect before you get out there and carry out your plan. New realtors waste time talking about getting the right car, the right outfit, the right marketing materials, the right website. They spend months wondering, "Should I sell houses or condos? Should I handle leases? What area is best?" They spend more time wondering in what office they should hang their license, whether they need more training, whether they are ready. There are thousands of questions, people, and situations that can be roadblocks, stopping you from doing one thing: executing. Don't let it happen. Engage, fall on your face, and don't be afraid to make mistakes. Don't obsess about getting everything right or worry about making a fool of yourself and looking stupid. That will paralyze you. Forget about all that and execute, and you will have an **Edge** over almost every agent out there. While most are *thinking* about what to do, you will be *doing* it.

For Steven Bochco, executing meant putting together a completed TV show. Not just writing a script or filming part of a show, but having a written, finished, completely done episode filmed and in the can. He said he never tried to get things perfect and half the time he wasn't sure if the material was good or not, but he knew he could get a finished project completed. This was his **Edge**! He talked about how the most important thing was to get the project done and hand it over to the network; then he had done his job. Whether the show was a hit or not was out of his control. Shows he thought would make it, didn't, and ones he thought wouldn't, ended up being hits. **His ability to detach from the outcome combined with ability to execute propelled him to become one of the greatest television creators of all time.**

GET IN OVER YOUR HEAD

The realtors that soar and last are the ones who embrace their imperfections and talk to people, whether they are ready or not. You will never be 100% ready. It's time to dive in, take the screw-ups as they come and remember that by just getting out there and getting in the ring and executing every day, you will put yourself ahead of 99% of all other realtors. While they are waiting for everything to be lined up and perfect, you will be getting knocked down and getting back up. You'll be learning, growing, laughing, and living life in the arena. You will be in the game, and let me tell you, this is where all the fun is.

Life is not a spectator sport.

Neither is selling houses. If you want to sell houses, then go sell one. You are just as capable as anyone else, but you have to dive in and swim to the deep end, and you are going to get in over your head. This is when you know you are executing. You now have the selling program that provides the tools you needed. When others say things like, "You are too new for this," or "You can't be here," and you find yourself ruffling some feathers, know in your heart that it's time to keep going. You may be beyond your comfort zone, but this is executing, my friends. This is when you are living large, and huge amazing things are about to come your way. Thank you, Mr. Bochco.

STAY COACHABLE FOREVER

Someone with average skills who gets on the right track and gets the right advice from the right coach, manager, or teacher will outperform someone with superlative skills who does not have access to the right track, the right guidance and the right coaches. The right track, the right guidance and the right help will lead you to the right opportunities. And even if you don't get ALL the right opportunities, your life will be a hell of a lot easier. You have to be willing to ask for help and directions, and that is the definition of being coachable. You have to be willing to humble yourself, realize that you may not have all the answers, and understand that to get better, you may have to ask for advice and help. (Just like I did with Tammy Olson, the girl who beat me in tennis.) For real estate agents, the Six Steps of **Selling on the Edge** are what I have found to be the best advice and roadmap for success in selling houses. Remember, though, that you may encounter other stuff out there that could be valuable to you, so it's important to keep an open mind forever and keep that desire to learn more. Stay thirsty, my friends.

Edge Rule: You can learn new things from anyone.

Chapter 25

BELIEVE IN YOURSELF TO BE YOURSELF

You have to be the first one to believe in yourself. Others will follow, but it starts with you.

Everyone has his or her unique talents and beautiful differences. Yet, for whatever reason, as life goes on, we lose track of who we are. We stop being ourselves. We try to be what we think everyone else wants us to be. Eventually we wake up one day, look in the mirror, and ask ourselves, Who am I? Who have I become? What am I doing? It's time to stop the madness and it's time to take the power back. It's time to own it and be you because I have news for you, you're back Jack!

THE MEMO

It's time to remind people who may be lost about the memo we all got the day we were born. The memo that stated:

There is no one in the world like you. There is only one you for a reason. Your way and your style of doing things will be exactly what the world is looking for. It is your unique differences that will change lives and change the world for the better. Always be yourself. Never doubt who you are, and always share your amazing authenticity with the world, no matter what. You are perfect exactly the way you are and always will be! You were born to be you. Don't ever forget it.

Edge Rule: You were born to be YOU.

Check your birth certificate. I promise you, it's on there somewhere. I am just here to remind you of this. If you can use this program to remember that and empower yourself to be YOU in all areas of your life, and then share that authenticity with everyone and everything, you can be assured that LIFE WILL RESPOND. Life will respond with all the abundance, appreciation, and love you will ever need. If I have done my job, I have helped you reset your clock, so to speak, and you are back to becoming the real you once again. The fired up you that can let loose and change lives! There is no duplicate.

> *"We are all inventors, each sailing out on a voyage of discovery, guided each by a private chart, of which there is no duplicate."*

> -Ralph Waldo Emerson

It was designed that way for a reason. The world needs your uniqueness and gifts front and center. Once you tap into the power of your own uniqueness and really let it shine, your life will change. Being you will not only change your life; it will help change the world, and isn't that the idea? This whole program was designed with one thing in mind: YOU. Yes, *the Edge* starts with gratitude and ends with having fun; however, YOU are everything in between. This is your time.

NOW IT IS YOUR TURN

You will know you are on the right path when someone asks for your help. There is no greater compliment or sign that you have arrived. I want you to be aware of that moment because it is coming and most people miss it. When someone asks you for your help, or what's your secret, or compliments you on your new positive vibe and uniqueness, I ask one favor of you. I ask that you tell them your secret and then help them! And by keeping this cycle of helping others going, maybe we all change a few lives together and hey you might even sell their house one day. KABLAM!

Life responds to those who can be themselves in all areas of their lives. There is flat-out nothing more attractive and engaging than someone who is not afraid to lay it all on the line and simply be themselves. Remember Joe "Big Country" Convery ? He was the master. Most people cannot do it because it exposes many nerves, makes them vulnerable, lets people see how they really are inside. Exposes their true self. And, yes, that can be scary. Because what if we get rejected or criticized or denied because we were being ourselves? Then, my friends, as you learned, you simply DIS-Qualify those naysayers and move on. The truth is that more and more people will be attracted to you, whether they know why or not.

DANCE

If this book has helped you, even in the slightest way, to bring out the you in you, then mission accomplished! If, in the end, I motivated you a little or you learned something new and you want to call me a motivational speaker or this a motivational program, OK, I can live with that. After twenty years of selling houses, being around thousands of talented people in the real estate world, and learning from some of the best coaches, teachers, leaders, friends and family in the world, I have given my all to delivering a program to you that I feel is the right guidance to put you on the right track, in the right environment, and among the right friends and support group, as you start your new journey selling houses. Taking on the exciting world that is residential real estate, keep the foundation close to the vest. The Four Cornerstones of Gratitude, Service, Humility and Forgiveness will always keep you grounded and centered as you continue to master the Six Steps: Be Yourself, Get Out There, DIS-Qualify, Focus, Own It, Have Fun – and the way to get really good at all of this… *Repeticion, Repeticion, Repeticion!! (French Accent!)*

I look forward to seeing you soar to new heights in your new career. You will soon be doing things that I have never done nor could have dreamed of doing. That is my wish for you and the reason I wrote this book. I wish you joy, prosperity, health, unlimited amounts of laughter and peace in your journey. It's the journey that matters in the end, not the destination and it's the joy we receive along the way by seeing progress not perfection, that makes life worth living.

Steve Jobs is famous for saying "here's to the crazy ones". I would agree with that all day long and I always added a little twist of my own with here's to the crazy ones, …*that are crazy enough to dance on the edge!* It really is where all the fun is, but do me a favor, don't tell just anyone ok? Deal? Remember the Edge Golden Rule: A! B! D! Always Be Dis-qualifying! 😊 Now get out there, close some big ass deals, send me your success stories via email below, and never stop dancing along the way. Remember, no one can do you like you. You are a miracle. There is no one else like you in the whole entire world. And *that* is a serious reason to celebrate.

So let's dance my friend.

Dance!

MARK JOHN WILLIAMS

Contact Mark: thinkwilliams@gmail.com

Summary of Edge Rules

(All Eighty-Frickin-Five of 'em!)

Edge Rule: You sell houses.
Edge Rule: Just finish it.
Edge Rule: No one can do you better than you.
Edge Rule: The only script we use is the truth
Edge Rule: Your first year in real estate, don't even attempt to work with friends or family.
Edge Rule: Time kills deals.
Edge Rule: You don't get what you are worth, you get what you negotiate.
Edge Rule: Like attracts like.
Edge Rule: Don't give in to negativity and cynicism.
Edge Rule: Choose gratitude.
Edge Rule: Humility - Never leave home without it.
Edge Rule: Never put a client in their place. Never.
Wil's Rule: Never react. Pause, wait, and then ...respond.
Edge Rule: Set your rocks down.
Edge Rule: Gratitude is like air. Breathe it in or die.
Edge Rule: Give more unconditionally of whatever it is you want.
Edge Rule: When you have nothing left to give, give thanks.
Edge Rule: If you feel it, say it.
Edge Rule: Only work with people you like working with.
Edge Rule: If you don't like doing it, stop doing it.
Edge Rule: Keep it simple.
Edge Rule: Relationship first. Sell second.
Edge Rule: Drive a low-profile car.
Edge Rule: If you are talking, you're losing.
Edge Rule: Relationship first, sell second. (or not at all)
Edge Rule: You decide who is IN and who is OUT.
Edge Rule: Always follow your instinct, your heart, and your gut.
Edge Rule: Your job is to find trauma victims.
Edge Rule: If you lose your sh*t, you will lose the deal.
Edge Rule: Develop your DQ not your IQ!
Edge Rule: No Trauma, No change.
Edge Rule: Don't abuse the system.
Edge Rule: Use the 90 percent rule.
Edge Rule: Trauma+Pre-OP+Insurance = Real Client
Edge Rule: No Free Surgery.
Edge Rule: Sales Triage steps must be done in order
Edge Rule: Gut check first, then run Sales Triage
Edge Rule: Never Operate without Trauma, Pre-Op, and Insurance.
Edge Rule: Actions trump words all day long.
Edge Rule: Real buyers have no problem showing you the money.
Edge Rule: Real sellers sign listing agreements.
Edge Rule: No ticky, No laundry.
Edge Rule: Always get the key.
Edge Rule: Loose lips sink ships.
Edge Rule: Sell and let sell.
Edge Rule: A sale is "final" when the commission check has been cashed and the check has cleared.
Edge Rule: Post-op diffuses remorse and prevents back-outs
Edge Rule: Take breaks.

Edge Rule: Learn it, use it, and make it your own.
Edge Rule: Use it or lose it.
Edge Rule: What you focus on expands.
Edge Rule: Focus on the "do", not the "want".
Edge Rule: How you feel doesn't matter. It's what you do that matters.
Edge Rule: Spend 80-percent of your time finding Trauma Victims
Edge Rule: Know your ideal customer.
Edge Rule: Avoid WMDs.
Edge Rule: Master step one and you will always get it done.
Edge Rule: Keep it Simple.
Edge Rule: If everyone else is doing it, stop doing it.
Edge Rule: Think triple win.
Edge Rule: Be Nice. (Even when you are having a bad day)
Edge Rule: When you close a deal, pay all your taxes immediately, no exceptions.
Edge Rule: It's not about the final destination. It's about those we meet along the way.
Edge Rule: To change it, own it.
Edge Rule: Nothing can be an excuse. Nothing.
Edge Rule: If you don't know what the problem is, look in the mirror.
Edge Rule: Champions do reality checks and ask for help.
Edge Rule: Your excuses are your own.
Edge Rule: You never, ever, leave your wingman.
Edge Rule: No one succeeds alone.
Edge Rule: Avoid the crabs.
Edge Rule: If nothing changes, nothing changes.
Edge Rule: Disappointment does not equal disaster.
Edge Rule: Earn their trust and you will earn the business.
Edge Rule: There is only one script for the Edge - The Truth.
Edge Rule: Whoever gets emotional first, goes home with product.
Edge Rule: Focus on the W.
Edge Rule: It's not important if clients like you. It is important they respect you.
Edge Rule: Recharging is NOT optional.
Edge Rule: Reward, Recharge, Repeat.
Edge Rule: Execute.
Edge Rule: You can learn new things from anyone.
Edge Rule: Beat to your own drum
Edge Rule: You were born to be you.
Edge Rule: For the love of God….No more Edge rules!

Special Thanks

Mom/Dad, Chris, Rachel, Nicole, Piper, Joe "Big Country" Convery, Convery Family, Mo, Sandra Beck, Uncle Bobby, Nick, Ilaria, Pene, Jackson, Doug, Nitz, C$, Gooshy, Vinh, Pistol, Dean Malevich, Liebajew, Deano, Billy, Eisenberger, Goldberg, Adeline, Phil Sr., John, Hilda 1 and 2, Uncle Wil, Williams group, Illies gang, Shulo group, Beste gang, Heron crew, Carol and Tom, Vincent Avenue Gang, Guglielmelli, SC, Dusty, Patrick, Geoff and Susie, Tim, Jen, Sofia, Hawk, Brom, JW, Seitz, Monte, Shido, Plut, Boosie, Big D, Little D, Cock, Knudy, Hamcracker, Goff, Dick, Amy O, T-Pappa, Kriades, Jude, Mel and Nigel, May, Sean B, Boxerbaum, Johnny, Moo, Moss, Jr., M3, M4, JTS, Frag, Shim, Merrie K, Bete, Bega, BD, T-Moore, Boogs, Etters, Mehoff, MJK, CAI, Chardsy, Bickford, Bill M, Bill W, Kalata, Jeff B, Bennington, Oyston, Welch, Tommy, Forte, Space Nugget, Liana, Jojo, Padraic and Cindy, Bobby V, Kou, The Blonigens, Kripp, Hess, Linda J, Linda E, Linda F, Combs, Dergs, Morris, Val, Shimizu, Christos, Svobods, Janice, Good Seanie, Ten, Tina, Cindy N, Arbab, T-Raider, Barns, Bobby P, Lars, Rieder, Daniels, Chad, Hammer, Schnookie, An, Jeff B, Joel O, Patricia, Bails, Wil C, Anita R, Sugarman, Mojo, Bottlik, Eduardo, Barry B, Barry D, Steven B, Robert, Jimmy, JPJ, Bonzo, Eddie, Jeff, Stone, Mike, Greg Palast, Leni Badpenny, Weisbrot, JD, AB, Kirky, Ginger, Bella, MP, Morgs, Gray, Dahl, Raff, Garv, Simmy, Jens, Brovy, Jandrich, OB, Coyote, Erik O, Log Cabin, Silverman, Hai, Kara, JJ, JC, Forlitti, Michelle L, Vince F, Denise C, Tony H, L.A. Kings, Pearl Jam, Maynard, Tool, Mamet, Gary Thorne, Bill Clemente, all the real estate agents out there, anyone thinking about getting their real estate license, and of course you, for giving my book a chance. Lastly, above all, God, without Whose help none of this would have ever been possible. Goodnight Everybody.

About the Author

Mark John Williams has sold homes in Los Angeles for over twenty years and is not only well-known and well-respected amongst his clients and peers, but he also prides himself on being known as one of the most fun residential real estate agents in Southern California. It wasn't always fun however. After a brutal start in the industry to the point where he almost didn't make it, Mark found himself broke, pushing thirty, and living in a friend's garage. It was so bad at one point even his close friends referred to him as "the worst real estate agent in Los Angeles." Jokingly of course, but not really lol. After years as a complete failure in the real estate world, it was do or die so Mark made a decision to give it one last shot. Only this time, things would be different. This time he was going to do things his way. Traditional training techniques and the fancy closing tips that the whole industry was teaching were not working for him. Mark decided to come up with his own selling system and it started first and foremost by being himself.

"I figured no one could do me better than me, so that might give me some kind of advantage. I simply started being myself in every situation."

No more trying to jam the square peg in a round hole and be like everybody else. "It was time to get get my Edge on! It was time to start doing things my way." T-shirt, Jeans, and Tennis shoes replaced the stuffy suit and tie. And certainly no more open houses on Sundays. Alleluia!

"I hated working on Sundays, so I simply stopped doing it."

"Whatever other agents were doing, I was going to do the complete opposite."

With authenticity, brutal honesty, and his Dad's advice of always develop relationships first, sell second, and throw in a little *Jack Reacher* in there, Mark set out on a mission to change the way people looked at real estate agents and the way agents looked at selling. Mark's new style and way of selling houses not only helped him go on to sell multi-million dollar homes and work with well-known celebrities from all over, but he did it all staying true to himself, sporting his T-shirt, jeans, and yes still even today driving his beat-up Jetta. "I love that car!" (Today, 2023, It's a Hyundai.)

"The truth is clients want a humble real estate agent they can trust, so be careful on what you drive. Many new agents go out and buy a luxury vehicle, get in debt to their eyeballs, thinking a fancy car is what gets clients. It doesn't. It can actually backfire. My suggestion: Keep your hoopty!"

Mark's fresh new twist on selling combined with the success he was having in southern California ultimately got the attention of some top residential real estate firms in the world. They began asking Mark to help train and develop their new agents. It was in helping these new agents where Mark began to discover another joy in life: Teaching. After more than a two decades now (as of 2023 version 2) of a successful selling career in the cut-throat markets of Los Angeles, Hollywood Hills, Beverly Hills and Malibu, CA the joy of teaching and helping others ultimately surpassed his passion for selling. On the advice of his old college Dean of Students to always write a book, Mark set out in 2010 to do just that. Locked in a remote sketch motel in the middle of the Rocky Mountains for six plus weeks, Mark began laying the outline for what is now Selling on the Edge. Today, 2023 a special improved and highly acclaimed TENTH YEAR ANNIVERSARY version2.0 that has been released and is in your hands! A timeless goldmine of material that is now at every real estate agent's fingertips. Take advantage of it!

Mark currently splits time between Los Angeles, CA and Minnesota. He spends two to three months a year in his hometown of Minnesota fishing, waterskiing, snowskiing, playing ice hockey, spending time with his family, friends, and still wondering if that girl from the airport is ever gonna call? "Alright fine, she's DQ'd! ...KABLAM!" 😊

Made in United States
North Haven, CT
21 June 2023

38070405R00182